D0890700

ßirchbark ßelles

Women
on the
Michigan Frontier

A frontier woman helps her husband out of a tight spot.

ßirchbark ßelles

Women
on the
Michigan Frontier

edited by
Larry B. Massie

The Priscilla Press
Allegan Forest, Michigan
1993

Copyright 1993 by Larry B. Massie

All rights are reserved. No portion of this publication may be reproduced without the express permission of the editor.

Please direct any questions or comments concerning this publication to:
Larry B. Massie
2109 41st St. Allegan Forest, MI. 49010
(616) 673-3633

Cover by Judi Miller Senior
Title Graphic by Devon Blackwood
Printing by Bookcrafters, Chelsea, MI.

ISBN: Soft Cover 0-9626408-7-5
       Hard Cover 0-9626408-8-3

First Edition - November 1993

For my birchbark belle, Priscilla, who canoed the St. Marys River with me the day we met.

LIBRARY
ALMA COLLEGE
ALMA, MICHIGAN

Some flowers that blossom in the Allegan Forest.

Table of Contents

PREFACE

Anna Jameson, an impetuous Irish beauty, sought to ease memories of her unhappy marriage to a cold Toronto judge by experiencing the wonders of the Upper Peninsula, still pristine in its unspoiled splendor. In the summer of 1837 she toured the far reaches of the newly created state of Michigan. At Sault Ste. Marie the native Chippewa named her "the woman of the bright foam" when she became the first white female to brave the roaring St. Marys Rapids in a flimsy birch bark canoe. Allegan raised Judi Senior has captured in watercolors Jameson's exhilaration in the cover illustration.

The summer before Jameson's northern tour, a sophisticated British lady named Harriet Martineau had climbed aboard a stagecoach at Detroit and bounced over the lower peninsula's abominable roads to Niles. Despite that bone jarring ride she too had marveled at the Eden-like beauty of oak openings and prairies emblazoned with wild flowers.

Cultivated New York school teacher Caroline Kirkland, on the other hand, found the crudities of life on the Michigan frontier little to her liking. She and her family lasted but briefly in their attempt to subdue the wilderness before retreating back to eastern civilization.

The travel narratives and essays written by these and some of the other leading literary ladies of their era preserve well crafted word pictures of the past. Equally valuable are the recollections penned by the women who put down roots on the Michigan frontier, the pioneers themselves.

Elizabeth Therese Baird retained the wide-eyed wonder of youth when as an elderly matron she described her magical childhood on Mackinac Island during the heyday of the fur trade. Sarah Bryan and Harriet Noble captured the hardship, fear and loneliness of mothers battling to keep their families alive and preserve their own sanity amid the Washtenaw County wilderness of the 1820s. Martha Gray recalled equally harrowing times in the Benzie County backwoods in the 1860s.

In *Birchbark Belles* I have gathered together the stories of 31 diverse women who had at least one thing in common - they experienced the Michigan Frontier. The stories are as they told them in now rare and valuable books, in pithy letters, in autobiographical essays published in newspapers and in addresses delivered at pioneer reunions. In some cases I have excerpted from lengthy narratives but otherwise these selections have been but little altered from the original wording.

For the most part archaic word spellings, grammar, paragraphing and punctuation have been retained. I have added notes which I hope will assist modern readers. The selections have been chosen to include some of the best descriptions, to range over as much of the state as possible, and to represent the varieties of women witnesses to the past and the differing genre in which they recorded their experiences. I have arranged the chapters chronologically within the general divisions of literary ladies and wolverine women. Inclusion within those categories, however, is not necessarily a judgement concerning their relative literary merits.

It is my hope that this volume will make these women's remarkable sagas more accessible so that all Michiganders can have the opportunity to appreciate an often overlooked aspect of their heritage.

Larry B. Massie
Allegan Forest, Michigan

In the Beginning

Imagine the lay of the land in the 1820s - two pristine peninsulas, majestic, natural, scarcely touched by the hand of man or woman. Millions of acres of virgin forest stretch seemingly forever - ancient white pine, tulip poplar, oak, walnut, hickory, bone-white sycamore, muscular beech - forest giants 150 to 200 feet tall reach for the sky. Waving grass and a rainbow of flowers perfume scattered prairies. Park-like oak openings, glacially chiseled valleys and ridges, towering sand dunes and densely tangled wet lands vary the terrain. Sparkling streams swimming with trout, sturgeon, and grayling lace the land. The peninsulas are studded with crystal clear lakes and lapped by great inland seas - more fresh water than anywhere else on the face of the earth and every drop of it pure and drinkable. Wildlife peoples the wilderness - beaver, otter and mink, rabbits, squirrels and raccoons, black bear, wildcats and panthers, deer herds and wolf packs, wild turkeys, trumpeter swans and whooping cranes, vees of geese, great blue herons and flocks of passenger pigeons that darken the skies.

To the native Potawatomi, Ottawa and Chippewa, who understand nature's ways, Michigan seems little short of the white man's Garden of Eden. It was a paradise worth fighting for and but a decade before the River Raisin had run red with American blood and fresh scalps had swung from many a warrior's belt. But now they are a conquered people, a remnant of a once dominant culture pushed to sign away ancestral domain for paltry payments.

Save for the old French settlements strategically situated at Detroit, Monroe, Mackinac Island and Sault Ste. Marie, and in the interior Pontiac, Bloomfield and a few other little settlements in Wayne, Oakland, St. Clair and Monroe counties, isolated trader's cabin are the only mark the white man has made on the forest primeval. What economy there is revolves around the Indian trade - fur for steel knives, copper kettles, gadgets, gaudy trinkets and fire water.

The stream of westward migration has all but bypassed Michigan Territory, branded an interminable swamp unfit for habitation. But in the early 1820s, immigrants make a few tentative forays into the interior of southern Michigan. In 1824, Washtenaw County feels the thud of the ax and the white man's plow first bites deeply into the virgin soil as the incipient communities of Ann Arbor and Dexter plant their roots. Word of the peninsula's fertile land, all you want for $1.25 an acre, filters back east. Then in 1825 comes an event of profound importance for Michigan's development - the opening of the Erie Canal. It becomes a great immigrant's highway and the sons and daughters of those who had pioneered western New York the generation before pull up stakes - lured by the cheap land on the Michigan frontier. They ride canal boats to Black Rock and Buffalo, steam across Lake Erie to Detroit and begin fanning out into the interior. Soon the trickle becomes a torrent - a land rush for "Michigania" of epic proportion. In the late 1820s and 1830s thousands of families load all their possessions in covered wagons and lumber off into the trackless wilderness, intent on carving out a new life in little log shanties amid the big trees.

Often miles from the nearest neighbor, beyond the reach of doctor and minister, they practice self sufficiency or do without. All experience some degree of hardship - hunger, cold, fear of wild animals and Indians, the torments of insects and malarial fevers - and some pay with their lives for the opportunity to tame a new land.

Those who survived earned well the title pioneer. Sometimes in later life they recorded their recollections of frontier life in the form of books, articles and addresses at pioneer reunions. Most who took the time to "put pen to paper" were men and consequently the role of the male pioneer has received most of the attention. But enough female pioneers also described experiences on the Michigan frontier so that their stories need not be eclipsed. These "Wolverine Women" deserve a chance to be heard once again and that is one of the purposes of this collection - to make available their amazing stories of a world forever gone, memories of isolation, hardship, sorrow and triumph recorded in their own words.

In addition to these wolverine women who cast their lot with Michigan and helped carve a state out of the wilderness, a variety of talented literary ladies, some of the era's most renowned, visited Michigan during its pioneer period and transition era. They were cultivated woman from the East, British and German tourists and travelers en route to the far West. They journeyed by Great Lakes steamer, birchbark canoe, stagecoach, horseback and rail. They met some of Michigan's most colorful personalities, Lewis Cass, Henry Rowe Schoolcraft, Susan Johnston and others. The descriptions they penned in their travel narratives, in particular, offer intimate glimpses into Michigan's past. What seemed mundane to pioneer residents often appeared novel to travelers and frequently provoked comment and comparison with their own cultural values. As a result travel narratives contain colorful accounts of early Michigan - detailed description of pioneer scenery, settlements, customs, personalities and events.

Together, the words of these literary ladies and wolverine women, offer a balanced picture of pioneer Michigan from a feminine perspective. Their stories ought not to be forgotten.

Detroit: 1824
by
Electa Sheldon Stewart

In 1845 Electa Sheldon wrote a fine account of her immigration to Detroit with her father, Ira Bronson, in 1824 and her subsequent childhood memories of life there. Not until 1892, however, would her article see publication in the *Michigan Pioneer Collections*.

Placing her article in this section rather than among those written by "wolverine women" is a subjective choice based on her literary career. She was born ca. 1817 in New York state. Following her move to Detroit at the age of seven and later childhood there, she married Berthier M. Sheldon, long time confidential clerk to shipping magnate Capt. Eber Ward. For two years beginning in 1853, she edited the *Western Literary Cabinet*, a monthly periodical for women published in Detroit. Curiously, she opposed woman's suffrage in its columns although she did advocate a broadening of women's avocations. When her husband died of cholera in 1854 she suspended publication of the magazine.

Before her magazine folded she had begun publication of a series of articles on the early history of Michigan, based largely on French archival sources which her friend, Lewis Cass, had collected while serving as minister to France in 1836-1842. She revised and supplemented these articles in her book, *The Early History of Michigan, From its First Settlement to the Year 1815*, published in New York in 1856. As a history of the state Sheldon's book was preceded only by James Lanman's 1839 *History of Michigan* and hers was the first to be based largely on primary sources. Her work enjoyed popularity and was reprinted several times.

Prior to her marriage to John Stewart in 1868 and relocation to Michigan Center in Jackson County, she helped found the Detroit Industrial School (for

neglected children) in 1857. She lost her second husband in 1890 and twelve years later Mrs. Electa M. Sheldon-Stewart died at the Home for the Friendless in Jackson.

My father emigrated with his family, consisting of my mother, my younger sister and myself, from Rochester, N.Y., to Detroit in September, 1824, when I was a child seven years old. I have indistinct recollections of a long night ride in a stage coach, and of our arrival in Buffalo before daylight; making this forced journey that we might be in time to take passage on the *Superior,*[1] the only steamer then on Lake Erie, which only made weekly trips.

From the time of our embarkation, till pioneer life lost its romance ten or twelve years later, almost every incident is vividly impressed on my memory. I have sometimes been surprised at the correctness of these memory pictures, when compared with the recollections of persons whose judgment was then mature, but the fact ceases to be remarkable when I consider that everything at the west was almost totally unlike the scenes to which I had been accustomed.

I had never before seen a large body of water; and as I stood on the steamer's deck, and saw Buffalo receding from view, and listened to the plash, plash of the steamer's wheels in the sparkling water, my childish mind was filled with commingled emotions of fear, wonder and delight.

The three days of our voyage were days of exquisite beauty; not a cloud cast its shadows on the placid waters, the sun looked down from the clear sky with a mellowed light, while the distant shore was partially veiled in the dreamy haze peculiar to autumn. Scarce a ripple disturbed the sleeping waters, and I recollect how ardently I wished for a little bit of a storm, that I might see how "white caps" looked dancing on the top of great waves; but no storm came and my love of adventure remained ungratified.

The most delightful part of our voyage, was our passage up the Detroit River. We did not stop at Malden, but we could plainly see the small, desolate looking town, and grass covered fort.[2] The only inhabitants of the place, seemed to be the red-coated soldiery, who stood gazing idly at the passing boat.

On Grosse Isle, now populous and highly cultivated, were only two farm houses; but the white, sandy beach, and the

15

green, sloping lawns, rising gradually from the shore; the small cultivated fields, and the still unbroken forest, formed a most pleasing landscape. At the upper end of the island was a rude hut, almost in the water, which my father told me was a fisherman's hut, and that was where they caught whitefish. That fishing ground was called Manitou Point.

Presently, all were startled by a loud, shrill whoop, which thrilled the nerves like an electric shock. Peals of most unearthly laughter next greeted our ears, and a succession of whoops and yells rent the air. I clung in terror to my father's hand, but he was not long in discovering the cause of this uproar; there, on the Canada shore opposite, was a band of young Indians evidently enjoying the surprise of the "pale faces." Some lay stretched on the lawn, their new blankets contrasting finely with the green carpet beneath them, others bounded gracefully along the shore, whooping and calling out to us in their own language, and trying the flight of their arrows in vain attempts to send some of those missiles on board. But the puffing steamer soon left them behind, and new objects drew our attention.

The scenery on the Canada shore was strangely beautiful. The bank of the river was high, but not precipitous and was covered with green sward to the water's edge. The face of the country as far back as the eye could reach, was level, and divested of forest trees, except now and then a clump of dwarf oaks standing near the edge of the river bank.

The low French-built farm houses were few in number, and half hidden by untrimmed shrubbery and apple trees of native growth; sometimes there was an inclosure of rude pickets, sometimes no fence of any kind.

There were no cornfields nor wheat stubbles, no great barns nor herds of cattle; nothing that looked like American thrift. Not a human being was seen after we passed the Indians, except now and then, a man mounted on a diminutive French pony, riding along with that peculiar indescribable gait which characterized the Canadians.

A small Catholic Cathedral[3] so old that its walls were supported by numerous props, stood near the river, and added to the aspect of desolation.

Yet the vast commons looked like shaven lawns and straggling fruit trees, unfenced and far away from human habitations, their boughs bending beneath their load of fruit, gave a certain mournful beauty to the landscape. A grove of lofty

16

trees on the very brink of the river just above the point opposite Springwells, excited general attention. At first, they were thought to be Lombardy poplars, and the gentlemen were discussing the question whether they were indigenous or transplanted, when, on nearer approach they were found to be pear trees.[4]

The view of the American side of the river was more cheerful. The shore, from Grosse Isle to near the suburbs of the city, was level and sandy, and the farms of the inhabitants were bounded by the river. These farms were very narrow, only a few rods wide in front and extending back a mile or more.

The farm houses all fronted the river. They were built in French style, large, one story high, with very steep roofs, and dormer windows. A few of them were painted white, and all of them were half hidden by tall lilac and rosebushes. A road separated the little yard in front of the house from the vegetable garden which extended to the water's edge. A wharf, formed of a single plank ran out into the river and was securely fastened. A stake was driven beside the wharf for the canoe or sailboat.

There was a sameness in arrangement, but an air of quiet comfort about these quaint looking houses.

At Springwells, three miles below the city, a windmill stood on the sand just at the edge of the water. The body of the mill was painted a dark red and contrasted well with the snow white sails or wings. Above, for a short distance, and below as far as the eye could reach, the white, sandy beach looked like a line of light dividing the water from the habitations of man.

"There is the residence of Governor Cass"[5] said a gentleman, pointing to a low, French-built house, half hidden by trees and shrubbery, standing like the others, not far from the river bank, and some distance below the city. I had never before seen a governor's house, but a governor was a great man, and, of course, his residence must be a magnificent, lordly castle like the pictures I had seen in books. My castle fell suddenly, when I saw that quaint old edifice; yet I afterwards learned that it was a delightful place of residence, with its rich internal adornments, and its lovely Christian mistress, and her daughters,[6] though the exterior was decidedly ancient.

Above the governor's dwelling, the houses were built a little farther from the river, and there were no more river side gardens; but the table land along the steep banks formed a beautiful park, where the weary citizens came to walk at evening, and happy children gambolled on the green carpet nature had spread, and played under the oaks that looked too diminutive to have had their birthplace by that mighty river.

The steamer announced her approach to the city by firing a cannon, which seemed to have called out the whole town. French women, wearing large, coarse straw hats, and carrying heavy baskets of fruit, were pressing their way through a crowd of men and boys; carts drawn by diminutive ponies, were backed up to the very edge of the wharf, their owners jabbering French and broken English "at the top of their voices." A little in the background the only coach was waiting to carry passengers to the only hotel in the city.[7] The captain, on board was giving orders concerning the lading, passengers were bustling around collecting their baggage, porters were disputing in French and English, making the scene a very fair representation of ancient Babel.

A few weeks after our arrival at Detroit, we were comfortably settled in a house owned by B.F. Witherell, standing on a large common northeast of the fort.

Detroit in 1824, was a very small town, ancient and venerable in its appearance. Its principal street, Jefferson Avenue, was lined on both sides with low, French houses whose unpainted fronts and moss covered roofs looked as if they had braved the storms of a century. Here and there, along the avenue, a newly painted shop showed that emigrants from "down east" were in town..

There were also two brick buildings on this street, one of which belonged to an English merchant, and the other was occupied by Gen. Hull[8] during the War of 1812.

The jail, the arsenal and the French Catholic Cathedral, were the only stone buildings in the city.

Not far from our house, the foundation of the court house was already laid, and the building, of brick, was completed the following summer.

Even then the bounds of the corporation were quite extensive, but the buildings except along Jefferson Avenue, were very scattering. There were but two church edifices in the city, the French cathedral, a massive stone structure, with five spires; and a small wooden church standing on the corner of Woodward Avenue and Larned Street, occupied by the Presbyterians. The Episcopalians worshiped in the old "council house," and the Baptists and Methodists in rooms hired for that

A view of Wind-Mill Point on the Detroit River in 1837.

purpose.

The greatest inconvenience felt the "down-easters" was the want of water; the only supply being from the river, and all the water used must be brought from the river in barrels by carmen, at an exorbitant price. Just think of drinking water, without ice, during the summer months, which had stood twenty-fours hours in a barrel.

A poor, but enterprising man by the name of Rufus Wells[9] originated the present extensive water works. He raised the water from the river to a reservoir on the bank, by *one-horsepower, literally,* and from thence it was carried in wooden logs over a small portion of the city. But his means were too limited for even the necessities of that time. He lost all, and other completed what his ingenuity and enterprise began.

About three hundred Indians, the remnants of two or three tribes, were constantly about the city during the day, trading away moccasins and baskets, and even their blankets for the white man's "fire water," and when hungry begging food at the house of the inhabitants. Toward evening they would begin to return to their wigwams in the forest, or "bush," as it was termed, all more or less intoxicated, and having to pass the scattered dwellings on the common, it was not unusual for us to be disturbed by their whoops and yells to a late hour of the night. My poor mother suffered much from fear of the Indians during the first year of our residence in Detroit.

I recollect one afternoon late in autumn, we saw a drunken Indian coming toward the house. Mother[10] dropped the widow shades and fastened the doors. We soon heard him trying to open the kitchen door; after a while he seemed to give up the attempt, and we thought he had gone, but scarcely had mother begun to breathe more freely, when the door flew open, and the great, powerful Indian, who had evidently tried the cooling effect of the wayside ditches, lay full-length on the clean floor. After lying some time, muttering to himself, he crawled along to the stove, leaving muddy marks of progress. Entreaties and threats were alike in vain to induce him to take leave. At last mother called to some French laborers who were passing, and begged their assistance. They listened to what she said, and then with a shrug of the shoulder and a muttered oath they passed on. Concluding the Frenchmen could not understand her, my mother sent for the sheriff who lived near us. He came immediately, and seizing the Indian by the collar, led him to the door, and very unceremoniously pitched him into the street.

Mr. Hunt laughed heartily when my mother told him the Frenchmen did not understand her. "Yes, they did understand you," said he, "but you have not lived long enough in Detroit to know that there are two classes of our French inhabitants. We have a class of polished and refined French people here, but the 'black French' as they are called, are said to be the descendants of intermarriages between the original French and Indians. They will never molest an Indian whatever he may be doing, though they themselves are perfectly inoffensive."

This explanation did not, of course, have a tendency to quiet my mother's fears; but a kind Providence has so constituted the human mind that it will become accustomed to almost any situation, and after a time my mother only regarded the Indians with emotions of compassion.

Old Fort Shelby[11] was still occupied by a small detachment of troops, and the morning and evening guns, and the cheerful reveille were quite enough to invest the fort with peculiar charms in the mind of an imaginative child. Our house was but a short distance outside the picketed fields, and the view of the green banks of the fort, the white cantonment, and the parading soldiers, marching to strains of exhilarating music was perfectly enchanting. A number of deaths occurred at the fort before the removal of the troops; their funeral services were very solemn. The departed was borne to his last resting place by his "companions in arms," marching to the mournful music of muffled drums, the coffin was lowered into the grave in oppressive silence, the solemn "burial service" committed "earth to earth and dust to dust," and volleys of minute guns were fired - a soldier's farewell.

In the summer of 1825, I think the troops were removed to Green Bay, and the fort and its adjoining ground speedily became a most delightful play ground for the children in the neighborhood. Often have my companions and myself, climbed up the steps made in the embankment at one corner of the fort, and enjoyed a romp around the top, then descending a few feet on the inside, we would run in the path of the sentinels, stop at every stand of the now dismantled cannon and peep through the port holes.

There were two or three log houses within the fort, and we used to wonder how the people could breathe shut up between the high green walls of the fort.

The first Sunday school I attended was in the old "council house," corner of Jefferson Avenue and Randolph Street. The rector was Rev. Mr. Cadle. After the removal of the troops he was appointed their chaplain, and left the city; and my sister and I commenced attending the Presbyterian Sunday school.

Mrs. Cass, was a devoted Christian, and a member of the Presbyterian Church, and every Sunday Governor Cass would bring his wife and daughters to church in an old fashioned cart, back the cart up to the church steps, unload his family, and drive away, coming for them at the close of the services. The governor like many another great man, seldom attended church. The calm, sweet face of Mrs. Cass, and her gentle manner, gave me my first impressions of the refining beauty of Christianity; for my parents, though strictly moral, did not become Christians until some years later.

The "Savoyard," a small stream in summer, and in the spring and autumn large enough to float canoes, was spanned by a bridge, on Woodward Avenue. I used to stop on the bridge on my home from school and watch the minnows in the bright clear water. What an ignominious fate awaited that beautiful stream; it is now the principal sewer of the city.

The market was a long shed like building, in the center of Woodward Avenue, extending from Jackson Avenue toward the river. Immense sturgeon were then caught in the river, below the city, and perhaps above, and were often landed on the sand at the foot of the avenue, below the market.

One day I saw a sturgeon so large that it was towed through the water, the boat would not hold it; and the strength of several men were needed to drag it on shore. I had never seen a sturgeon before, and was quite sure that this immense fish must be a *whale*.

When we had lived in Detroit two years we moved into a house on Jefferson Avenue, two doors from the old Campau house, and from our back piazza we had a fine view of the river. I never wearied of watching the white winged vessels as they sailed up and down the beautiful stream; the canoes paddled by the Canadian women bringing loads of fruit and vegetable to market, and the little sail boats tossing on the water. I wanted no other pastime. Every pleasant evening in summer, all along the river, canoes were launched, and gay parties rowed up and down the stream, meeting and exchanging salutations, or side by side trying the strength and speed of their oarsmen.

The large birch canoe of Gov. Cass with its crimson canopy in the center, was always an object of special attraction to the spectators on shore.

Just as the sun disappeared below the horizon, from some canoe would arise the sweet notes of the vesper hymn, one and another would catch the strain, till over the placid river floated waves of almost heavenly melody.

One song would succeed another, till the gathering shadows beckoned the happy hearted singers to their homes.

The original St. Anne's Church as built by Father Richard.

Detroit to Mackinac Island by Ship: 1830
by
Juliette Kinzie

We now turn to an account of a steam ship voyage from Detroit to Mackinac Island in 1830 and a description of life on the island during the heyday of the fur trade. The author, 24-year-old Juliette Augusta Magill Kinzie, had, the month previous to her voyage, married John H. Kinzie at her home in New Hartford, New York. Kinzie, agent of Indian Affairs at Fort Winnebago, east of present day Portage, Wisconsin, was escorting his bride to her new home at the fort where she would spend the succeeding three years. They had tarried for some time at Detroit, where Kinzie had many friends and relative, before embarking on the *Henry Clay,* a state of the art steamer and one of six vessels which comprised the Lake Erie Steamboat Line fleet.

Mrs. Kinzie's description of the voyage appeared as the first chapter of her *Wau-Bun,The "Early Day" in the North-West*, first published in New York in 1856. The remainder of the 498 page volume contains picturesque descriptions of Chicago, life at Fort Winnebago, Indian legends and a classic account of the Chicago massacre of 1812 which Kinzie heard from her mother-in-law and other survivors of the tragedy. One of the most popular mid western travel narratives, *Wau Bun* was reprinted many times in the 19th and 20th centuries.

A cultured and well educated woman, Mrs. Kinzie would become one of the leading members of Chicago society, where she and her husband settled in 1833. There they would achieve a modest fortune through the sale of the 102 acre family homestead in the form of lots in the Kinzie Addition.

Mrs. Kinzie had first ventured into print in 1844 with her anonymously published pamphlet,

Narrative of the Massacre at Chicago. This she also reprinted in *Wau Bun.* Following her husband's death in 1865, Kinzie published a novel, *Walter Ogilby* (Philadelphia, 1869). A second novel, *Mark Logan, the Bourgeois* (Philadelphia, 1887) appeared after her own death in 1870.

It was on a dark, rainy evening in the month of September, 1830, that we went on board the steamer *Henry Clay,* to take passage for Green Bay. All our friends in Detroit had congratulated us upon our good fortune in being spared the voyage in one of the little schooners, which at this time afforded the ordinary means of communication with the few and distant settlements on lakes Huron and Michigan.

Each one had some experience to relate of his own or of his friends' mischances in these precarious journeys - long detentions on the St. Clair flats - furious head winds off Thunder Day, or interminable calms at Mackinac or the Manitous. That which most enhanced our sense of peculiar good luck, was the true story of one of our relatives having left Detroit in the month of June and reaching Chicago in the September following, having been actually three months in performing what is sometimes accomplished by even a sail vessel in four days.

But the certainty of encountering similar misadventures would have weighed little with me. I was now to visit, nay more, to become a resident of that land which had, for long years, been to me a region of romance. Since the time when, as a child, my highest delight had been in the letters of a dear relative [12] describing to me his home and mode of life in the "Indian country," and still later, in his felicitous narration of a tour with General Cass, in 1820, to the sources of the Mississippi - nay, even earlier, in the days when I stood at my teacher's knee, and spelled out the long word Mich-i-li-mack-i-nac, that distant land, with its vast lakes, its boundless prairies, and its mighty forests, had possessed a wonderful charm for my imagination. Now I was to see it - it was to be my home!

Our ride to the quay, through the dark by-ways, in a cart, the only vehicle which at that day could navigate the muddy, unpaved streets of Detroit, was a theme for much merriment, and not less so, our descent of the narrow, perpendicular stair-way by which we reached the little apartment called the ladies' cabin. We were highly delighted with the accommodations, which, by comparison, seemed the very climax of comfort and convenience; more especially as the occupants of the cabin consisted, beside myself, of but a lady and two little girls.

Nothing could exceed the pleasantness of our trip for the first twenty-four hours. There were some officers, old friends, among the passengers. We had plenty of books. The gentlemen read aloud occasionally, admired the solitary magnificence of the scenery around us, the primeval woods, or the vast expanse of water unenlivened by a single sail, and then betook themselves to their cigar, or their game of eucre, to while away the hours.

For a time the passage over Thunder Bay was delightful, but alas! it was not destined, in our favor, to belie its name. A storm came on, fast and furious - what was worse, it was of long duration. The pitching and rolling of the little boat, the closeness, and even the sea sickness, we bore as became us. They were what we had expected, and were prepared for. But a new feature of discomfort appeared, which almost upset our philosophy.

The rain, which fell in torrents, soon made its way through every seam and pore of deck or moulding. Down the stair-way, through the joints and crevices, it came, saturating first the carpet, then the bedding, until finally we were completely driven, "by stress of weather," into the gentlemen's cabin. Way was made for us very gallantly, and every provision resorted to for our comfort, and we were congratulating ourselves on having found a haven in our distress, when lo! the seams above opened, and down upon our devoted heads poured such a flood, that even umbrellas were insufficient protection. There was nothing left for the ladies and children but to betake ourselves to the berths, which in this apartment, fortunately remained dry; and here we continued ensconced the live long day. Our dinner was served up to us on our pillows. The gentlemen chose the dryest spots, raised their umbrellas, and sat under them, telling amusing anecdotes, and saying funny things to cheer us until the rain ceased, and at nine o'clock in the evening we were gladdened by the intelligence that we had reached the pier at Mackinac.

We were received with the most affectionate cordiality by Mr. and Mrs. Robert Stuart, 13 at whose hospitable mansion we had been for some days expected.

The repose and comfort of an asylum like this, can be best appreciated by those who have reached it after a tossing and drenching such as ours had been. A bright, warm fire, and countenances beaming with kindest interest, dispelled all sensations of fatigue or annoyance.

After a season of pleasant conversation, the servants were assembled, the chapter of God's word was solemnly read, the hymn chanted, the prayer of praise and thanksgiving offered, and we were conducted to our place of repose.

It is not my purpose here to attempt a portrait of those noble friends whom I thus met for the first time. To an abler pen than mine, should be assigned the honor of writing the biography of Robert Stuart. All who have enjoyed the happiness of his acquaintance, or still more, a sojourn under his hospitable roof, will carry with them, to their last hour, the impression of his noble bearing, his genial humor, his untiring benevolence, his upright, uncompromising adherence to principle, his ardent philanthropy, his noble disinterestedness. Irving[14] in his "Astoria," and Franchere[15] in his "Narrative," give many striking traits of his early character, together with events of his history of a thrilling and romantic interest, but both have left the most valuable portion unsaid, his after-life, namely, as a Christian gentleman.

MICHILIMACKINAC! that gem of the Lakes! How bright and beautiful it looked as we walked abroad on the following morning! The rain had passed away, but had left all things glittering in the light of the sun as it rose up over the water of Lake Huron, far away to the east. Before us was the lovely bay, scarcely yet tranquil after the storm, but dotted with canoes and the boats of the fishermen already getting their nets for the trout and whitefish, those treasures of the deep. Along the beach were scattered the wigwams or lodges of the Ottawas who had come to the island to trade. The inmates came forth to gaze upon us. A shout of welcome was sent forth, as they recognized Shaw-nee-aw-kee,[16] who from a seven years' residence among them, was well known to each individual.

A shake of the hand, and an emphatic "Bon-jour bon-jour," is the customary salutation between the Indian and the white man.

"Do the Indians speak French?" I inquired of my husband. "No; this is a fashion they have learned of the French traders during many years of intercourse."

This early woodcut view of Mackinac Island appeared in *Harper's Magazine.*

Not less hearty was the greeting of each Canadian engage' as he trotted forward to pay his respects to "Monsieur John," and to utter a long string of felicitations, in a most incomprehensible *patois*. I was forced to take for granted all the good wishes showered upon "Madame John," of which I could comprehend nothing but the hope that I should be happy and contented in my "vie sauvage."

The object of our early walk was to visit the Mission-house and school which had been some few years previously established at this place, by the Presbyterian Board of Missions. It was an object of especial interest to Mr. and Mrs. Stuart, and its flourishing condition at this period, and the prospects of extensive future usefulness it held out, might well gladden their philanthropic hearts. They had lived many years on the island, and had witnessed its transformation, through God's blessing on Christian efforts, from a worldly, dissipated community to one of which it might almost be said, "Religion was every man's business." This mission establishment was the beloved child and the common centre of interest of the few Protestant families clustered around it. Through the zeal and good management of Mr. and Mrs. Ferry,[17] and the fostering encouragement of the congregation, the school was in great repute, and it was pleasant to observe the effect of mental and religious culture in subduing the mischievous, tricky propensities of the half-breed, and rousing the stolid apathy of the genuine Indian.

These were the palmy days of Mackinac.[18] As the headquarters of the American Fur Company, and the entrepot of the whole North-West, all the trade in supplies and goods on the one hand, and in furs and products of the Indian country on the other, was in the hands of the parent establishment or its numerous outposts scattered along lakes Superior and Michigan, the Mississippi, or through still more distant regions.

Probably few are ignorant of the fact, that all the Indian tribes, with the exception of the Miamis and the Wyandots, had, since the transfer of the old French possessions to the British Crown, maintained a firm alliance with the latter. The independence achieved by the United States did not alter the policy of the natives, nor did our government succeed in winning or purchasing their friendship. Great Britain, it is true, bid high to retain them. Every year the leading men of the Chippewas, Ottawas, Potawatamies, Menomonees, Winnebagoes, Sauks and Foxes, and even still more remote tribes, journeyed from their distant homes to Fort Malden [19] in Upper Canada, to receive their annual amount of presents from their Great Father across the water. It was a master policy thus to keep them in pay, and had enabled those who practised it to do fearful execution through the aid of such allies in the last war between the two countries.

The presents they thus received were of considerable value, consisting of blankets, broadcloths or *strouding,* calicoes, guns, kettles, traps, silver works (comprising arm-bands, bracelets, brooches, and earbobs), looking glasses, combs and various other trinkets distributed with no niggardly hand.

The magazines and store houses of the fur company were the resort of all the upper tribes for the purchase of all such articles as they had need of, including, those above enumerated, and also ammunition, which, as well as money and liquor, their British friends very commendably omitted to furnish them.

Besides their furs, various in kind and often of great value - beaver, otter, marten, mink, silver-gray and red fox, wolf, bear, and wild cat, musk-rat, and smoked deer skins - the Indians brought for trade maple sugar in abundance, considerable quantities of both Indian corn and petit-ble, [20] beans and the folles avoines, [21] or wild rice, while the squaws added to their quota of merchandize a contribution in the form of moccasins, hunting pouches, mococks, or little boxes of birch bark embroidered with porcupine quills and filled with maple sugar, mats of a neat and durable fabric, and toy models of Indian cradles, snow shoes, canoes, etc., etc.

It was no unusual thing, at this period, to see a hundred or more canoes of Indians at once approaching the island, laden with their articles of traffic; and if to these we add the squadrons of large Mackinac boats constantly arriving from the outposts, with the furs, peltries, and buffalo-robes collected by the distant traders, some idea may be formed of the extensive operations and important position of the American Fur Company, as well as of the vast circle of human beings either immediately or remotely connected with it.

It is no wonder that the philanthropic mind, surveying these races of uncultivated heathen, should stretch forward to the time when, by an unwearied devotion of the white man's energies, and an untiring sacrifice of self and fortune, his red brethren might rise in the scale of social civilization, when Education and Christianity should go hand in hand, to make "the wilderness blossom as the rose."

Little did the noble souls at this day rejoicing in the success of their labors at Mackinac, anticipate that in less than a quarter of a century there would remain of all these numerous tribes but a few scattered bands, squalid, degraded, with scarce a vestige remaining of their former lofty character, their lands cajoled or wrested from them, the graves of their fathers turned up by the ploughshare, themselves chased farther and farther towards the setting sun, until they were literally grudged a resting place on the face of the earth! [22]

Our visit to the Mission school was of short duration, for the *Henry Clay* was to leave at two o'clock, and in the meantime we were to see what we could of the village and its environs, and after that, dine with Mr. Mitchell, an old friend of my husband. As we walked leisurely along over the white gravelly road, many of the residences of the old inhabitants were pointed out to me. There was the dwelling of Madame Laframboise, an Ottawa woman,[23] whose husband had taught her to read and write, and who had ever after continued to use the knowledge she had acquired for the instruction and improvement of the youth among her own people. It was her custom to receive a class of young pupils daily at her house, that she might give them lessons in the branches mentioned, and also in the principles of the Roman Catholic religion, to which she was deeply devoted. She was a woman of a vast deal of energy and enterprise, of a tall and commanding figure, and most dignified deportment. After the death of her husband, who was killed while away at his trading post by a Winnebago named White Ox, she was accustomed to visit herself the trading posts, superintend the clerks and engages, and satisfy herself that the business was carried on in a regular and profitable manner.

The Agency-house, with its unusual luxuries of piazza and gardens, was situated at the foot of the hill on which the fort was built. It was a lovely spot, notwithstanding the stunted and dwarfish appearance of all cultivated vegetation in this cold northern latitude.

The collection of rickety, primitive looking buildings, occupied by the officials of the fur company, reflected no great credit on the architectural skill of my husband, who had superintended their construction, he told me, when little more than a boy.

There were, besides these, the residences of the

Dousmans, the Abbotts, the Biddles, the Drews, and the Lashleys,[24] stretching away along the base of the beautiful hill, crowned with the white walls and buildings of the fort, the ascent to which was so steep, that on the precipitous face nearest the beach staircases were built by which to mount from below.

My head ached intensely, the effect of the motion of the boat on the previous day, but I did not like to give up to it; so after I had been shown all that could be seen of the little settlement in the short time allowed us, we repaired to Mr. Mitchell's.

We were received by Mrs. Mitchell, an extremely pretty, delicate woman, part French and part Sioux, whose early life had been passed at Prairie du Chien, on the Mississippi. She had been a great belle among the young officers at Fort Crawford;[25] so much so, indeed, that the suicide of the post surgeon was attributed to an unsuccessful attachment he had conceived for her. I was greatly struck with her soft and gentle manners, and the musical intonation of her voice, which I soon learned was a distinguishing peculiarity of those women in whom are united the French and native blood.

A lady, then upon a visit to the mission, was of the company. She insisted on my lying down upon the sofa, and ministered most kindly to my suffering head. As she sat by my side, and expatiated upon the new sphere opening before me, she inquired:

"Do you not realize very strongly the entire deprivation of religious privileges you will be obliged to suffer in your distant home?"

"The deprivation," said I, "will doubtless be great, but not entire; for I shall have my prayer book, and though destitute of a church, we need not be without a mode of worship."

How often afterwards, when cheered by the consolations of this precious book in the midst of the lonely wilderness, did I remember this conversation, and bless God that I could never, while retaining it, be without "religious privileges."

We had not yet left the dinner table, when the bell of the little steamer sounded to summon us on board, and we bade a hurried farewell to all our kind friends, bearing with us their hearty wishes for a safe and prosperous voyage.

A finer sight can scarcely be imagined than Mackinac, from the water. As we steamed away from the shore, the view came full upon us, the sloping beach with the scattered wigwams, and canoes drawn up here and there, the irregular, quaint looking houses, the white walls of the fort, and beyond one eminence still more lofty, crowned with the remains of old Fort Holmes. [26] The whole picture completed, showed the perfect outline that had given the island its original Indian name, Mich-i-li-mack-i-nac, the Big Turtle.

As we passed the extreme western point of the island, my husband pointed out to me, far away to the north west, a promontory which he told me was Point St. Ignace. It possessed great historic interest, as one of the earliest white settlements on this continent. The Jesuit missionaries had established here a church and school as early as 1607, the same year in which a white settlement was made at St. Augustine, in Florida, and one year before the founding of Jamestown, Virginia. [27]

All that remains of the enterprises of these devoted men, is the remembrance of their labors, perpetuated, in most instances, only by the names of the spots which witnessed their efforts of love in behalf of their savage brethren. The little French church at Sandwich, opposite Detroit, alone is left, a witness of the zeal and self sacrifice of these pioneers of Christianity.

Passing "Old Mackinac," on the main land, which forms the southern border of the straits, we soon came out into the broad waters of Lake Michigan. Every traveller, and every reader of our history, is familiar with the incidents connected with the taking of the old fort by the Indians, in the days of Pontiac, How, by means of a game of ball, played in an apparently friendly spirit outside the walls, and of which the officers and soldiers had come forth to be spectators, the ball was dexterously tossed over the wall, and the savages rushing in, under pretext of finding it, soon got possession and massacred the garrison. [28]

The little Indian village L'Arbre Croche gleamed far away south, in the light of the setting sun. With that exception, their was no sign of living habitation along the vast and wooded shore. The gigantic forest trees, and here and there the little glades of prairie opening to the water, showed a landscape that would have gladdened the eye of the agriculturist, with its promise of fertility; but it was evidently untrodden by the foot of man, and we left it, in its solitude, as we took our course westward across the waters.

The rainy and gusty weather, so incident to the equinoctial season, overtook us again before we reached the mouth of Green Bay, and kept us company until the night of our arrival upon the flats, about three miles below the settlement.

Here the little steamer grounded "fast and hard." As almost every one preferred braving the elements to remaining cooped up in the quarters we had occupied for the past week, we decided to trust ourselves to the little boat, spite of wind, rain, and darkness, and in due time we reached the shore.

The Indians pitched their teepees on the beach at Mackinac Island when they arrived there for annual treaty payments.

Jackson to Cass County by Horseback: 1835
by
An Unknown Diarist

In 1852, Elizabeth Ellet published *Pioneer Women of the West,* "the story of the wives and mothers who ventured into the western wilds and bore their part in the struggles and labors of the early pioneers." The compilation contains much of Michigan interest including the following extract from a woman's diary kept during a horseback trip with her husband across southern Michigan in 1835. Unfortunately, Ellet does not name the author of the diary, noting only that she is "a highly gifted and accomplished lady, now residing in the western part of New York." Despite that frustrating omission, an extract is included here because it offers a classic account of life on the Michigan frontier as witnessed by a sensitive and articulate observer.

Ellet herself was one of America's most prolific female writers of her era. Born Elizabeth Fries in Sodus Point, New York, in 1818, she received her education at the Aurora, New York, female academy. Following her marriage to chemistry professor William Henry Ellet in 1835, she began to write for periodicals. Her best known work, *Women of the American Revolution* appeared in three volumes in 1851. *Pioneer Women of the West* was written as a sequel to carry forward the story of heroic women's contributions to the development of America. Over a literary career which spanned five decades, Ellet would produce nearly 20 volumes of poetry, history, biography, travel narratives, and in particular works about women.

Bronson[29] (now Kalamazoo), May 28th, 1835. Owing to the uniform progress of journeying day after day from Jacksonburgh[30] to Marshall, a distance of thirty-six, and from Marshall hence, of thirty-seven miles, 'the little lines of yesterday' have well nigh faded without being noticed. The memory of the beautiful, and of such beauty - a forest in its wildness - is so much more powerful than distinct, and having the same characteristics, presents so much uniformity that but little record can be made. On our route we passed over some twenty miles through the wild woods, without seeing a human being. The foliage was just bursting from its numberless sheaths into rich drapery, our pathway was literally strewn with flowers, the horses pressing them at every step, while the birds in their leafy homes, deluged the otherwise unbroken stillness with wild and delicious melody. The silence of the deep forest, during the brief intervals of these untaught lays seems strangely oppressive; yet ere you can analyze its unwonted power, earth's lyre, with its myriad tones, is struck again, and you are roused to the liveliest sympathy. I had somewhat the feeling of Milton's Eve, differently applied. She asked, 'Wherefore all night long shine these? My heart-query was, 'Wherefore all this wealth of varied note and strain? But the same answered, 'These feathered songsters know of home, and love, and sweet companionship, and joyously give thanks for gift of being, telling to each other, and to Him who made them, of the blessing of life.' 31

This day we first saw the Kalamazoo River32 a narrow, dark stream. We stopped at a small log cabin, which on its shingle sign advertised 'Entertainment for man and beast;' doubtless after the fashion of the settlements the proprietors had left, and we were grateful for any shelter from the noonday sun. I noticed, while sitting in an inner room, to which, as a lady traveller, I was ceremoniously conducted, that the landlord eyed my husband with singular, yet irresolute attention. I did not fancy, however, that he had ever seen him before. He was an odd looking personage; rather slight in his general proportions, and short in stature; he had large, prominent features, overshadowed by a shock of coarse yellow hair, faded and worn, that gave him a wild and savage aspect, particularly as this hair and his complexion seemed scarcely to vary a shade in tint. After repeated advances, accompanied with stolen and hurried glances at my husband, he rushed out from his so called bar, and broke out into a sort of earnest thanksgiving, blessing him for having ejected him from one of the small pieces of land contracted to settlers in western New York. He went on to say that he did not at first recognize him, but he did now, and could tell him that sending him from that farm was one of the best things that ever happened to him; that after he was sent away because he could not pay a cent on his land, he came to this place, and would not give ten acres of it for fifty like that he left in the State of New York. Setting aside the intrinsic value so earnestly put forth, this new and much prized possession was truly a beautiful spot. The dark current of the river was rushing with arrowy swiftness past the trail on which he had piled his log dwelling. A fine piece of rising ground formed the back ground, which was imperfectly subdued by cultivation, while a little to the west a scene lay revealed that might do for a glimpse of fairy land. A small lake, with its sparkling waters, reposed like a jewel in its dark green setting. The forest, on the one side, was enlivened with the luxuriance of the dogwood, now in full blossom as far as the eye could reach. The large white flowers dispensed in such profusion, gave more the aspect of a boundless garden of lilies, than the unsuspected treasures of an uncultivated wilderness. There were clear openings on the other side, the meadow-like ground being just sprinkled with trees, as if arrayed for picturesque landscape beauty, affording wider vistas from the foliage only making itself seen in delicate tracery, not being yet quite unfolded. 'Many an elf and many a fay here might hold their pastime gay.'

Our landlady for the hour seemed to share fully her husband's feelings of self-gratulation, though she told me it was pretty hard times when they had to live in and under their ox wagon during the early spring days, while the logs were felled and put up for their home. This log house would be quite an object of interest to persons unaccustomed to the pristine dwellings of the western territories. It seemed to consist of three distinct buildings, probably put up at different periods, to meet the increasing demands of ambition as prosperity more abounded. What was evidently the first pile of logs, was used as a bar room of the roughest construction. This also served as a counter for the ready change business of this much frequented inn. The boards, or rather planks of the floor, were hewn, and laid down so unequally as to be perilous to an unwary or even rapid step. Directly in the rear was the kitchen, in which the culinary implements and table necessaries were arranged, evidently with an attempt at order without the recognized law thereunto of anything in heaven or earth. The cooking apparatus was so simple, and the vessels for various uses so few in number, as to excite my wonder and admiration at woman's homely tact and skill; and wayworn traveller though I was, the preparation for our noonday meal was almost as engrossing as the partaking there of after it was prepared. A third division of the house served as a parlor for our hostess, and as an occasional bedroom for 'special people'- a phrase which I found quite current as a designation for the more fastidious class of travellers, who now began to pass through this hitherto almost unknown territory. Above the main part of these buildings extended a sort of garret, lighted by a window of four small panes in one end, and the opening of the ladder way the only mode of entrance. This was the dormitory of India rubber like capacity for the multitudes who in this season of land speculation, did here nightly congregate.

On the fifth of June, we pursued our journey toward the southeastern part of the territory, intending to take a look at Lake Michigan from the mouth of the St. Joseph's River. Our way lay through forests and openings similar to those through which we had passed for days, but afterwards we struck into the more heavily timbered land, which the growth of the advancing season had clad with cumbrous garments of foliage, closing up the vistas of beauty and light; in places denying the summer sun its right to rest upon the flowers and shrubs it had but lately warmed into being. At nearly noon, we came upon the edge of a large prairie,[33] the largest in the territory, which although much smaller than those spread farther westward, had still all the distinctive features of those vast and undulating plains. The landscape was expanded and beautiful, and yet one can scarcely make intelligible the penetrating sentiment of its beauty. Perhaps the first influence consisted in the sense of relief from the pent up feeling we had experienced in the close pressure as it were, of the deep, dark forest from which we emerged. In the centre of this plain was a collection of innumerous boughs like an island in the midst of circling waters. The prairie was begirt by a belt of timbered land, though the outline was so dim in the distance, as rather to look like a lazy cloud resting for support upon the verge of the horizon. We gave our horses the reins, and they cantered merrily across the rich plain, the whole covered in this early summer with short and close grass. Innumerable flowers raised their variegated heads between the tiny meshes of network woven by the wild pea, while the butterflies, with their bright tints and quick fluttering wings, were perpetually upspringing, startled by our approach. After crossing the prairie we again struck into the forest, having previously stopped at the island inn[34] for some refreshment.

Towards evening, as was our wont, we felt that we must

look along our way for some lodging for the night. Our custom had been, except in the villages, not to seek accommodation at the inns scattered at irregular distance along the road. The new settlers continually moving in toward their purchases, and the number of speculators in pursuit of locations on which to raise, no dwellings, but future fortunes, so completely filled them up, as to render it an impossibility to find for a lady even momentary seclusion, much less repose. Our practice was as soon as we found the shadows beginning to lengthen, to stop at the first decent log house and ask for a drink of water. Getting the water afforded time and opportunity for reconnoitering; and if the tin cup or basin in which the draught was offered looked clean, and the premises in any way inviting by comparison, we made the request that we could be accommodated for the night. We had not on this evening seen any houses, the tract of country through which we had been passing for some hours being without settlement.

On coming up to some woodmen whose gleaming axes told that their whereabouts was near at hand, we stopped, and after exchanging mutual glances of inquiry, my husband asked if they could tell us where we could find a tavern? They looked at each other and then askance at us. The question was repeated again; they looked bewildered, when my husband thoughtfully changed his phrase and said 'Where can I stay tonight, and have good care taken of my horse?' The answer then came quickly 'Oh, at Nicholas B_'s, the Hooshier's, he has a first rate place, and takes in every night a great many folks.' We made two or three further inquiries and passed on, with our expectations considerably raised in prospect of the promised accommodation.

Just after sunset, we reached the place designated by the woodman, and peering through the gloaming, I espied a good-sized frame barn, with an enclosure, and all the appearance of a well stocked barn and rick. I fairly screamed with delight, so important to our further journey was the welfare of our horses, and so certain did the indication seem of a comfortable resting place for my own wearied limbs. We soon came out of the forest, upon the edge of a small prairie;[35] there stood the barn in very truth, but I looked around in vain for the house which I had pictured in such glowing colors to myself, as presenting some comparison in size and comfort to the barn. A sudden chill of loneliness came over us. There lay the prairie, about three hundred acres in extent, shrubless and bare, except the patches of recent cultivation, which however, in the dim light, gave but little indication of richness or growth. The trees shut us in completely, and after traversing the deep forest as we had been for hours, we could not even let imagination picture a livelier or brighter scene beyond. Night came rapidly on, while we stood baffled, without a present sign of human existence. Our horses had for a mile or two been lagging perhaps in memory of the morning scamper and noon-day refreshment; and now the whole group seemed peculiarly sensible of the influence of solitude, which in us soon resolved itself into utter dreariness. A fresh glance of scrutiny, however, enabled us to descry a very small hut jutting into the woods, as uninviting a log house as we had seen in all our wanderings. We both looked at it for some moments without speaking, so completely paralyzed were all our high raised expectations. I then exclaimed, 'We cannot stay in that hovel.' But fastidiousness was soon displaced by eagerness with me, when my husband calmly said 'We must find shelter there or in the barn, for no further can we go to-night.' We urged our horses to the door; a well stood directly in front of it, a rare treasure in a new settlement, and after grateful notice of this, my husband entered the dwelling. He asked the woman civilly, 'if she could accommodate us for the night.' Her answer came quick in utterance and shrill in tone. 'I suppose I shall have to, any way.' Such was our welcome. But necessity here giving no scope to pride, or even wonted self-respect, obliged me to dismount and receive the favor so grudgingly bestowed. The woman was perhaps about thirty years of age, plain in feature, and old fashioned beyond my memory in attire. Her dress was a thick striped material, woven to defy time and its ravages. It was unlike any fabric to which I had been accustomed. It fitted the figure almost closely, low in the neck, with sleeves just coming below the elbow. The dress was extremely short waisted, without a particle of fullness in the skirt, save the ordinary plaiting just behind essential to convenience. She had on no shoes or stockings, and a faded bandana handkerchief was tied loose knot around her neck. Her hair was bound straight about her head, and fastened with some sort of a metal comb, just large enough to perform its office.

On my entrance a wooden chair was handed me, after being hurriedly dusted; it was low and rickety, but it instantly bestowed the promise of rest, which I so much craved after sitting so many hours in the saddle. My husband, without entering the hut, went on the woman's vague direction to find the landlord, that our horses, whose prospects of accommodation were so far beyond ours, might speedily receive attention. As soon as he was gone, I essayed an acquaintance with my hostess, and soon believed that her want of courtesy at our reception proceeded more from a fear of not being able to make us comfortable, than from vexation at the present trouble. Two children, the eldest of them not more than two year of age, divided her care with the present bustle of preparing a meal and entertaining me by rapid talking. Her face became almost pleasant with the interest it soon showed in transforming me into a newspaper, from which she could extract without much trouble the information desired by woman, let her nook of the world be ever so obscure, or her connection with the things without ever so slight. I had in my daily progress become quite used to this sort of questioning, and in some instances had to make my tarrying a lasting memorial of usefulness, by drawing patterns of certain garments, collars, caps, etc., with a coal on the floor or table, where paper could not be had, so that when cloth could be procured the latest mode might be used in its fashioning. While thus engaged in conversation, growing in self importance every moment, and quite forgetting that I was an unwished for guest, I took a survey of the house. It was, of course, built of logs, fourteen feet by sixteen; its sides five feet six inches in height, and the roof covered with strips of bark. A few scattering boards made the floor. It had not the ordinary stick and round chimney common to log houses, but a sort of box was made of split logs at one end of the room; this was filled in with dirt and ashes, and the fire built in the centre of it. An opening in the ill-made roof permitted the smoke to find egress, though occasional puffs during the process of getting supper, advised us of its loitering presence. After my survey of the room itself, I began to take notice of the furniture, and more especially of its sleeping facilities. Two bedsteads, each sustained by one post - quite an anomaly in my previous experience of cabinet furniture; a large chest, which had evidently borne journeying when the essay at house-keeping was made away from the paternal home; a small box of home manufacture, and some other absolute essentials to the wants of even the poorest dwelling, constituted its wealth. I must add a note of description of the bedsteads. Two sides were formed by the projection of the logs of which the hut was made into the room; the one post supported the other two pieces,

41

which were on the other ends inserted into the sides of the house. Feather beds were heaped high upon them, and these were covered with blue and white woolen coverlets, doubtless part of the portion brought by the young wife to her husband. Small pillows, with clean looking cotton pillow cases, completed their decoration.

I had noticed that my hostess, during her bustle and constant chat with me, had gone frequently to the door, and looked anxiously into the increasing darkness, I of course supposed from no other motive than a desire to find out whether my husband had found hers, and secured attention for our horses. But not so interested was she in her stranger guests. At another visit to the low door, her anxiety could not be restrained, and she exclaimed, 'I wonder where my children can be! They ought to have been here more than an hour ago; they are always out of the way when I want them.' I looked aghast. More children! How many - how old! What could be done with them! I had been puzzling myself to know how six of us could be accommodated in the two beds, and in this tiny room; and now an indefinite number to be expected, how could we be made even tolerably comfortable? Speculation - quiet though it was - was soon to be ended by more precise apprehension, when four children, three boys and a girl, came rushing from the woods into the house, animated by all the buoyancy of hungry little mortals just liberated from a day's confinement and control. It being quite dark without, the light, small as it was within the dwelling, formed a strong contrast, and the little urchins were so suddenly arrested upon perceiving a stranger, that they stood like so many statues, incapable of thought or movement. The remonstrance of the mother quickly restored them, and then began importunate demands for something to eat. Thus there were six children, the father and mother, with ourselves, to be stowed away for the night. It was in vain for me to speculate upon the probable disposition of these numbers, so trusting as I had often done before to the elastic capabilities of these log houses, I determined to bide my time.

Our host came in with my husband, both bending low in passing through the door. My husband gave a wistful glance at me, and seemed reassured when a widened rather than a lengthened face was turned upon him. Truth to tell, I was almost convulsed with laughter at some of the previous proceedings of my hostess. The ill jointed planks which served for our floor, were quickly brushed hither and thither with an Indian broom (made of wood finely splintered); the flying dust seeming to have no particular destination, save to seek new places of deposit. The children were repeatedly hushed and pushed into sundry nooks and corners, while the cooking of the supper went on. The little urchins peered at the stranger, and anon played tricks with each other, when a sudden burst, caused by outbreaking mischief, would occasion a new effort at quieting. In process of time our supper was served, and ere long we gathered to the meal. The table was an oaken plank, supported by three stout sticks put into bored holes, for legs. A table cloth being altogether a superfluous luxury, we dispensed with it; some bread, baked in an open kettle, pork fried in the same utensil, and tea with maple sugar, formed the variety presented to us. Neither milk or butter were afforded, and yet we were at a regular house of entertainment, kept by a large landed proprietor. Strange to say, the meal was quite palatable, eaten with a healthful appetite after a day's ride on horseback of some thirty-five miles. Soon after tea, the children being fed by pieces put into their hands during the time we were supping, I ventured to hint, that as I was very tired I should like to go to bed. The woman went to the chest which I had before noticed, took out two clean sheets, spread them upon one of the feather beds, and again put on the woolen coverlet, although it was a June night, a fire burning briskly, and ten persons were to inhabit the small apartment. Immediately after the bed was prepared, the hostess said in an authoritative tone to her husband, 'Nicholas, the lady wishes to go to bed; turn your face to the wall.' Nicholas, as if accustomed to this nightly drill, wheeled swiftly about and stood as still as if suddenly become one of the scanty articles of furniture.

This said Nicholas looked somewhat like a barbarian, his bushy head and unshaven beard presenting quite a wild appearance. He however seemed intelligent enough for his locality and business, and took most excellent care of our horses.. My toilet for the night was very speedily made, and I threw myself on the bed, having first removed the odious coverlet. Still no new developments were made in reference to the accommodation of the youthful group; ere long, however, sundry signs of sleepiness appeared, betokened by fretfulness and some quarrelling, and then the mother proceeded to lift out two trundle beds made of pieces of board nailed together. The absence of rollers made the operation rather laborious, but the husband and father vouchsafed not his aid. It was finally done by the woman alone, and into these five of the little ones were speedily placed. Very soon after, the dim, flickering light was put out, and we were left utterly abandoned, as I feared, to suffocation. I remonstrated decidedly against the shutting of the door, but was told there was fear of the wolves; and indeed before morning our ears were saluted with the shrill, though somewhat smothered howl of these prowlers of the forest. I bore the heat and bad air for several hours, and then in desperation for want of a pure breath, I commenced picking the chinking out from between the logs at the side of the bed, and in this way secured for myself a breathing place, amid the enjoyment of which I fell asleep, and awaked not until the broad sunbeams were laughing in my face.

Elizabeth Ellet in 1850.

Detroit to Michigan City by Stage: 1836
by
Harriet Martineau

Two major roads traversed southern Michigan during the pioneer era. The southern most route, which approximated the present course of US-12, was begun in 1825. Known as the Military Road or the Chicago Road, it linked Detroit with Fort Dearborn. The other immigrant highway laid out in 1830 was known as the Territorial Road. It branched off the Chicago Road at Ypsilanti and followed close to the present I-94 to its terminus at St. Joseph.

By 1835 stagecoaches provided transportation from Detroit to Chicago. The following summer Harriet Martineau climbed aboard a stagecoach at Detroit and set off on a ride across the territory on the Chicago Road.

The description she penned of her experiences demonstrated that a stage journey on Michigan's abominable roads was little better, if not worse, than horseback travel.

Martineau, a sophisticated British literary lady, toured much of America in 1835 and 1836. She recorded her impressions in *Society in America* (2 vols. London, 1837) and *Retrospect of Western Travel* (3 vols. London, 1838). Ralph L. Rusk, author of *The Literature of the Middle Western Frontier* (New York, 1925) observed that her books "contained probably the most important view of the West by an English author during the last years of the pioneer period." Yet because she was outspokenly critical of much of what she saw during her travels, her books wounded the vanity of many Americans.

Born in Norwich, England, in 1802, Martineau suffered an unhappy childhood. Her parents were ultra-religious and Puritanically suppressive, and she was born without the sense of smell and taste. At the age of twelve she began loosing her hearing and as she became increasingly deaf resorted to the use of a huge ear trumpet. She began writing religious articles when she was in her early 20s. A series she wrote on political economy in the early 1830s first won her a popular following. During the remainder of her life she published scores of volumes of children's stories, religious essays, history, biography, political economy, morals, tour guides and travel narratives. With the exception of the latter, most have been long forgotten. Yet during her lifetime her writings enjoyed tremendous popularity. It has been said that she was "the perfect expression of her age," the Victorian era, that is.

The selection which follows appeared in *Retrospect of Western Travel.*

We landed at Detroit, from Lake Erie, at seven o'clock in the morning of the 13th of June, 1836. We reached the American[36] just in time for breakfast. At that long table, I had the pleasure of seeing the healthiest set of faces that I had beheld since I left England. The breakfast was excellent, and we were served with much consideration: but the place was so full, and the accommodations of Detroit are so insufficient for the influx of people who are betaking themselves thither, that strangers must patiently put up with much delay and inconvenience till new houses of entertainment are opened. We had to wait till near one o'clock before any of us could have a room in which to dress; but I had many letters to write, and could wait; and before I had done, Charley[37] came with his shining face and clean collar, to show me that accommodation had been provided. In the afternoon, we saw what we could of the place, and walked by the side of the full and tranquil river St. Clair.[38] The streets of the town are wide and airy; but the houses, churches, and stores, are poor for the capital city of a Territory or State. This is a defect which is presently cured, in the stirring northern regions of the United States. Wooden planks, laid on the grass, form the pavement in all the outskirts of the place. The deficiency is of stone, not of labour. Thousands of settlers are pouring in every year: and of these, many are Irish, Germans or Dutch, working their way into the back country; and glad to be employed for a while at Detroit, to earn money to carry them further. Paving stones will be imported here I suppose, as I saw them at New Orleans, to the great improvement of the health and comfort of the place. The block wood pavement, of which trial has been made in a part of Broadway, New York, is thought likely to answer better at Detroit than any other kind, and is going to be tried.

The country round Detroit is as flat as can be imagined; and indeed, it is said that the highest mountain in the state boasts only sixty feet of elevation. A lady of Detroit once declared, that if she were to build a house in Michigan, she would build a hill first. The Canada side of the river looks dull enough from the city; but I cannot speak from a near view of it, having been disappointed in my attempts to get over to it. On one occasion, we were too late for the ferry boat; and we never had time again for the excursion.

A cool wind from the northern lakes blows over the whole face of the country, in the midst of the hottest days of summer: and in the depth of winter, the snow never lies deep, nor long. These circumstances may partly account for the healthiness of the row of faces at the table of the American.

The society of Detroit is very choice; and, as it has continued so since the old colonial days, through the territorial days. There is every reason to think that it will become, under its new dignities, a more and more desirable place of residence. Some of its inferior society is still very youthful; a gentleman, for instance, saying in the reading-room, in the hearing of one of our party, that though it did not sound well at a distance, lynching was the only way to treat Abolitionists: but the most enlightened society is I believe, equal to any which is to be found in the United States. Here we began to see some of the half-breeds, of whom we afterwards met so many at the north. They are the children of white men who have married squaws; and may be known at a glance, not only by the dark complexion, but by the high cheek-bones, straight black hair, and an indescribable mischievous expression about the eyes. I never saw such imps and Flibbertigibbets as the half-breed boys that we used to see rowing or diving in the waters, or playing pranks on the shores of Michigan.

We had two great pleasures this day; a drive along the quiet Lake St. Clair, and a charming evening party at General Mason's.[39] After a pilgrimage through the State of New York, a few exciting days at Niagara, and a disagreeable voyage along Lake Erie, we were prepared to enjoy to the utmost the novelty

The north side of Detroit's Jefferson Avenue and Griswold Street looked like this in 1837.

of a good evening party; and we were as merry as children at a ball. It was wholly unexpected to find ourselves in accomplished society on the far side of Lake Erie; and there was something stimulating in the contrast between the high civilization of the evening, and the primitive scenes that we were to plunge into the next day. Though we had to pack up and write, and be off very early in the morning, we were unable to persuade ourselves to go home till late; and then we talked over Detroit as if we were wholly at leisure.

The scenery of Lake St. Clair was new to me. I had seen nothing in the United States like its level green banks, with trees slanting over the water, festooned with the wild vine; the groups of cattle beneath them; the distant steam-boat, scarcely seeming to disturb the gray surface of the still waters. This was the first of many scenes in Michigan which made me think of Holland; though the day of canals has not yet arrived.

June15th. An obliging girl at the American provided us with coffee and biscuits at half-past five, by which time our "exclusive extra" was at the door. Charley had lost his cap. It was impossible that he should go bare-headed through the state; and it was lucky for us that a store was already open where he was furnished in a trice with a willow-hat. The brimming river was bright in the morning sun; and our road was, for a mile or two thronged with Indians. Some of the inhabitants of Detroit, who knew the most about their dark neighbours, told me that they found it impossible to be romantic about these poor creatures. We, however, could not help feeling the excitement of the spectacle, when we saw them standing in their singularly majestic attitudes by the roadside, or on a rising ground; one with a bunch of feathers tied at the back of the head; another with his arms folded in his blanket; and a third, with her infant lashed to a board, and thus carried on her shoulders. Their appearance was dreadfully squalid.

As soon as we had entered the woods, the roads became as bad as, I suppose, roads ever are. Something snapped, and the driver cried out that we were "broke to bits." The teambolt[40] had given way. Our gentlemen, and those of the mail stage, which happened to be at hand, helped to mend the coach; and we ladies walked on, gathering abundance of flowers, and picking our way along the swampy corduroy road. In less than an hour, the stage took us up, and no more accidents happened before breakfast. We were abundantly amused while our meal was preparing at Danversville. [41] One of the passengers of the mail stage took up a violin, and offered to play to us. Books with pictures were lying about. The lady of the house sat by the window, fixing her candlewicks into the moulds. In the piazza sat a party of emigrants, who interested us much. The wife had her eight children with her; the youngest, puny twins. She said she had brought them in a wagon four hundred miles; and if they could only live through the one hundred that remained before they reached her husband's lot of land, she hoped they might thrive; but she had been robbed, the day before, of her bundle of baby things. Some one had stolen it from the wagon. After a good meal, we saw the stage passengers stowed into a lumber wagon; and we presently followed in our more comfortable vehicle.

Before long, something else snapped, the splinter-bar[42] was broken. The driver was mortified; but it was no fault of his. Juggernaut's car would have been "broke to bits" on such a road. We went into a settler's house, where we were welcomed to rest and refresh ourselves. Three years before, the owner bought his eighty acres of land for a dollar an acre. He could now sell it for twenty dollars an acre. He shot, last year, a hundred deer, and sold them for three dollars a piece. He and his family need have no fears of poverty. We dined well, nine miles before reaching Ypsilanti. The log houses, always comfortable when well made, being easily kept clean, cool in summer, and warm in winter, have here an air of beauty about them. The hue always harmonizes well with the soil and vegetation. Those in Michigan have the bark left on, and the corners sawn off close; and are thus both picturesque and neat.

At Ypsilanti, I picked up an Ann Arbor newspaper. [43] It was badly printed; but its contents were pretty good; and it could happen nowhere out of America, that so raw a settlement as that at Ann Arbor, where there is difficulty in procuring decent accommodations, should have a newspaper.

It was past seven before we left the inn at Ypsilanti, to go thirteen miles further. We departed on foot. There was a bridge building at Ypsilanti; but, till it was ready, all vehicles had to go a mile down the water-side to the ferry, while the passengers generally preferred crossing the foot bridge, and walking on through the wood. We found in our path, lupins, wild geraniums, blue-eye grass, blue iris, wild sunflower, and many others. The mild summer night was delicious, after the fatigues of the day. I saw the youngest of golden moons, and two bright stars set, before we reached Wallace's Tavern, [44] where we were to sleep. Of course, we were told that there was no room for us; but, by a little coaxing and management, and one of the party consenting to sleep on the parlour floor, everything was made easy.

June 16th. We were off by half-past six; and, not having rested quite enough, and having the prospect of fourteen miles before breakfast, we, with one accord, finished our sleep in the stage. We reached Tecumseh by half-past nine, and perceived that its characteristic was chair making. Every other house seemed to be a chair manufacturer. One bore the inscription, "Cousin George's Store:" the meaning of which I do not pretend to furnish. Perhaps the idea is, that purchasers may feel free and easy, as if dealing with cousin George. Everybody has a cousin George. Elsewhere, we saw a little hotel inscribed, "Our House;" a prettier sign than "Traveller's Rest," or any other such tempting invitation that I am acquainted with. At Tecumseh, I saw the first strawberries of the season. All that I tasted in Michigan, of prairie growth, were superior to those of the west, grown in gardens.

Charley was delighted today by the sight of several spotted fawns, tamed by children. If a fawn be carried a hundred yards from its bush, it will follow the finder, and remain with him, if kindly treated. They are prettiest when very young, as they afterwards lose their spots.

We fairly entered the "rolling country" today: and nothing could be brighter and more flourishing that it looked. The young corn was coming up well in the settlers' fields. The copses, called "oak openings," looked fresh after the passing thunder showers; and so did the rising grounds, strewed with wild flowers and strawberries. "The little hills rejoiced on every side." The ponds gleaming between the hills and copses, gave a park-like air to the scenery. The settlers leave trees in their clearings; and from these came the song of the wood-thrush; and from the dells the cry of the quail. There seemed to be a gay wood-pecker in every tree.

Our only accident today was driving over a poor hog: we can only hope it died soon. Wherever we stopped, we found that the crowds of emigrants had eaten up all the eggs; and we happened to think eggs the best article of diet of all on a journey. It occurred to me that we might get some by the way, and carry them on to our resting place. All agreed that we might probably procure them: but how to carry them safely over such roads was the question. This day we resolved to try. We made a solemn stir for eggs in a small settlement; and procured a dozen. We each carried one in each hand, except Charley, who was too young to be trusted. His two were wrapped up each in a bag. During eight miles of jolting, not one was hurt; and we delivered them to our host at Jonesville with much satisfaction. We wished that some of our entertainers had been as rich as a Frenchman at Baltimore, who, talking of his poultry yard, informed a friend that he had "fifty head of hen."

At Jonesville, the ladies and Charley were favoured with a large and comfortable chamber. The gentlemen had to sleep with the multitude below; ranged like walking-sticks, or umbrellas, on a shop counter.

June 17th. The road was more deplorable than ever today. The worst of it was, that whenever it was dangerous for the carriage, so that we were obliged to get out, it was, in proportion, difficult to be passed on foot. It was amusing to see us in such passes as we had to go through today. I generally acted as pioneer, the gentlemen having their ladies to assist; and it was pleasant to stand on some dry perch and watch my companions through the holes and pools that I had passed. Such hopping and jumping; such slipping and sliding; such looks of despair from the middle of a pond; such shifting of logs, and carrying of planks, and handing along the fallen trunks of trees! The driver, meantime, was looking back provokingly from his box having dragged the carriage through; and far behind stood Charley, high and dry, singing or eating his bit of bread, till his father could come back for him. Three times this day was such a scene enacted; and, the third time, there was a party of emigrant ladies to be assisted, too. When it was all over, and I saw one with her entire feet cased in mud, I concluded we must all be very wet, and looked at my own shoes: and lo! even the soles were as dry as when they were made! How little the worst troubles of traveling amount to, in proportion to the apprehension of them? What a world of anxiety do travellers suffer let they should get wet, or be without food! How many really faint with hunger or fall into an ague with damp and cold? I was never in danger of either the one or the other, in any of the twenty-three States which I visited.

At one part of our journey today, where the road was absolutely impassable, we went above a mile through the wood, where there was no track, but where the trees are blazed to serve as guide posts, summer and winter. It was very wild. Our carriage twisted and wound about to avoid blows against the noble beech stems. The waters of the swamp plashed under our wheels, and the boughs crunched overhead. An overturn would have been a disaster in such a place. We travelled only forty-two miles this long day; but the weariness of the way was much beguiled by singing, by a mock oration, story telling, and other such amusements. The wit and humour of Americans, abundant under ordinary circumstances, are never, I believe, known to fail in emergencies, serious or trifling. Their humour helps themselves and their visitors through any Sloughs of Despond, as charitably as their infinite abundance of logs through the swamps of their bad roads.

We did not reach Sturgis's Prairie[45] till night. We had heard so poor an account of the stage house, that we proceeded to another, whose owner has the reputation of treating his guests magnificently, or not at all. He treated us on *juste milieu* principles. He did what he could for us; and that could not be called magnificent. The house was crowded with emigrants. When, after three hours' waiting, we had supper, two full grown persons were asleep on some blankets in the corner of the room, and as many as fifteen or sixteen children on chairs and on the floor. Our hearts ached for one mother. Her little girl, two years old, had either sprained or broken her arm, and mother did not know what to do with it. The child shrieked when the arm was touched, and wailed mournfully at other times. We found in the morning, however, that she had had some sleep. I have often wondered since how she bore the motion of the wagon on the worst parts of the road. It was oppressively hot. I had a little closet, whose door would not shut, and which was too small to give me room to take off the soft feather bed. The window would not keep open without being propped by the tin water jug; and though this was done, I could not sleep for the heat. This reminds me of the considerate kindness of an hotel keeper in an earlier stage of our journey. When he found that I wished to have my window open, there being no fastening, he told me he would bring his own toothbrush for a prop, which he accordingly did.

June 18th. Our drive of twelve miles to breakfast was very refreshing. The roads were the best we had travelled since we left New York State. We passed through a wilderness of flowers; trailing roses, enormous white convolvulus, scarlet lilies, and ground ivy, with many others, being added to those we had before seen. Milton must have travelled in Michigan before he wrote the garden parts of "Paradise Lost." Sturgis's and White Pigeon Prairies are highly cultivated, and look just like any other rich and perfectly level land. We breakfasted at White Pigeon Prairie, and saw the rising ground where the Indian chief lies buried whose name has been given to the place. [46]

The charms of the settlement, to us, were a kind landlady, an admirable breakfast, at which eggs abounded, and a blooming garden. Thirty-seven miles further brought us to Niles, where we arrived by five in the afternoon. The roads were so much improved that we had not to walk at all; which was well, as there was much pelting rain during the day.

Niles is a thriving town on the river St. Joseph, on the borders of the Potowatomi territory. Three years ago, it consisted of three houses. We could not learn the present number of inhabitants; probably because the number is never the same two days together. [47] A Potowatomi village stands within a mile; and we saw two Indians on horseback, fording the rapid river very majestically, and ascending the wooded hills on the other side. Many Indian women were about the streets; one with a nose-ring; some with plates of silver on the bosom, and other barbaric ornaments.

Such a tremendous storm of thunder and lightning came on, with a deluge of rain, that we were prevented seeing anything of the place, except from our windows. I had sent my boots to a cobbler, over the way. He had to put on India rubbers, which reached above the knee, to bring his work home; the street was so flooded. We little imagined for the hour the real extent and violence of this storm, and the effect it would have on our journeying.

The prairie strawberries, at breakfast this morning, were so large, sweet, and ripe that we were inclined for more in the course of the day. Many of the children of the settlers were dispersed near the road-side, with their baskets, gathering strawberries; they would not sell any: they did not know what mother would say if they went home without any berries for father. But they could get enough for father, too, they were told, if they would sell us what they had already gathered. No; they did not want to sell. Our driver observed, that money was "no object to them." I began to think that we had, at last, got to the end of the world; or rather, perhaps, to the beginning of another and a better.

June 19. No plan could be more cleverly and confidently laid than ours was for this day's journey. We were to travel through the lands of the Potowatomi, and reach the shores of the glorious Lake Michigan, at Michigan City, in time for an early supper. We were to proceed on the morrow round the southern extremity of the lake, so as, if possible to reach Chicago in one day. It was wisely and prettily planned: and the plan was so far followed, as that we actually did leave Niles some time before six in the morning. Within three minutes, it began to rain again, and continued, with but few and short intervals, all day.

We crossed the St. Joseph by a rope ferry, the ingenious management of which, when stage coaches had to be carried over, was a perpetual study to me. The effect of crossing a rapid river by a rope ferry, by torch-light, in a dark night, is very striking; and not the less so for one's becoming familiarized with it, as the traveller does in the United States. As we drove up the steep bank, we found ourselves in the Indian territory. All was very wild; and the more so for the rain. There were many lodges in glades, with the red light of fires hanging around them. The few log huts looked drenched; the tree stems black in the wet; and the very wild flowers were dripping. The soil was sandy; so that the ugliest features of a rainy day, the mud and puddles, were obviated. The sand sucked up the rain, so that we jumped out of the carriage as often as a wild-flower of peculiar beauty tempted us. The bride-like, white convolvulus, nearly as large as my hand, grew in trails all over the ground.

The poor, helpless, squalid Potowatomi are sadly troubled by squatters. It seems hard enough that they should be restricted with a narrow territory, so surrounded by whites that the game is sure soon to disappear, and leave them stripped of their only resource. It is too hard that they should also be encroached upon by men who sit down, without leave or title, upon lands which are not intended for sale. I enjoyed hearing of an occasional alarm among squatters, caused by some threatening demonstrations by the Indians. I should like to see every squatter frightened away from Indian lands, however advantageous their squatting may be upon lands which are unclaimed, or whose owners can not defend their own property. I was glad to hear today that a deputation of Potowatomi had been sent to visit a distant warlike tribe, in consequence of the importunities of squatters, who wanted to buy the land they had been living upon. The deputation returned, painted, and under other hostile signals, and declared that the Potowatomi did not intend to part with their lands. We stopped for some milk, this morning, at the "location" of a squatter, whose wife was milking as we passed.

The gigantic personage, her husband, told us how anxious he was to pay for the land which repaid his tillage so well; but that his Indian neighbours would not sell. I hope that, by this time, he has had to remove, and leave them the benefit of his house and fences. Such an establishment in the wild woods is the destruction of the game, and those who live upon it. [48]

Despite being nearly deaf and lacking the senses of taste and smell Harriet Martineau was a keen observer of the Michigan frontier.

Mackinac Island to Sault Ste. Marie by Canoe: 1836
by
Anna Jameson

Some of the choicest accounts of Detroit, Mackinac Island and Sault Ste. Marie during the 1830s came from the pen of Anna Jameson. She wrote colorful descriptions of those places and in particular, her work offers sensitive and sympathetic accounts of Indians.

Born in Dublin, Ireland, in 1794, Anna Brownell Murphy developed into an impetuous, independent and gifted child. When she was 26 she met Robert Jameson,a young lawyer. Within a few months they were engaged, but he soon broke it off. Heart sick, she secured a job as a governess to a wealthy family and they went on a grand tour of Europe. Then in 1825 she married Jameson. This proved a big mistake. Most of her long unhappy marriage would be spent separated from her husband.

Jameson launched her literary career in 1826 with *The Dairy of an Ennuyee* based on a journal of her European travels. She followed that success with numerous volumes of essays about women, art and travel books. She also became friends with a coterie of the leading British writers of the period.

In 1833, her husband was appointed a high ranking judge in Canada. He left for his post there without his wife. Three years later, against her better judgement, she joined him in Toronto. Eight months later she returned to England, permanently separated from the judge. But, fortunately for those who continue to savor her clear and lively descriptions, she recorded the incidents of her tour of Canada and the Great Lakes in *Winter Studies and Summer Rambles* (3 vols. London, 1838). While visiting Mackinac Island, Jameson was befriended by the Henry Rowe Schoolcraft family, and in particular

by his beautiful half-Chippewa wife, Jane, We join Jameson there on a hot June day in 1836, just prior to her embarking on a canoe trip with Jane Schoolcraft to Sault Ste. Marie, where Jameson will become the first European female to shoot the Sault Rapids.

I was sitting last Friday, at sultry noon tide, under the shadow of a schooner which had just anchored alongside the little pier sketching and dreaming - when up came a messenger, breathless, to say that a boat was going off for the Sault Ste. Marie, in which I could be accommodated with a passage. Now this was precisely what I had been wishing and waiting for, and yet I heard the information with an emotion of regret. I had become every day more attached to the society of Mrs. Schoolcraft,[49] more interested about her; and the idea of parting, and parting suddenly, took me by surprise, and was anything but agreeable. On reaching the house, I found all in movement, and learned, to my inexpressible delight, that my friend would take the opportunity of paying a visit to her mother and family, and with her children, was to accompany me on my voyage.

We had but one hour to prepare packages, provisions, everything--and in one hour all was ready.

This voyage of two days was to be made in a little Canadian bateau rowed by five *voyageurs* from the Sault. The boat might have carried fifteen persons, hardly more, and was rather clumsy in form. The two ends were appropriated to the rowers, baggage, and provisions; in the center there was a clear space, with a locker on each side, on which we sat or reclined, having stowed away in them our smaller and more valuable packages. This was the internal arrangement.

The distance to the Sault, or, as the Americans call it, the *Sou,* is not more than thirty miles[50] over land, as the bird flies; but the whole region being one mass of tangled forest and swamp, infested with bears and mosquitoes, it is seldom crossed but in winter, and in snow shoes. The usual route by water is ninety-four miles.

At three o'clock in the afternoon, with a favorable breeze, we launched forth on the lake, and having rowed about a mile from the shore, the little square sail was hoisted, and away we went merrily over the blue waves.

For a detailed account of *voyageurs*, or Canadian boatmen, their peculiar condition and mode of life, I refer you to Washington Irving's "Astoria;" what he describes them to *have been,* and what Henry[51] represents them in his time, they are even now, in these regions of the upper lakes. But the *voyageurs* in our boat were not favorable specimens of their very amusing and peculiar class. They were fatigued with rowing for three days previous, and had only two helpless women to deal with. As soon, therefore, as the sail was hoisted, two began to play cards on top of a keg, the other two went to sleep. The youngest and most intelligent of the set, a lively, half-breed boy of eighteen, took the helm. He told us with great self-complacency that he was *captain,* and that it was already the third time that he had been elected by his comrades to this dignity but I cannot say he had a very obedient crew.

About seven o'clock we landed to cook our supper on an island which is commemorated by Henry as the Isle des Outardes, and is now Goose Island.[52] Mrs. Schoolcraft undertook the general management with all the alertness of one accustomed to these *impromptu* arrangements, and I did my best in my new avocation - dragged one or two blasted boughs to the fire - the least of them twice as big as myself - and laid the cloth upon the pebbly beach. The enormous fire was to keep off the mosquitoes, in which we succeeded pretty well, swallowing, however, as much smoke as would have dried us externally into hams or red herrings. We then returned to the boat, spread a bed for the children, (who were my delight,) in the bottom of it, with mats and blankets, and disposed our own, on the lockers on each side, with buffalo skins, blankets, shawls, cloaks and whatever was available, with writing case for a pillow.

After sunset the breeze fell: the men were urged to row, but pleaded fatigue, and that they were hired for the day, and not the night, (which is the custom). One by one they sulkily abandoned their oars, and sunk to sleep under their blankets, all but our young captain; like Ulysses, when steering away from Calypso --

Placed at the helm he sat, and watched the skies,
Nor closed in sleep his ever watchful eyes.

He kept himself awake by singing hymns, in which Mrs. Schoolcraft joined him. I lay still, looking at the stars and listening:

when there was a pause in the singing, we kept up the conversation, fearing lest sleep should overcome our only pilot and guardian. Thus we floated on beneath that divine canopy "which love had spread to curtain the sleeping world;" it was a most lovely and blessed night, bright and calm and warm, and we made some little way, for both wind and current were in our favor.

As we were coasting a little shadowy island, our captain mentioned a strange circumstance, very illustrative of Indian life and character. A short time ago a young Chippewa hunter, whom he knew, was shooting squirrels on this spot, when by some chance a large blighted pine fell upon him, knocking him down and crushing his leg, which was fractured in two place. He could not rise, he could not remove the tree which was lying across his broken leg. He was in a little uninhabited island, without the slightest probability of passing aid, and to lie there and starve to death in agonies, seemed all that was left to him. In this dilemma, with all the fortitude and promptitude of resource of a thorough-bred Indian, he took out his knife, cut off his own leg, bound it up, dragged himself along the ground to his hunting canoe, and paddled himself home to his wigwam on a distant island, where the cure of his wound was completed. The man is still alive.

Mrs. Schoolcraft told me of a young Chippewa who went on a hunting expedition with his wife only; they were encamped at a considerable distance from the village when the woman was seized with the pains of child-birth. This is in general a very easy matter among the Indian women, cases of danger or death being exceedingly rare; but on this occasion some unusual and horrible difficulty occurred. The husband, who was described to me as an affectionate, gentle spirited man, much attached to his wife, did his best to assist her; but after a few struggles she became insensible, and lay, as he supposed, dead. He took out his knife, and with astonishing presence of mind, performed on his wife the Cesarean operation, saved his infant, and ultimately the mother, and brought them both home on a sleigh to his village at the Sault, where, as Mrs. Schoolcraft told me, she had frequently seen both the man and woman.

We remained in conversation till long after midnight; then the boat was moored to a tree, but kept off shore, for fear of the mosquitoes, and we addressed ourselves to sleep. I remember lying awake for some minutes, looking up at the quiet stars, and around upon the dark weltering waters, and at the faint waning moon, just suspended on the very edge of the horizon. I saw it sink - sink into the bosom of the lake, as if to rest, and then with a thought of far off friends, and a most fervent thanksgiving, I dropped asleep. It is odd that I did not think of praying for protection, and that no sense of fear came over me; it seemed as if the eye of God himself looked down upon me; that I was protected. I do not say I thought this any more than the unweaned child in its cradle; but I had some such feeling of unconscious trust and love, now I recall those moments.

I slept, however, uneasily, not being yet accustomed to a board and a blanket; *ca viendra avec le temps.* About dawn I awoke in a sort of stupor, but after bathing my face and hands over the boat side, I felt refreshed. The voyageurs, after a good night's rest, were in better humour, and took manfully to their oars. Soon after sunrise, we passed round that very conspicuous cape, famous in the history of northwest adventurers, called the "Grand Detour," half way between Mackinaw and the Sault. Now, if you look at the map, you will see that our course was henceforth quite altered; we had been running down the coast of the main land towards the east; we had now to turn short round the point, and steer almost due west; hence its most fitting name, the Grand Detour.[53] The wind, hitherto favorable, was now dead against us. This part of Lake Huron is studded with little islands, which, as well as the neighbouring main land, are all uninhabited, yet clothed with the richest, loveliest, most fantastic vegetation, and no doubt swarming with animal life.

I cannot, I dare not, attempt to describe the strange sensation one has, thus thrown for a time beyond the bounds of civilized humanity, or indeed any humanity; nor the wild yet solemn reveries which come over one in the midst of this wilderness of woods and waters. All was so solitary, so grand in its solitude, as if nature unviolated sufficed to herself. Two days and nights the solitude was unbroken; not a trace of social life, not a human being, not a canoe, not even a deserted wigwam, met our view. Our little boat held on its way over the placid lake and among green tufted islands; and we its inmates, two women, differing in clime, nation, complexion, strangers to each other but a few days ago, might have fancied ourselves alone in a new-born world.

We landed to boil our kettle, and breakfast on a point of the island of St. Joseph's. This most beautiful island is between thirty and forty miles in length, and nearly a hundred miles in circumference, and towards the center the land is high and picturesque. They tell me that on the other side of the island there is a settlement of whites and Indians. Another large island, Drummond's Isle, was for a short time in view. We had also a settlement here, but it was unaccountably surrendered to the Americans. If now you look at the map, you will wonder, as I did, that in retaining St. Joseph's and the Manitoulin islands, we gave up Drummond's Island. Both these islands had forts and garrisons during the war.

By the time breakfast was over, the children had gathered some fine strawberries; the heat had now become almost intolerable, and unluckily we had no awning. The men rowed languidly, and we made but little way; we coasted along the south shore of St. Joseph's through fields of rushes, miles in extent, across Lake George, and Muddy Lake;[54] (the name, I thought, must be a libel, for it was as clear as a crystal and as blue as heaven; but they say that, like a sulky temper, the least ruffle of wind turns it as black as ditchwater, and it does not subside again in a hurry,) and then came a succession of openings spotted with lovely islands, all solitary. The sky was without a cloud, a speck - except when the great fish-eagle was descried sailing over it blue depths - the water without a wave. We were too hot and too languid to converse. Nothing disturbed the deep noon tide stillness, but the dip of the oars, or the spring and splash of a sturgeon as he leapt from the surface of the lake, leaving a circle of little wavelets spreading around. All the islands we passed were so woody, and so infested with mosquitoes, that we could not land and light our fire, till we reached the entrance of St. Marys River, between Neebish Island and the main land.

Here was a well known spot, a sort of little opening on a flat shore, called the *Encampment,*[55] because a party of boatmen coming down from Lake Superior, and camping here for the night, were surprised by the frost, and obliged to remain the whole winter till the opening of the ice in the spring. After rowing all this hot day till seven o'clock against the wind, (what there was of it,) and against the current coming rapidly and strongly down from Lake Superior, we did at length reach this promised harbour of rest and refreshment. Alas! there was neither for us; the moment our boat touched the shore, we were enveloped in a cloud of mosquitoes. Fires were lighted instantly, six were burning in a circle at once; we were well nigh suffocated and smoke dried - all in vain. At last we left the voyageurs to boil the kettle, and retreated to our boat, desiring then to make us fast to a tree by a long rope; then, each of us taking an oar - I only wish you could have seen us - we pushed off from the land, while the children were sweeping away the enemy with green boughs. This being done, we commenced supper, really half famished, and were too much engrossed to look about us. Suddenly we were again surrounded by our adversaries; they came upon us in swarms, in clouds, in myriads, entering our eyes, our noses, our mouths, stinging till the blood followed. We had, unawares, and while absorbed in our culinary operations, drifted into the shore, got entangled among the roots of trees, and were with difficulty extricated, presenting all the time a fair mark and a rich banquet for our detested tormentors. The dear children cried with agony and impatience, and but for shame I could almost have cried too.

I had suffered from these plagues in Italy; you too, by this time, may probably know what they are in the southern countries of the old world; but 'tis a jest, believe me, to encountering a forest full of them in these wild regions. I had heard much, and much was I forewarned, but never could have conceived the torture they can inflict, nor the impossibility of escape, defence, or endurance. Some amiable person, who took an especial interest in our future welfare, in enumerating the torments prepared for hardened sinners, assures us that they will be stung by mosquitoes all made of brass, and as large as black beetles - he was an ignoramus and a bungler; you may credit me, that the brass is quite an unnecessary improvement, and the increase of size equally superfluous. Mosquitoes, as they exist in this upper world, are as pretty and perfect a plague as the most ingenious amateur sinner-tormentor ever devised. Observe, that a mosquito does not sting like a wasp, or a gad-fly; he has a long proboscis like an awl, with which he bores your veins, and pumps the life blood out of you, leaving venom and fever behind. Enough of mosquitoes - I will never again do more than allude to them; only they are enough to make Philosophy go hang herself, and Patience swear like a Turk or a trooper.

Well, we left this most detestable and inhospitable shore as soon as possible, but the enemy followed us and we did not soon get rid of them; night came on, and we were still twenty miles below the Sault.

I offered an extra gratuity to men, it they would keep to their oars without interruption; and then, fairly exhausted lay down on my locker and blanket. But whenever I woke from

63

uneasy, restless slumbers, there was Mrs. Schoolcraft, bending over her sleeping children, and waving off the mosquitoes, singing all the time a low, melancholy Indian song; while the northern lights were streaming and dancing in the sky, and the fitful moaning of the wind, the gathering clouds, and chilly atmosphere, foretold a change of weather. This would have been the *comble de malheur*. When daylight came, we passed Sugar Island, where immense quantities of maple sugar are made every spring, and just as the rain began to fall in earnest, we arrived at the Sault Ste. Marie. On one side of the river, Mrs. Schoolcraft was welcomed by her mother; and on the other, my friends, the McMurrays,[56] received me with delighted and delightful hospitality. I went to bed - Oh! the luxury! - and slept for six hours.

Enough of solemn reveries on star-lit lakes, enough - too much - of self and self-communings; I turn over a new leaf, and this shall be a chapter of geography, and topography, natural philosophy, and such wise-like things. Draw the curtain first, for if I look out any longer on those surging rapids, I shall certainly turn giddy - forget all the memoranda I have been collecting for you, lose my reckoning, and become unintelligible to you and myself too.

This river of St. Mary is, like the Detroit and the St. Clair, properly a strait, the channel of communication between lake Superior and Lake Huron. About ten miles higher up, the great ocean-lake narrows to a point; then, forcing a channel through the high lands, comes rushing along till it meets with a downward ledge, or cliff, over which it throws itself in foam and fury, tearing a path for its willows through the rocks. The descent is about twenty-seven feet in three quarters of a mile, but the rush begins above, and the tumult continues below the fall, so that, on the whole, the eye embraces an expanse of white foam measuring about a mile each way, the effect being exactly that of the ocean breaking on a rocky shore; not so terrific, nor on so large a scale, as the rapids of Niagara, but quite as beautiful - quite as animated.

What the French call a *saut*, (leap,) we term a fall; the Sault Ste. Marie is translated into the falls of St. Mary. By this name the rapids are often mentioned, but the village on their shore still retains its old name, and is called the Sault. I do not know why the beautiful river and its glorious cataracts should have been placed under the peculiar patronage of the blessed Virgin; perhaps from the union of exceeding loveliness with

Old Fort Brady was constructed at Sault Ste. Marie in 1822.

irresistible power; or, more probably, because the first adventurers reached the spot on some day hallowed in the calendar. [57]

The French, ever active and enterprising, were the first who penetrated to this wild region. They had an important trading post here early in the last century, and also a small fort. They were ceded, with the rest of the country, to Great Britain, in 1762. I wonder whether, at that time, the young king or any of his ministers had the least conception of the value and immensity of the magnificent country thrown into our possession, or gave a thought to the responsibilities it brought with it! - to be sure they made good haste, both king and ministers, to get rid of most of the responsibility. The American war began, and at its conclusion the south shore of St. Mary's, and the fort, were surrendered to the Americans.

The rapids of Niagara, reminded me of a monstrous tiger at play, and threw me into a sort of ecstatic terror; but these rapids of St. Mary suggest quite another idea; as they come fretting and fuming down, curling up their light foam, and wreathing their glancing billows round the opposing rocks, with a sort of passionate self-will, they remind me of an exquisitely beautiful women in a fit of rage, or of Walter Scott's simile--"one of the Graces possessed by a Fury;" - there is no terror in their anger, only the sense of excitement and loveliness; when it has spent this sudden, transient fit of impatience, the beautiful river resumes all its placid dignity, and holds on its course, deep and wide enough to float a squadron of seventy-fours,[58] and rapid and pellucid as a mountain trout stream.

Here, as everywhere else, I am struck by the difference between the two shores. On the American side there is a settlement of whites, as well as a large village of Chippewas; there is also a mission (I believe of the Methodists) for the conversion of the Indians. The fort, which has been lately strengthened, is merely a strong and high enclosure, surrounded with pickets of cedar wood; within the stockade are the barracks, and the principal trading store. This fortress is called Fort Brady, after that gallant officer.[59] The garrison may be very effective for aught I know, but I never beheld such an unmilitary looking set. When I was there today, the sentinels were lounging up and down in their flannel jackets and shirt sleeves, with muskets thrown over their shoulders - just for all the world like ploughboys going to shoot sparrows; however, they are in keeping with the fortress of cedar posts, and no doubt both answer their purpose very well. The village is increasing into a town, and the commercial advantages of its situation must raise it ere long to a place of importance.

On the Canada side, we have not even these demonstrations of power or prosperity. Nearly opposite to the American fort there is a small factory belonging to the North-West Fur Company; below this, a few miserable log-huts, occupied by some French Canadians and voyageurs in the service of the company, a set of lawless *mauvais sujets,* from all I can learn. Lower down stands the house of Mr. and Mrs. McMurray, with the Chippewa village under their care and tuition, but most of the wigwams and their inhabitants are now on their way down the lake, to join the congress at the Manitoulin Islands. A lofty eminence, partly cleared and partly clothed with forest, rises behind the house, on which stand the little missionary church and schoolhouse for the use of the Indian converts. From the summit of this hill you look over the traverse into Lake Superior, and the two giant capes which guard its entrance. One of these capes is called Gros-Cap, from its bold and lofty cliffs, the yet unviolated haunt of the eagle.   The opposite cape is more accessible, and bears an Indian name, which I cannot pretend to spell, but which signifies "the place of the Iroquois' bones;" [60] it was the scene of a wild and terrific tradition. At the time that the Iroquois (or Six Nations) were driven before the French and Hurons up to the western lakes, they endeavoured to possess themselves of the hunting grounds of the Chippewas, and hence a bitter and lasting feud between the two nations. The Iroquois, after defeating the Chippewas, encamped, a thousand strong, upon this point, where, thinking themselves secure, they made a war feast to torture and devour their prisoners.   The Chippewas from the opposite shore beheld the sufferings and humiliation of their friends, and roused to sudden fury by the sight, collected their warriors, only three hundred in all, crossed the channel, and at break of day fell upon the Iroquois, now sleeping after their horrible excesses, and massacred every one of them, men, women, and children. Of their own party they lost but one warrior, who was stabbed with an awl by an old women who was sitting at the entrance of her wigwam, stitching moccasins: thus runs the tale. The bodies were left to bleach on the shore, and they say that bones and skulls are still found there.

67

Here, at the foot of the rapids, the celebrated whitefish of the lakes is caught in its highest perfection. The people down below,[61] who boast of the excellence of the whitefish, really know nothing of the matter. There is no more comparison between the whitefish of the lower lakes and the whitefish of St. Marys than between plaice and turbot, or between a clam and a Sandwich oyster. I ought to be a judge, who have eaten them fresh out of the river four times a day, and I declare to you that I never tasted anything of the fish kind half so exquisite. If the Roman Apicius had lived in these latter days, he would certainly have made a voyage up Lake Huron to breakfast on the whitefish of St. Marys River, and would not have returned in dudgeon, as he did, from the coast of Africa. But the epicures of our degenerate times have nothing of that gastronomical enthusiasm which inspired their ancient models, else we should have them all coming here to eat whitefish at the Sault, and scorning cockney white bait. Henry declares that the flavor of the whitefish is "beyond any comparison whatever," and I add my testimony thereto - *probatum est!*

I have eaten tunny in the gulf of Genoa, anchovies fresh out of the bay of Naples, and trout of the Salz-kammergut, and divers other fishy dainties rich and rare, - but the exquisite, the refined whitefish, exceeds them all; concerning those cannibal fish (mullets were they, or lampreys?) which Lucullus fed in his fish ponds, I cannot speak, never having tasted them; but even if they could be resuscitated, I would not degrade the refined, the delicate whitefish by a comparison with any such barbarian luxury.

But seriously, and *badinage* apart, it is really the most luxurious delicacy that swims the waters. It is said by Henry that people never tire of them. Mr. MacMurray tells me that he has eaten them every day of his life for seven years, and that his relish for them is undiminished. The enormous quantities caught here, and in the bays and creeks round Lake Superior, remind me of herrings in the lochs of Scotland; besides subsisting the inhabitants, whites and Indians, during the great part of the year, vast quantities are cured and barrelled every fall, and sent down to the eastern states. Not less than eight thousand barrels were shipped last year.

These enterprising Yankees have seized upon another profitable speculation here; there is a fish found in great quantities in the upper part of Lake Superior, called the *skevat,*[62] so exceedingly rich, luscious, and oily, when fresh, as to be quite uneatable. A gentleman here told me that he had tried it, and though not very squeamish at any time, and then very hungry, he could not get beyond the first two or three mouthfuls; but it has been lately discovered that this fish makes a most luxurious pickle. It is very excellent, but so rich even in this state, that like the tunny *marinee*, it is necessary either to taste abstemiously, or die heroically of indigestion. This fish is becoming a fashionable luxury, and in one of the stores here I saw three hundred barrels ready for embarkation. The Americans have several schooners on the lakes employed in these fisheries; we have not one. They have besides planned a ship canal through the portage here, which will open a communication for large vessels between Lake Huron and Lake Superior, as our Welland Canal has united Lake Erie with Lake Ontario. The ground has already been surveyed for this purpose. When this canal is completed, a vessel may load in the Thames and discharge her burthen at the upper end of Lake Superior. I hope you have a map before you, that you may take in at a glance this wonderful extent of inland navigation. Ought a country possessing it, and all the means of life besides, to remain poor, oppressed, uncultivated, unknown?

But to return to my beautiful river and glorious rapids, which are to be treated, you see, as a man treats a passionate beauty - he does not oppose her, for that were madness - but he gets round her. Well, on the American side, further down the river, is the house of Tanner, [63] the Indian interpreter, of whose story you may have heard - for, as I remember, it excited some attention in England. He is a European of unmixed blood, with the language, manners, habits of a Red-skin. He had been kidnapped somewhere on the American frontier when a mere boy, and brought up among the Chippewas. He afterwards returned to civilized life, and having relearned his own language, drew up a very entertaining and valuable account of his adopted tribe. He is now in the American service here, having an Indian wife, and is still attached to his Indian mode of life.

Just above the fort is the ancient burial place of the Chippewas. I need not tell you of the profound veneration with which all the Indian tribes regard the places of their dead. In all their treaties for the cession of their lands, they stipulate with the white man for the inviolability of their sepulchres. They did the same with regard to this place, but I am sorry to say that it has not been attended to, for in enlarging one side of the fort, they have considerably encroached on the cemetery. The outrage excited both the sorrow and indignation of some of my friends here, but there is no redress. Perhaps it was this circumstance that gave rise to the allusion of the Indian chief here, when in speaking of the French he said, "They never molested the places of our dead!" [64]

The view of the rapids from this spot is inexpressibly beautiful, and it has besides another attraction, which makes it to me a frequent lounge whenever I cross the river; but of this by-and-bye. To complete my sketch of the localities, I will only add, that the whole country around is in its primitive state, covered with the interminable swamp and forest, where the bear and the moose-deer roam - and lakes and living streams where the beaver builds his hut. The cariboo, or reindeer, is still found on the northern shores. The hunting grounds of the Chippewas are in the immediate neighbourhood, and extend all round Lake Superior. Beyond these, on the north, are the Chippewyans; and on the south, the Sioux, Ottagamies,[65] and Pottowattomies.

I might here multiply facts and details, but I have been obliged to throw these particulars together in haste, just to give you an idea of my present situation. Time presses, and my sojourn in this remote and interesting spot is like to be of short duration.

One of the gratifications I had anticipated in coming hither - my strongest inducement perhaps - was an introduction to the mother of my two friends, of whom her children so delighted to speak, and of whom I had heard much from other sources. A woman of pure Indian blood, of a race celebrated in these regions as warriors and chiefs from generation to generation, who had never resided within the pale of what we call civilized life, whose habits and manners were those of a genuine Indian squaw, and whose talents and domestic virtues commanded the highest respect, was, as you may supposed, an object of the deepest interest to me. I observed that not only her own children, but her two sons-in-law Mr. MacMurray and Mr. Schoolcraft, both educated in good society, the one a clergyman and the other a man of science and literature, looked up to this remarkable woman with sentiments of affection and veneration.

As soon, then, as I was a little refreshed after my two nights on the lake, and my battles with the mosquitoes, we paddled over the river to dine with Mrs. Johnston:[66] she resides in a large log house[67] close upon the shore; there is a little portico in front with seats, and the interior is most comfortable.

Indians dipping for whitefish in the St. Marys rapids.

The old lady herself is rather large in person, with the strongest marked Indian features, a countenance, open, benevolent, and intelligent, and a manner perfectly easy - simple, yet with something of motherly dignity, becoming the head of her large family. She received me most affectionately, and we entered into conversation - Mrs. Schoolcraft, who looked all animation and happiness, acting as interpreter. Mrs. Johnston speaks no English, but can understand it a little, and the Canadian French still better; but in her own language she is eloquent, and her voice, like that of her people, low and musical; many kind words were exchanged, and when I said anything that pleased her, she laughed softly like a child. I was not well, and much fevered, and I remember she took me in her arms, laid me down on a couch, and began to rub my feet, soothing and caressing me. She called me Nindannis, daughter, and I called her Neengai, mother, (though how different from my own fair mother, I thought as I looked up gratefully in her dark Indian face!) She set before us the best dressed and best served dinner I had seen since I left Toronto, and presided at her table, and did the honours of her house with unembarrassed, unaffected propriety. My attempts to speak Indian, caused, of course, considerable amusement; if I do not make progress, it will not be for want of teaching and teachers.

After dinner we took a walk to visit Mrs. Johnston's brother, Wayishky, whose wigwam is at a little distance, on the verge of the burial ground. The lodge is of the genuine Chippewa form, like an egg cut in half lengthways. It is formed of poles stuck in the ground, and bent over at top, strengthened with a few wattles and boards; the whole is covered over with mats, birch bark, and skins; a large blanket formed the door or curtain, which was not ungracefully looped aside. Wayishky, being a great man, has also a smaller lodge hard by, which serves as a storehouse and kitchen.

Rude as was the exterior of Wayishky's hut, the interior presented every appearance of comfort, and even elegance, according to the Indian notions of both. It formed a good sized room: a raised couch ran all round like a Turkish divan, serving both for seats and beds, and covered with very soft and beautiful matting of various colours and patterns. The chests and baskets of birch bark, containing the family wardrobe and property; the rifles, the hunting and fishing tackle, were stowed away all round very tidily; I observed a coffee-mill nailed up to one of the posts or

72

stakes; the floor was trodden down hard and perfectly clean, and there was a place for a fire in the middle: there was no window, but quite sufficient light and air were admitted through the door, and through an aperture in the roof. There was no disagreeable smell, and everything looked neat and clean. We found Wayishky and his wife and three of their children seated in the lodge, and as it was Sunday, and they are all Christians, no work was going forward. They received me with genuine and simple politeness, each taking my hand with a gentle inclination of the head, and some words of welcome murmured in their own soft language. we then sat down.

The conversation became very lively; and, if I might judge from looks and tones, very affectionate. I sported my last new words and phrases with great effect, and when I had exhausted my vocabulary - which was very soon - I amused myself with looking and listening.

Mrs. Wayishky (I forget her proper name) must have been a very beautiful woman. Though now no longer young, and the mother of twelve children, she is one of the handsomest Indian women I have yet seen. The number of her children is remarkable, for in general there are few large families among the Indians. Her daughter Zah-gah-see-ga-quay, (the sunbeams breaking through a cloud,) is a very beautiful girl, with eyes that are a warrant for her poetical name - she is about sixteen. Wayishky himself is a grave, dignified man about fifty. He told me that his eldest son had gone down to the Manitoulin Island to represent his family, and receive his quota of presents. His youngest son he had sent to a college in the United States, to be educated in the learning of the white men. Mrs. Schoolcraft whispered me that this poor boy is now dying of consumption, owing to the confinement and change of living, and that the parents knew it. Wayishky seemed aware that we were alluding to his son, for his eye at that moment rested on me, and such an expression of keen pain came suddenly over his fine countenance, it was as if a knife had struck him, and I really felt it in my heart, and see it still before me - that look of misery.

After about an hour we left this good and interesting family. I lingered for a while on the burial ground, looking over the rapids, and watching with a mixture of admiration and terror several little canoes which were fishing in the midst of the boiling surge, dancing and popping about like corks, The canoe used for fishing is very small and light; one man (or woman more commonly) sits in the stern, and steers with a paddle; the fisher places himself upright on the prow, balancing a long pole with both hands, at the end of which is a scoop net. This he every minute dips into the water, bringing up at each dip a fish, and sometimes two. I used to admire the fishermen on the Arno, and those on the Lagune, and above all the Neapolitan fishermen, hauling in their nets, or diving like ducks, but I never saw anything like these Indians. The manner in which they keep their position upon a footing of a few inches, is to me as incomprehensible as the beauty of their forms and attitudes, swayed by every movement and turn of their dancing, fragile barks, is admirable.

George Johnston,[68] on whose arm I was leaning, (and I had much ado to reach it,) gave me such a vivid idea of the delight of coming down the cataract in a canoe, that I am half resolved to attempt it. Terrific as it appears, yet in a good canoe, and with experienced guides, there is no absolute danger, and it must be a glorious sensation.

Mr. Johnston had spent the last fall and winter in the country, beyond Lake Superior, towards the forks of the Mississippi, where he had been employed as American agent to arrange the boundary line between the country of the Chippewas and that of their neighbours and implacable enemies, the Sioux. His mediation appeared successful for the time, and he smoked the pipe of peace with both tribes; but during the spring this ferocious war has again broken out, and he seems to think that nothing but the annihilation of either one nation or the other will entirely put an end to their conflicts; "for there is no point at which the Indian law of retaliation stops, short of the extermination of one of the parties."

I asked him how it is that in their wars the Indians make no distinction between the warriors opposed to them and helpless women and children? How it could be with a brave and manly people, that the scalps taken from the weak, the helpless, the unresisting, were as honourable as those torn from the warrior's skull? And I described to him the horror which this custom inspired - this, which of all their customs, most justifies the name *savage!*

He said it was inseparable from their principles of war and their mode of warfare; the first consists in inflicting the greatest possible insult and injury on their foe with the least possible risk to themselves. This truly savage law of honour we might call cowardly, but that, being associated with the bravest contempt of danger and pain, it seems nearer to the natural law. With regard to the mode of warfare, they have rarely pitched battles, but skirmishes, surprises, ambuscades, and sudden forays into each other's hunting grounds and villages. The usual practice is to creep stealthily on the enemy's village or hunting encampment, and wait till just after the dawn; then, at the moment the sleepers in the lodges are rising, the ambushed warriors stoop and level their pieces about two feet from the ground, which thus slaughter indiscriminately. If they find one of the enemy's lodges undefended, they murder its inmates, that when the owner returns he may find his hearth desolate; for this is exquisite vengeance! But outrage against the chastity of women is absolutely unknown under any degree of furious excitement.

This respect of female honour will remind you of the ancient Germans, as described by Julius Caesar: he contrasts in some surprise their forbearance with the very opposite conduct of the Romans; and even down to this present day, if I recollect rightly, the history of our European wars and sieges will bear out this early and characteristic distinction between the Latin and Teutonic nations. Am I right, or am I not?

To return to the Indians. After telling me some other particulars, which gave me a clearer view of their notions and feelings on these points than I ever had before, my informant mildly added, "It is a constant and favourite subject of reproach against the Indians - this barbarism of their desultory warfare; but I should think more women and children have perished in one of your civilized sieges, and that in late times, than during the whole war between the Chippewa and Sioux, and that has lasted a century."

I was silent, for there is a sensible proverb about taking care of our own glass windows: and I wonder if any of the recorded atrocities of Indian warfare or Indian vengeance, or all of them together, ever exceeded Massena's retreat from Portugal, and the French call themselves civilized. [69] A war party of Indians, perhaps two or three hundred, (and that is a very large number,) dance their war dance, go out and burn a village, and bring back twenty or thirty scalps. They are savages and heathens. We Europeans fight a battle, leave fifty thousand dead or dying by inches on the field, and a hundred thousand to mourn them desolate; but we are civilized and Christians. Then only look into the motives and causes of our bloodiest European wars as revealed in the private history of courts: the miserable, puerile, degrading intrigues which set man against man - so horridly disproportioned to the horrid result! And then see the Indian take up his war hatchet in vengeance for some personal injury, or from motives that rouse all the natural feelings of the natural man within him! Really I do not see that an Indian warrior, flourishing his tomahawk, and smeared with his enemy's blood, is so very much a greater savage than the pipe clayed, padded, embroidered personage, who, without cause or motive, has sold himself to slay or be slain: one scalps his enemy, the other rips him open with a sabre; one smashes his brains with a tomahawk, and the other blows him to atoms with a cannonball: and to me, femininely speaking, there is not a needle's point difference between the one and the other. If war be unchristian and barbarous, then war as a science is more absurd, unnatural, unchristian, than war as a passion.

The more I looked upon those glancing, dancing rapids, the more resolute I grew to venture myself in the midst of them. George Johnston went to seek a fit canoe and a dexterous steersman, and meantime I strolled away to pay a visit to Wayishky's family, and made a sketch of their lodge, while pretty Zah-gah-see-gah-qua held the umbrella to shade me.

The canoe being ready, I went up to the top of the portage, and we launched into the river. It was a small fishing canoe about ten feet long, quite new, and light and elegant and buoyant as a bird on the waters. I reclined on a mat at the bottom, Indian fashion, (there are no seats in a genuine Indian canoe;) in a minute we were within the verge of the rapids and down we went with a whirl and a splash! The white surge leaping around me - over me. The Indian with astonishing dexterity kept the head of the canoe to the breakers, and somehow or other we danced through them. I could see, as I looked over the edge of the canoe, that the passage between the rocks was sometimes not more than two feet in width, and we had to turn sharp angles - a touch of which would have sent us to destruction - all this I could see through the transparent eddying waters, but I can truly say, I had not even a momentary sensation of fear, but rather of giddy, breathless, delicious excitement. I could even admire the beautiful attitude of a fisher, past whom we swept as we came to the bottom. The whole affair, from the moment I entered the canoe till I reached the landing place, occupied seven minutes, and the distance is about three quarters of a mile.

My Indians were enchanted, and when I reached *home,*

my good friends were not less delighted at my exploit: they told me I was the first European female who had ever performed it, and assuredly I shall not be the last. I recommend it as an exercise before breakfast. Two glasses of champagne could not have made me more tipsy and more self-complacent! As for my Neengai, she laughed, clapped her hands, and embraced me several times. I was declared duly initiated and adopted into the family by the name Wah-sah-ge-wah-no-qua. They had already called me among themselves, in reference to my complexion and my travelling propensities, O-daw-yaun-gee *the fair changing moon, or rather, the fair moon which changes her place;* but now, in compliment to my successful achievement, Mrs. Johnston bestowed this new appellation, which I much prefer. It signifies *the bright foam,* or more properly, with the feminine adjunct qua, *the woman of the bright foam;* and by this name I am henceforth to be known among the Chippewas.

A marble likeness of Anna Jameson in later life.

Pinckney: 1837-1843
by
Caroline   Kirkland

Few women who wrote of their Michigan experience did so with the literary skill and humor of Caroline Kirkland. Her often reprinted *A New Home - Who'll Follow!* (New York, 1839) remains a most readable Michigan classic.

Born Caroline Matilda Stansbury in New York in 1801, as a child she developed a flair for languages. Her love of reading allowed her to gain an education uncommon for women of her time. As a teenager she began teaching in New York. In 1828 she married William Kirkland, a myopic and nearly deaf professor of classical literature. Seven years later the Kirkland's immigrated to Michigan where they taught at the newly established Detroit Female Academy.

Soon Prof. Kirkland caught the land fever then raging across the peninsula and he acquired control of 1,300 acres in southern Livingston County. There he founded the settlement of Pinckney. In the summer of 1837 his wife and their four children joined Kirkland at Pinckney. The sophisticated eastern lady found neither the crudities of log cabin life nor the peculiarities of her frontier neighbors to her liking. She described her many humorous experiences in *A New Home - Who'll Follow!* (New York, 1839), published under the pseudonym Mary Clavers. The book won enthusiastic praise from eastern reviewers but when copies found their way to Pinckney and residents readily reorganized themselves among the characters she had lampooned, Kirkland soon found herself *persona non grata*. Ostracized and nearly bankrupt, the Kirklands returned to New York in 1843.

Shortly thereafter when her nearly blind and deaf husband accidently walked off a New York wharf and drowned, Kirkland began supporting the family solely through her writing. Among her publications were two additional books about her Michigan debacle.

In 1847 Kirkland began editing a popular ladies journal called the *Union Magazine*. Among its hand-colored fashion plates, sentimental poetry and temperance tales appeared a series written by Kirkland entitled "Western Sketches," based also on her Michigan recollections. The following "Western Sketch," "The Justice," which has not previously appeared in book form, demonstrates clearly that excessive litigation is not solely a 20th century abomination.

Some people think litigation an evil, but a few in the western country seem to count it among their pleasures. The calm tenor of rural life is seldom interrupted by any thing in the way of amusement, that is to say, of what the uneducated world calls amusement. Day succeeds day with scarce a variation in toil; and the Sabbath is spent either in a continuation of the same toils, in the pursuit of game, or in attendance on some place of worship, whence all that is beautiful and attractive, whether in sights or sounds, is shut out, and a poor, barren, lifeless or fanatical presentation of religion too often the only resource. The substitute for music on such occasions is the nasal twang caught of some itinerant singing master, one of a class of people who may be said to *infest* the back country. This music, being destitute of all that moves the soul or excites the fancy, scarcely deserves the name.

As for beauty to delight the eye, it abounds everywhere out of doors. Rich foliage, a resplendent sky seen through an atmosphere of Italian transparency silver, streams and lakes at every turn, overflowing fertility that makes the fields 'to laugh and sing' all these, and more than we can enumerate are there. But where is the taste which can enjoy such things, and appropriate them, and incorporate them, day by day, with the very being? Where no culture is, a taste for the beautiful, though not wholly extinct in any human heart, is obscure and almost impotent. You remark, "A fine sunset!" "Yes;" will be the reply, "I hope we a'nt goin' to have rain till after the wheat' ten." "What a beautiful view!" you say again. "Poor property, though," will be the response. The unopened mind is ignorant alike of its needs and its capabilities. It feels indeed a lack of something essential, and it tries to supply the want by - what? reading? watching the chasing clouds? listening to the music of brook and bird? Ah no! It tries whiskey, perhaps, or tobacco, or camp-meeting, or election, or a law-suit. It would have faith in culture, if it knew what culture is. It would sometimes find consolation and interest in religion, if religion were presented as Christ presented it to those who came about him, in simplicity under the open sky. But for lack of what should be, it accepts what should not be. Mere animal excitement nay, even the rousing of the angry and destructive passions, is preferred to apathy.

This is the only method in which we are able to account for the frequency of petty law-suits, where law is dear and land cheap; where cattle may pasture upon 'a thousand hills,' like the herds of the patriarchs, without trenching upon anybody's rights; where 'grass grows and water runs' unclaimed by anybody but the government, which disturbs no one; and above all, where the most valuable of all earthly possessions is time, since that alone is wanting to do all that must needs be done before the wilderness can blossom as the rose, and where the price of a man's day is therefore higher than in almost any other part of the world. Yet, all these utilitarian considerations will not hinder the most pains-taking, money scraping, penurious old clod-compeller, from going to law about a length of fence, a stick of timber, the right to water cattle in a particular spot, the price of a plough-point, or the setting of a saw. It is surprising to see the energy and perseverance that will be wasted in this way. The man who could not be persuaded to mend a broken latch to keep the cows out of the garden, or to stop a leak that lets the rain in upon his bed, is the very one who will be punctual as the sun at the Justice' Court, whether his own cause is coming on or not; as anxious to see the side he espouses come off the triumphant winner of fifty cents, as if the title to his own farm hung upon the result. And long observation has convinced us that, in a majority of such cases, mere longing for excitement is the moving cause, one which can be remedied only by the sedulous introduction of means of real solid culture among this people, too able, too noble, to bear the stagnation of ignorance without some effort, however insane, for mental action.

The Justice' Court is held sometimes in the tavern, sometimes (rarely) in the school-room, but usually near the domestic hearth in the family room, where the Lares and Penates may sit in judgement, if they will, on the decisions of their

80

protege'. The mother gathers up her sewing and her babies, brushes the hearth, puts the table in its place, and then withdraws to the 'bed-room,' not but the Justice' Court has a bed in it, too, as that is considered no disqualifying circumstance (Q. did the 'lit de justice' arise from some primitive custom of the sort?) There the dame sits, jogging the cradle and darning the stockings; coming into court now and then, to look for scissors, or to skim the pot which sings over the fire, the lawyers and witnesses civilly making way for her, unless the stage of pleadings is too absorbingly interesting to allow them to observe her presence. The baby may cry, or Johnny fall down and break 'his precious nose,' nobody calls 'silence!' since that is past hoping for. If the older and more unruly of the children will hang about too pertinaciously, the justice may call out now and then, 'Mother! can't you take these 'young'uns' away? they bother me!' And the mother calls, and they obey, it they have a mind to.

The Justice' Court being held in this unceremonious sort of way, nothing is easier than to get sight of one at any time when a cause of any interest is coming on. Such causes excite a good deal of talk in the neighborhood, and, as we have before said, draw together all the men, of whatever occupation. By the convenient vicinity of the 'bed-room' the lady of the public functionary may hold her levee at the same time with his court, and give her gossips the advantage of all the pleadings, as well as of the earliest knowledge of the decision. If the parties are well-off, they generally employ young lawyers from the neighboring villages, and these, called to plead before a plain, and often very ignorant farmer, delight in not only throwing learned dust into his eyes, by the use of Latin more barbarous even than that of the law-books, but also in tickling his ears by the incessant repetition of 'Your Honor!' a sound delicious in proportion to its novelty, and the shortness of the period during which it will probably be enjoyed, justice-ships shifting like the clouds, where all are equally anxious for the office and equally eligible to it.

As may be supposed, under these circumstances, decisions are often so monstrously unjust and improper that the whole public voice cries out at once against them; in which case a new trial is inevitable, and more loss of time and money, more ill-blood, and more disappointment follow, both parties growing more angry as the dispute proceeds, and as the result appears less certain. Testimony, in bringing forward new points, brings upold grievances; treachery is developed, party feelings are

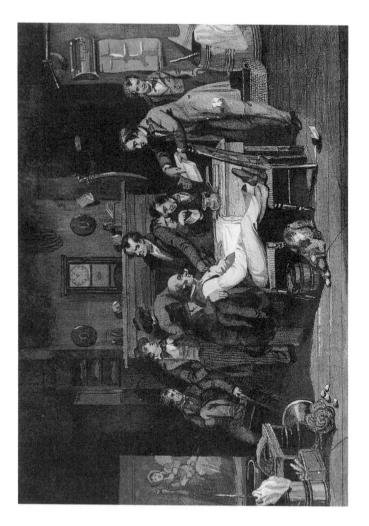

Caroline Kirkland illustrated her article with this steel engraving of a Michigan log cabin trial.

raised, family secrets dragged to light; and the end of all is, too often, sorely-wounded feelings, life-long enmity, and perhaps secretly-nourished schemes of revenge. Some, to be sure, look at a law-suit as a sort of game, and take the winning or losing as coolly as if it were only at their favorite 'checkers;' but it is rare to see two men who can shake hands heartily after a law-suit, and turn off the matter with a laugh.

Much mischief is done by a mean, unscrupulous class of lawyers, not a whit behind those whose venomous faces haunt the Tombs,[70] laying in wait for the unwary and the wretched. In a country which is the land of golden promise for adventurers, it is not to be wondered at that this kind of harpy should find entrance and support, even in a quiet and honest community. Such infest every society where law as a profession has been established, witness Dickens' account of Messrs. Dodson and Fogg, who incited Mrs. Bardell to sue for breach of promise, promising to do their part 'on spec,' and then throwing her into prison for the costs.[71] A case of this kind which fell under our knowledge, shows that law-rogues are identical, everywhere.

A man who was known as an exceedingly rude, quarrelsome and litigious fellow, complained that several acres of his 'mash' were flooded by the setting-back of the water of a mill which had just been built in the neighborhood. As the fact was evident, the owner of the mill offered compensation, and proposed to submit the amount to arbitration. This was indignantly rejected. The land had cost its possessor ten shillings[72] per acre, bought of the government. It was wet land, always, and useless except for mowing, when the hay would bring perhaps five dollars annually. But the price demanded was considerably over one hundred dollars the acre. This being out of the question, the mill-owner resolved to let the law decide the matter, whenever his neighbor should see fit to sue, as he loudly threatened to do.

At this stage of proceedings, a lawyer of the class to which we have alluded, hearing of the angry talk of the litigant, succeeded in making him believe that it was easy for him to oblige the owner to pay the thousand dollars demanded, or take down his mill, an alternative always insisted upon in the course of these discussions. Thus excited, the man, keen enough in most matters, was so blind as to begin by giving the lawyer, who professed to be entirely disinterested, but wishing security for form's sake,though he promised never to demand payment if

83

unsuccessful, a lien upon part of his farm, quite secure that what he was to gain would make him too rich to care for a farm, his lawyer assuring him that the mill, then in full operation, would eventually fall into his hands.

The delays of the law deferred the trial for some time. The threats were louder than ever, and the lawyer more assiduous as the cause was deferred; the passions of the quarreller became more exasperated, and the cunning tempter at his ear offering fresh hopes, piece after piece of his farm was mortgaged for costs of the suit. Meanwhile the mill-owner, not being very sure that justice would have her bandage on when the time of trial came, felt anxious to settle the matter without a resort to her ladyship; and taking a friend with him, and a bag containing two hundred and fifty silver dollars, (those being the days of 'Wild-Cat Banks,') by way of tangible evidence of his desire for a settlement, called once more on his loud talking neighbor, and made a final effort at an adjustment, though at a cost which judicious people thought five times the worth of the land in question. This offer was rejected with scorn, and the old alternative of 'a thousand dollars or take down your mill' was repeated as the ultimatum.

But at this time of rapid emigration, when the building of mills was felt to be the making of the country, while the evil complained of in this case, the flooding of more land than was allowed for in the formation of ponds, gave rise to frequent litigation by sharpers, it had been found necessary to take the circumstances of the case into consideration in deciding similar causes, lest, as there were few scientific mill-wrights, whose knowledge would secure their employers against these unlucky accidents, the erection of mills should be checked, and so great evil ensue. When the matter did at last come to trial, therefore, and lawyers were heard on both sides, the Court awarded seventeen dollars damages to J.M., being the value of the hay which he might have cut from his marsh in three years during which the trespass had existed.

In six months from that time, J.M. was turned off his farm by his lawyer and the store-keeper who had furnished his family with goods during the time when he neglected his business to pursue his law-suit; and he disappeared from the neighborhood to begin the world anew, further west, with the axe on his shoulder almost his sole possession.

The owner of the mill now wished to buy the flowed land

of the store-keeper, into whose hands it had fallen; but it was too precious a bone of contention to be give up at any price. He preferred holding it, not knowing, as he said, what might happen; that is to say, looking forward to some snug bit of litigation in the future. So we may hear of it again some day.

The suits brought in Justices' Courts are often ludicrously small in their commencements, though they not unfrequently become formidable before they are finished. We have seen a suit for seventy-five cents swell to a hundred dollars on each side, and the litigants, bull-dog like, as loth to quit their hold as ever. Mere passionate quarrels, leading to blows, are common ground of law-suits, the combatants sometimes pleading each his own cause in person. Cases occur in which the women are brought in as witnesses and these are generally uncommonly rich ones, affording talk for miles round long after. The ladies are even occasionally the heroines of court-scenes, being 'bound over to keep the peace" when they have been too belligerent in act or threat. The poor husband cuts a melancholy figure on these occasions.

But we must leave something for our artist to tell, and we doubt not the reader will discover his meaning without any amplification of ours.

Caroline Kirkland, literary lady on the frontier.

Detroit to Mackinac Island by Ship: 1840

by
Eliza Steele

With the advent of regularly scheduled steam boats splashing over the waters of lakes Huron and Michigan a trip to the north country became part of a fashionable Great Lakes tour. Mrs. Eliza Steele, a prim New York author of religious books, traveled from Detroit to Mackinac Island as part of her 4,000 mile summer tour "through the Great Lakes, the prairies of Illinois, the rivers Illinois, Mississippi, and Ohio; and over the Alleghany Mountains to New York in 1840."

She recorded her impressions gathered during that trip in the form of letters published in *A Summer Journey in the West* (New York, 1841).

Based on her own experiences, Steele found it necessary to caution her female readers never to attempt travel to such remote places, unescorted, as Anna Jameson had. Though she was "reluctant to censure one so gifted." Steele's own prose, in fact, did not measure up to Jameson's writing, and at times she seems to be confused as to where she is. Yet her book offers some fine descriptions of Detroit, a voyage up the St. Clair River and Lake Huron and Mackinac Island. Unfortunately Steele's boat continued on to Chicago along the Wisconsin side of Lake Michigan. We join Mrs. Steele as she approaches Detroit on the morning of July 2, 1840.

Land began to appear upon our western quarter, and soon the state of Michigan became visible. The mouth of Detroit River was soon after seen here, five miles wide from the Canadian shore to Michigan. At Amherstburg, a small Canadian town, we stopped about seven o'clock, for the purpose of taking on wood. The flashing of bayonets and the red uniform, as the sentinel walked up and down the wharf, told us we were in land belonging to another nation. Fort Malden is passed soon after.

Upon a platform, in front of the fortress, a file of soldiers were going through their exercises, their brilliant scarlet dresses and arms, prettily flashing back the morning sun. A boat, filled with red-coated soldiers, was passing over to an island to relieve the guard which stood upon a romantic point, near his little sentry box. A large ship came rapidly down the river, with all its sails out, looking like a huge bird of prey winging his flight to the shore, adding to the variety of the scene. Detroit is a beautiful river, connecting lakes St. Clair and Erie. Its width is generally about a mile - opposite Detroit city three-fourths of a mile. The shores are very beautiful, cultivated upon each side, with several pretty islands in the centre. Upon the Canadian side we observed several French settlements, their windmills upon every point giving a novel and unique effect to the scene. We did not reach Detroit until ten o'clock, although it is only 19 miles from the mouth of the river, owing to our delay in taking on wood. The city appeared well, covering a plateau of ground elevated 40 feet above the river. Three steamboats were in sight as we approached, one being a ferry boat to the town of Sandwich, opposite. As we were to remain here some time we landed and walked about the city. The city stands upon a plain which commands an extensive view of the river and surrounding country. A broad street runs through the centre called Jefferson Avenue, lined on each side with shops and hotels. At the upper end are several handsome dwellings surrounded with gardens. The churches are common in their appearance, except the Catholic, which I must say was uncommon. It is a large building of unpainted wood, having two odd looking steeples exactly alike, in the centre of the front; at the back is a dome having on each side a belfry.[73] Adjoining this is the residence of the bishop, a large brick building. I was disappointed in the appearance of this city. It was built by the French, you know, in 1670,[74] and being so much older than Rochester or Buffalo, we naturally supposed it would be larger than it is. But the same causes do not operate here which influence the prosperity of the other cities. It has not the old and settled state of New York behind it, nor the great canal. Michigan, of which Detroit is the capital, has been recently settled, and that only in the southern parts. The fur trade was for years its main dependence, and that has of late fallen off very much. As man invades the recesses of the forest, the animals retreat before him. Detroit has, however, felt the wind in her sails, and is rapidly following after her southern sisters. Of this, the increase of population is proof 2,222 being their number in 1830, and 1839, 9,278. Several railroads are planned out, which, when the river and lakes are filled with ice, will be of much service. Of these, the Detroit and St. Joseph[75] are the principal - leading from this city across the state to Lake Michigan, a distance of 194 miles; 33 miles are completed. Many persons take this route to Chicago, in preference to the more extensive one around the lakes. Besides these, there are contemplation the Detroit and Pontiac; Shelby and Detroit,[76] etc. Michigan will soon fill up, as its population has increased since 1830, seven hundred per cent; then it was 28,600, and now, in 1840, they count 211,205. Detroit will then be the great depot of the lakes, and bids fair to rival the neighboring cities. Here we landed our German emigrants, who were bound to the rich plains of Michigan. Upon the wharf were men busily engaged packing white fish salted, with barrels, fifty of which we took on board. The white fish is a delicious fish, something the form of our shad, averaging from 4 to 10 lbs. and sometime weigh 14 lbs. There is a great trade of this fish upon the lakes. 30,000 barrels were exported from Cleveland this season. While passing the city, when we had resumed our voyage, we observed several rows of handsome ware houses, many of which seemed as if newly erected. We also noticed a large brick building erected for the hydraulic works which supply the city with water,[77] it being in these lakes fit for cooking, washing and drinking.

Ten miles from Detroit the river gradually expands into Lake St. Clair. A pretty lake - a most sweet lake - appearing small among its larger sisters, and yet it is 90 miles in circumference. The waters are cool and transparent, fringed with the graceful ash, the linden, 'tasseled gentle,' the beech, and the stately liorio dendron,[78] and many other varieties. We felt reluctant to enter and ruffle the glassy surface, and disturb the profound repose which reigned around. The shores are low and there are no houses in sight. A wood cutter's hut, and at its extremity, a lighthouse, were the only signs of life we saw. The trees were throwing their flickering shadows upon the placid water, or leaning over, as if to admire their own reflection so perfectly painted upon the mirrored surface.

In which the massy forest grew,
as if in upper air;
More perfect both in shape and hue,
Than any waving there.

If you do not choose to emigrate to any of those charming spots I have mentioned along the road; if Auburn, or Rochester, or Cleveland do not lure you perhaps you would like to come to the picturesque shores of St. Clair, and weave you a bower 'in some sweet solitary nook' under those trees of 'ancient beauty;' or erect a picturesque hermitage with a pet skull, and moralize and spiritualize your hours away. I have heard many declare they could better worship their Creator in the fields and woods than in temples made with hands and can 'look from nature up to nature's God.'

The shores of St. Clair, being low, display the rise which has taken place in these northern lakes. That there is a rise and fall in this singular mass of fresh water has been observed for many years; and many opinions have been hazarded as to its cause. Some of the Indians declare there is a regular rise and fall every seven years; while the scientific traveller, Darby,[79] tells us there is a rise once in fifty years. A person, upon whose knowledge we could rely, told us at Buffalo, one year, while he resided upon the banks of the St. Lawrence, the current ran out of Lake Ontario at the rate of ten miles, and the next year the lake had unaccountably risen, and ran thirteen miles an hour. It must have been one of those extraordinary floods, of course much higher, which caused the lakes to overflow, as I have mentioned above - that is if it were not a diluvial torrent. The captain of our steamboat, who had navigated these lakes for several years, a man of intelligence and integrity, agreed with the Indians in the belief of a gradual rise and fall in seven years. During these last two years the water has risen to the height of five or six feet. Our captain pointed to many spots, upon the shore, where the water had overflowed the land. Upon one pretty place a farm house had been abandoned, and a fine apple orchard, standing two years in the water, had been destroyed; and now, while all around was green, their limbs were bare and leafless. A very intelligent man, a settler upon the river St. Clair, pointed to several noble maple and beech trees, as we passed the Michigan shore, whose gradual decay he had watched, while making his spring and fall trips in order to purchase goods in New York. It was pitiable, he said, to behold such goodly trees, 'green robed senators of ancient woods' sinking beneath the subtle destroyer, as some noble heart withering away at the touch of affliction! He watched them with an interest he would a friend consuming under a slow decay - their glorious beauty dimmed and faded, until a lifeless skeleton alone remained.

"a huge oak dry and dead,
Still clad with relics of its trophies old,
Lifting to heaven its aged hoary head,
Whose foot on earth hath got but feeble hold."

This man's history interested us much, and I will relate it for your edification. He was a native of our city of New York, one of a large family straightened for means. While quite young he had married, and struggled for years to support his family respectably, but sickness and 'bad times' rendered his lot a gloomy one. Hearing so often of the happiness and prosperity of 'the west,' he resolved to remove thither, and accordingly bought a tract of land upon St. Clair River, then farther west than it now is. He came here twenty years since, with a wife and several young children, and a mere trifle in money. A little village has now risen around him, of which he is the owner. He has built a good tavern for travellers, which he rents out; has erected a saw-mill; a few shops and houses, and a little church. His children are married and settled around him; and he is, as he expressed himself, "independent of the world." Once a year he goes to New York or Buffalo, to purchase goods for his shop. How much better is this state of things than to remain, struggling for a morsel, among the hungry crowd of a large city. I asked him if he never repented renouncing a city life. 'No, indeed!' he answered 'I go there once or twice a year to transact business, but hurry away, for I feel as if in prison. I want elbow room, and never breathe free until threading my green lakes and vast forests again. I am glad to leave such fictitious existence, where each man models his conduct upon that of his neighbor, and dare not act as his spirit prompts him.'

We had passed into St. Clair River, and about sun down dropped this man and his goods at his little village, which was seated upon a green slope, cut out of the forest, upon the Michigan shore. The houses were surrounded by little gardens and seemed comfortable. The sign of the village inn was swinging in the summer breeze; a traveler had just alighted from his horse in front of the piazza, and the steam from his mill was rising high above the trees tinted purple in the evening light. From a shop door a young man, probably his son, accompanied by a neighbor, stepped forth to greet him; while, from the honeysuckle covered porch of a neat cottage a woman, whom I fancied his wife, was looking eagerly out to watch his approach.

Every thing denoted industry, cheerfulness, and independence. Soon after leaving the village of Clay,[80] we observed a ship at anchor near the shore, quite a picturesque object. It proved to be the Milwaukee, a ship of three hundred tons burthen, bound from Buffalo to Chicago. It was waiting for wind, or steam, to enable it to enter Lake Huron, as this lake pours into the river St. Clair with so strong a current, that vessels can seldom stem it without a strong wind. She was soon attached to our steamboat, and we both passed swiftly along. What a superb western sky! The sun has long left us, and yet we scarcely miss its light, so golden and so brilliant is the mantle he has left behind him. It is nearly nine o'clock, and yet I can see to write this; but fatigue drives me to my cabin, and forces me to say adieu until tomorrow.

July 3rd. - Still in the river St. Clair. We stopped some hours in the night at Newport,[81] to take in a supply of wood. The captain purchased eighty cords at $1.50 a cord. He told us it was his opinion the steamboats upon these waters would soon be obliged to burn coal, although surrounded by such a world of trees, as there is so much time wasted in stopping for it. I did not regret our detention, as I was anxious to lose no part of a scenery to me so novel and pleasing. This is a beautiful river about sixty miles long, and half a mile broad, having several little towns upon it. Cottrellville and Palmer[82] we had also passed in the night; the latter a thriving place, from which a railroad is contemplated to Romeo, twenty-six miles, there to meet the Shelby and Detroit railroad. A communication will thus be continued with Detroit through the winter. The country upon the Canadian shore is wild and uninhabited, while the Michigan side of the river is frequently adorned with fields of grass or wheat, or thrifty orchards. The houses are plain, but seemed surrounded by every comfort. Our course ran quite near this shore, so close, that I might fancy myself transported into the midst of a farm yard, with all its morning business going on. A pretty white wood house is before me now, surrounded by fields and barns, having a row of cherry trees in front whose fruit is glistening red in the morning sun. In the barn yard a man is chopping wood, to cook the breakfast, I suppose - another is busy hoeing in a potato field, a boy is leading a horse down to the river for water, while numerous other children are arrested in their play and stand open mouthed gazing at us, ducks are dabbling in the wavelets, pigs are rooting up the turf, a flock of geese are running down the bank at us with

A Chippewa belle in the 1920s.

beaks and wings extended in a warlike attitude - while a sober cow chews her cud under a large hickory nut tree. The next moment all is gone, to give place to the silent groves of oak, maple and ash. Upon a long narrow island near the Canadian shore, my eyes were attracted by what seemed a row of haystacks. I enquired the meaning, and was told I was looking upon an Indian village, and these were wigwams. I was delighted to behold a veritable Indian lodge, and to see real Indians, instead of those half civilized beings I had met at Niagara. They are a body of Chippeway Indians who reside upon Warpole Island[83] under the care of a missionary of the Methodist church. Their wigwams consisted of poles meeting at top, around which, coarse matting, formed of reeds is fastened. From the apex of these cones smoke was rising, telling of culinary operations going on within. Around each lodge was a small patch of potatoes or corn. A small church, with the missionary cottage and a few log cabins, were in the midst. Groups of Indians were lounging upon the bank gazing at us, while others unconcernedly pursued their usual occupations of fishing or hoeing. How much more graceful were those wild sons of the forest, than the civilized men I had observed upon the shores I had passed. Their mantles of cloth of blanket stuff, trimmed with gay colors, were gracefully thrown around them, and their ornamented leggins or moccasins glittered as they walked. How dignified is the tread of an Indian! We remarked as we passed the island, many in various occupations and attitudes, yet they never moved awkwardly, nor sprang, nor jumped in a clumsy manner. The missionary cottage was an object of great interest to us. I had often read of these self denying disciples of Jesus, but never before looked upon the scene of their labors. Here in this lonely shore, away from all they love their friends and home and almost shut out from the face of civilized man, they spend their days in laboring to ameliorate the lot of these unhappy children of the forest. In bring them to the feet of their master, they are indeed conferring a blessing upon them past all return. As a recompense for the bright land their fathers have taken from the bereaved Indian, they are leading them to another, brighter and more lasting.

A small settlement is formed at the mouth of Black River, called Port Huron, which is to be the termination of another canal across the state.

Here we found another vessel waiting for wind. It was the

brig *Rocky Mountain,* bound to Green Bay, being attached to our other side we passed 'doubly armed.' Near the point where the river leaves Lake Huron stands Fort Gratiot,[84] an United States military station whose white walls and buildings, over which the American flag was waving, looked out brightly from among the dark forest of the Michigan shore. A line of blue coats were going through their morning drill; and a few cannons looked out fiercely upon us. A small white Gothic church, and a cottage stood near; the whole making a pretty cabinet picture. The river now narrowed to a quarter of a mile, upon each side a point - the American side crowned by a lighthouse, and the Canadian by a cluster of Indian cabins. A bark canoe, paddled by five Indians, pushed off the shore and came after us with the greatest rapidity, their long black hair flying wildly behind them. Our two vessels retarded our motion a little, so that the Indians overtook us, and kept at our side for some distance. They used their paddles with astonishing quickness, and we were surprised to see them in their 'light canoe' keep pace with our large steamboat. It was however for a short distance only - they were soon fatigued with such great exertion, and turned towards the point, and sprang out, or rather stepped out with the greatest dignity, drew the canoe to the shore, and then squatted down upon the bank evidently enjoying their race. I use the above inelegant word, as being very expressive of their posture. The Indian never sits down as we do - with his feet close beside each other, and his body erect, he sinks slowly down - his blanket is then thrown over his head and around his feet, so that nothing is seen except his dark glaring eyes. Through the narrow pass before mentioned, between the two points, the waters of Huron run with a swift current. Here we were furnished with another evidence of the rise of these waters.

An officer of the army and his wife were our fellow voyagers, very intelligent and agreeable persons. They had been stationed at Fort Gratiot a few years since, and had frequently roved over the beach around the lighthouse in search of the pretty silecious pebbles, agate, camelian, and calcedony, which are often found upon these shores. To their surprise, they now found their favorite point, 'curtailed of its fair proportions' by a rise of nearly five feet of water. Our steamboat and its two 'tenders' passed between the points out of St. Clair River, and we found ourselves at once in a large and shoreless lake, with nothing in front, between us and the bright blue sky, which touched the green waters in the far horizon beyond. The transition is so sudden from the narrow opening, to the boundless lake as to produce a grand and exciting effect. Once out upon the calm waters of Huron, our two guests were loosened from their tackles, and spreading their huge wings, they passed one to each shore, and we soon left them far behind. About an hour after, the bell of our steamboat startled the still lake with its clamors, denoting the approach of some vessel. We looked out in time to see the noble steamboat *Great Western* rush past us as if upon the wings of a whirlwind. She was on her way from Chicago to Buffalo. Her bell answered ours, and the deck was crowded with passengers. One of these standing alone by himself, and taking his hat off attracted our notice and we discovered in him an old acquaintance from New York. These meetings in a distant land are very interesting, carrying our feelings at once to the home we had left. This steamboat is one of the largest upon the lakes, is finished in a style of great elegance, and is said to be as long as the English steamship of the same name.

This whole day since ten o'clock we have been passing through Huron under a cloudless sky. The lake is two hundred and fifty-five miles long, and its waters are of a deeper tint than those we have passed, owing to its great depth, as we are sailing over nine hundred feet of water, while in some places it is said to be unfathomable. The color is dark olive almost black, and it is only when the sun shines through the waves that we can perceive they are green.

In the afternoon we were off Saginaw Bay, an indentation in the coast of Michigan running seventy or eighty miles deep and forty wide, making the lake here very broad; in one spot we were out of sight of the land. A river of the same name flows into the bay, upon which, about twenty-three miles from its mouth, is a small town. A canal is proposed from this bay across the state to Lake Michigan, at Grand or Washtenog River. How shall I convey to you an idea of the liveliness which sat upon earth, air, and water this afternoon! Certainly that sunset upon Lake Huron is the most beautiful I have ever beheld. The vast and fathomless lake, bounded by the heavens alone, presented an immense circle, 'calm as a molten looking glass,' - to quote from my favorite Job - surrounded by a band of fleecy clouds, making a frame work of chased silver. Slowly and gracefully sank the orb, the white clouds gently dispersing at his approach, and leaving their monarch a free and glorious path. As he drew near that crystal floor, all brilliancy faded from the face of the lake, save one bright pathway from the sun to us--like the bridge of Giamschid leading from earth to heaven. The sun which I had always been accustomed to see above, was now below me, near the water, on the water, under the water! A veil of purple is thrown over it, and now the sun sleeps on Lake Huron. The gold and rose which painted the western sky have gone. Darkness has stolen over the world below, and we turn our eyes above. What a high and noble dome of loveliest blue! Upon one side there hangs a crescent of the purest pearly white, while at its side steals forth one silver star, soon followed, as saith Ezekiel, by 'all the bright lights of heaven,' until night's star embroidered drapery is canopied around us. What bosom is insensible to this gorgeous firmament? Who hath not felt the 'sweet influence of the Pleiades' while gazing at this starry roof above?

We have seen nature in all its power and grandeur, while tossed on Erie's waves, or listening to the thunder of Niagara; but here she is at rest in all her quiet loveliness; and would her worshippers behold her in her fairest mood, let them come and gaze at evening on Lake Huron.

July 4th - The sun and I arose at the same time. When I left my state room, as if waiting to greet me, it arose majestically from the bosom of the water, flooding the lake with light. No land was descried upon the east, but we were near the Michigan shore off Thunder Bay. The Shanewaging Islands[85] which stretch across it were distinctly visible, and presented various beauties of shape and tint. All trace of man has now disappeared, for the northern part of Michigan has never been settled owing to the intense cold of the winters. We have passed a long line of coast without any inhabitant (except a forlorn woodman's hut in one spot) stretching for two hundred and fifty miles, covered with boundless forests, in whose green recesses there are paths 'which no fowl knoweth, and which the vultures eye hath not seen.' Here is the home of the bear, the elk, and the moose, deer and upon the aspen, oak, and maple trees, sport the blue bird, the robin, and yellow hammer, undisturbed by the foot of man. We have now passed the bounds of civilization, and our vessel is the only spot of life in this vast region of forest and water.

From the entrance of Lake Huron to Mackinac, there were but two places where man was visible. At the mouth of the

Zappa River[86] soon after entering the lake, there is a cabin where a woodman resides in the summer season to supply the steamboats; and at Presque Isle where we stopped in the afternoon there is another cluster of cabins, and wood piles. Our captain did not stop at this latter place, as he did not like their wood, it being chiefly swamp ash. The shore is low, covered with trees, having below, a beach of yellow sand, until just before coming in sight of Michilimackinac when the land becomes a little elevated. Ten miles this side of the last mentioned place, we passed Bois Blanc, a large wooded island, taking its name of *'white wood'* from the silver barked birch tree. This island belongs to government, and its only inhabitants, save a few straggling Ottawas are the family of the lighthouse keeper whose pretty tenement, and stately lighthouse, appear upon a projecting point. There is also a farm upon the island given by government to the missionaries of Michilimackinac, who sometimes maintain a farmer upon it.

O Mackinac, thou lonely island, how shall I describe thy various beauties! Certainly for situation, history, and native loveliness, it is the most interesting island in our states. We approach it through an avenue of islands, Drummond and Manitoulin, dimly seen on our east, and Bois Blanc, and Round, in our western side. Stretching across our path, far away in front of us, is Mackinac, painted against the clear blue sky. The island of Michilimackinac, or Mackinaw, or Mackinac as it is commonly spelt and pronounced, is a high and bold bluff of limestone about three hundred feet above the water, covered with verdure. Its name signifies in the Indian tongue great turtle, as it is something of the figure of this animal. At the foot of the bluff are strewed the buildings of the town. Among the most conspicuous of these are, the agency house and gardens, residence of Mr. Schoolcraft, Indian Agent, and the church and mission house. Along the beach were several Indian wigwams, while numerous pretty bark canoes were going and coming, as this is the Indian stopping place. A very beautiful, and conspicuous object was the United States fort, presenting at a distance the appearance of a long white line of buildings inserted into the top of the island high above the town. As we approached, its picturesque block houses and the pretty balconied residences of the officers came out to view, having the banner of the 'stripes and stars' waving over them. While gazing at this fair picture, suddenly a brilliant flame, and volumes of white smoke arose above the fort, while a booming sound told us they were firing their mid day salute in honor of the day. This added much to the beauty and grandeur of the scene. As our boat was to remain there for some hours, we disembarked and ascended to the fort to visit our friends the commanding officer and his family. We found them sitting upon their balcony, looking down upon the newly arrived steamboat. After the first greetings and mutual enquiries were over, we were shown all it was thought would interest us.

The view from our friend's balcony was beautiful in the extreme. The bay in front, the lovely islands around covered with a luxurious vegetation, the town spread out at our feet, the Indian lodges, and the canoes skimming the bright waters, each called forth our expressions of admiration. Passing into the interior of the fort, and through the fine parade ground and a large gateway, we found ourselves upon the summit of the island. Our path lay through copses of white birch, maple, and various other trees, and over green sward covered with strawberries and a variety of wild flowers, among which was a fine scarlet lilium superbum, blue bells, and kinni kanic, or Indian tobacco, and a pretty plant called Indian strawberry. Suddenly the silver tones of woman's voice, sounded near, and in a fairy dell we came upon a tent, surrounded by a party of ladies and gentlemen, busily engaged preparing for a fete in honor of the day. Among them was the daughter of our host, and some of the celebrated family of Schoolcraft. We were presented to the party, and were quite chagrined our limited time would not permit us to accept their invitation to remain and partake of their festivities. The grace and beauty of Mrs. Schoolcraft made great impression upon us. To me she was peculiarly interesting from the fact of her being descended from the native lords of the forest; for you know I have always taken the greatest interest in the fate of our Indian tribes. From the accent, the deep brunette of her smooth skin, and her dark hair and eyes, I should have taken her for a Spanish lady. From the tent we wound our way up to a high peak of the island. When near the summit, we left a grove, and saw before us one of the most picturesque and singular objects imaginable. It was a high arched rock of white limestone, stretching across a chasm before us, making a pretty natural bridge, through which we gazed far down into the waves of Huron, at least two hundred feet below. The surprise, the beauty and novelty of this striking object, brought forth expressions of admiration from us. The white arch was adorned with tufts of wild flowers, and shrubbery.

Ascending the arch, we gazed down upon the white beach below, whose pebbles could be here distinctly seen under the limpid water although many feet deep and out upon the fair waters, and the pretty islands, which "__like rich and various gems inlay the unadorned bosom of the deep."

We were obliged to be satisfied with a hasty view of this charming scene, as our time was limited; and we turned reluctantly towards our boat, without visiting the ruins of Fort Holmes, upon the high summit of the island. While passing through the town we observed several antique houses which had been erected by the French, who first settled this place in 1673.

These are frail dilapidated buildings, covered with roofs of bark. Upon the beach a party of Indians had just landed, and we stood while they took down their blanket sail, and hauled their birch bark canoe about twenty feet long, upon the shore. These are the Menominees or wild rice eaters, the ugliest Indians I had ever seen - also Winabagoes, with dark skin, low foreheads and shaggy hair, and having no pretentions to dress. I saw a chief however afterwards who was gaily bedizened with tinsel, beads, and paint, having one side of his face a light pea green, and the other cheek scarlet. We watched them erect their lodges which was done very soon - a few poles were placed in a circle, one end of each stood in the earth, while the others met at the top - coarse matting was folded around these, leaving an opening for a door, over which a blanket was hung. Some matting being spread upon the floor inside, the children and moveables were placed inside, and the canoe drawn up near it. We visited some of the shops and laid up a store of Indian articles, which are made by these poor people and sold here. Among them were small baskets called mococks, made of birch bark embroidered with porcupine quills, stained different colors - this was filled with maple sugar.

It is pleasant to meet friends so far from home, but I think the pleasure is almost counter balanced by the pain of parting. This we felt keenly, when the planks had withdrawn, and our friends had been forced to leave us, as we gazed after them winding their way up to the fort, the shores, and waters around seemed more desolate, more lonely than before.

Just before the steamboat started we had an opportunity of judging of the boasted transparency of this water, its depth having prevented this on our voyage. I looked down into it from the boat, where it was twenty feet deep, and could scarcely believe there was anything but air between us and those shining pebbles below. We had also an opportunity of hearing some Indian music. Upon the shore sat a group of unearthly beings, one of whom struck several taps upon a sort of drum, accompanied by the others, in what sounded like a wolf recitative - at the end of this all united in a yell which died away over the lake, much in the style of a howling blast accompanied by the shrieks of a drowning traveller. Our fishing party left us here to go up the Sault St. Mary into Lake Superior, spending their summer days among the picturesque scenery of that magnificent lake. We bade adieu with much regret to this pretty island, whose green terraces, fort and picturesque town, Indian lodges, and light canoes, made a beautiful scene - but the most interesting point in the view, was that white handkerchief waving farewell from the fortress balcony.

Upon a green slope of the Michigan shore, a pile of ruins were pointed out as the site of old Fort Mackinac, which was taken by Pontiac with a stratagem and afterwards every one within were massacred. How must those unfortunates have felt, upon this desolate shore, hundreds of miles away from their country, and at the mercy of savages. A band of Chippewa's or Ojibwa's were just passing in canoes thirty feet in length. This tribe stands higher in rank than the others, and their language, like the French, is the polite tongue among the Indian tribes. They have a ruler whose office has been hereditary for ages. He is called Mudjikiwis, and they pride themselves much upon his and their own rank and lineage. There is an anecdote, related by Schoolcraft, of one of this tribe, which if you have never seen, will amuse you. Chief Waishki, alias the Buffalo, was presented by the commissioners of the Treaty of Fond du Lac, with a medal as a badge of distinction. "What need have I of this?" he said haughtily. 'It is known whence I am descended!' These canoes are the prettiest and lightest things imaginable. They are formed of the bark of the birch tree, sewn together with a thread made from fine roots of cedar split. The bark is soaked to make it more pliable. Sometimes they are very gaily painted and ornamented. The paddles are of light wood.

Our captain placed before us at dinner a very fine lake trout, which he had purchased at Mackinac. It was two feet long, and very delicious. Fine salmon are also taken in these lakes. We were now upon the great Lake Michigan, which stretches from here three hundred and twenty miles, to the Illinois shore, and is nine hundred feet deep. Our course lay near the Michigan shore, which presented high bluffs and points of limestone, with banks of pebbles, and high jagged hills, or *dunes* of sand. These pebbles and sand are said to be thrown up by the northwestern winds, but I should rather imagine them left up by the floods which have swept over the land. Upon our right were Fox and Beaver isles, beyond which, Green Bay runs into Wisconsin, one hundred and three miles. This northern shore of Michigan is uninhabited, and covered with dense forests. The ledges and masses of white limestone upon some of these islands looked like fortresses or other buildings.

July 5th. Sunday upon the lake. When I left my cabin, I found the morning was misty, and the sun looking like the yolk of an egg, was bobbing up and down upon the water. It had just peeped above the waves, which, dashing about, sometimes obscured it from our view. We were lying at one of the Manitou Islands, taking in wood. This is a pretty crescent shaped islet, covered with trees. In the centre we were told is a lake with is unfathomable, and supposed to be connected with Lake Michigan. It is filled with the large trout, salmon and white fish of the lakes. There is a woodman's hut, and several large piles of wood upon the shore. 'Oh that the woodman would spare those trees.' Soon the pretty island will be denuded and forlorn. It is a sacred island - the Indians imagining it to be the residence of their Manitou, never dare to land there, as they believe such an intrusion would be followed by the anger of their Deity. One Indian, who despised such superstition ventured upon the shore, and was never heard of since. The forests and lake in the interior, they imagine is the abode of the blessed after death, whose hours will there pass in hunting and fishing. The Manitoulin Islands in Lake Huron, are also sacred; but they are much larger than these, one of them being fifty-five miles in length. I secured a handful of pebbles from the shore, which, like those of other lakes, are agate, chalcedony and other sileceous minerals. Upon the shores of Lake Superior these are found very fine, mixed with trachte, lava, and other volcanic rocks, and with masses of native copper. I had brought with me a package of well selected tracks,[87] which I opened this morning, and laid a few upon the table of the ladies saloon. Soon after, a pretty little girl knocked at my state-room door, saying her mother wished to know if I had any more tracts, as she should like to read one. I asked her where were those I laid upon the table? Those, she replied, some ladies were reading. I gave her several. The chambermaid next appeared begging for some; and then the cabin boy came with the same request. While I was selecting one which I thought might suit him, I observed a brawny dusky figure, with his shirt sleeves rolled up, and his person begrimed with soot and smoke, gazing earnestly towards us. 'That's Tom, one of the firemen,' said the cabin boy with a snigger; 'he heard you had books to lend and wants one dreadfully.' I beckoned to him, and he came forward with alacrity, while behind him I discerned several other grim visaged beings peeping out from their compartment toward us. I gave him a package to distribute among his fellows; and during the day had the pleasure of observing the greater part of the crew and passengers busily engaged with my books.

During our long voyage, those who had books had read them out, and those who had none, were getting very weary, so that they eagerly received anything in the shape of reading. But some of them, I trust, read them for the sake of the benefit they hoped to receive from their contents. It was a source of great satisfaction to behold so many persons engaged in themes of high import to their soul's best interest. These seeds were sown with a prayer for their success; and who can tell what immortal plants may spring up in some of their hearts, growing to a tree of life, and bearing fruit to flourish in the garden of paradise. Let me urge you never to travel without these, or other useful books to distribute on your way - like the girl in the fairy tale of our youth, is shedding gems and treasures in your path. There is no library in this boat as upon our Hudson and Eastern steamboats, and we were often amused with the alacrity with which our books were snatched up when we laid them down for a stroll, or to look at some object upon the shores. When we returned we were always sure to receive them again, and felt no vexation, as we knew they meant no impoliteness, and would be willing to lend us their own in return. My companion had never been used to such socialisms in his country, and was quite amused at this free and easy sort of thing. Our books were some of them French, and upon one occasion we found them in the hands of a simple hearted son of the forest, to whom books were so rare a treasure he could not resist examining them. He returned it with a smile, and said, shaking his head, 'how you can make any sense out of that I can't see, for I cannot read a word of it.'

Arch Rock was already a famous Mackinac Island attraction in 1840.

Mackinac Island: 1843
by
Margaret Fuller

Three years after Mrs. Steele had visited Mackinac Island, Margaret Fuller, one of the most distinguished literary women of her era, arrived there. Fuller also was making a pleasure cruise. In her book, *Summer On the Lakes in 1843* (Boston, 1844), she recorded the events of her voyage from Detroit to Chicago by steamer, then back to Mackinac Island and Sault Ste. Marie. At the Sault she emulated Anna Jameson's feat and also shot the rapids in an Indian canoe.

Fuller's book offers picturesque descriptions of Mackinac Island, in particular. She wrote with the true eye of an artist. She also devotes many pages to sympathetic discussions of the Indians.

Born in Cambridgeport, Massachusetts, in 1810, Fuller began her intellectual development early, studying Latin at the age of six and Greek when she was 13. Following the death of her father she taught school to support seven siblings. In 1835 she met Ralph Waldo Emerson and a friendship developed. She visited him at Concord and was involved with the Brook Farm communal experiment although she did not live there. She ultimately became friends with many of the leading eastern intellectuals and in 1839 she began her famous "conversations" with a group of cultivated Boston society women who met at Elizabeth Peabody's. Fuller helped edit the transcendentalist *Dial* and wrote for Horace Greeley's *New York Tribune,* winning a reputation as one of the best American critics. She also wrote articles advocating various reforms including woman's rights. Her first book, *Summer on the Lakes,* was followed by *Woman in the Nineteenth Century* (1845), a philosophical discussion of the woman's reform movement.

During a tour of Europe in 1846 she visited

Carlyle, Wordsworth and other literary greats. She settled in Rome the following year and married Giovanni Angelo, Marquis Ossoli, giving birth to a son in 1848. Her husband figured in the Italian struggle for independence against the French and she actively assisted him and performed heroic hospital work. When the French captured Rome in June, 1849, the Ossolis fled to the mountains and then took refuge in Florence. They sailed for America in May, 1850, but tragically their vessel was wrecked in a gale off Fire Island and the entire family drowned.

Late at night we reached this island of Mackinac, so famous for its beauty, and to which I proposed a visit of some length. It was the last week in August, at which time a large representation from the Chippewa and Ottawa tribes are here to receive their annual payments from the American government. As their habits make travelling easy and inexpensive to them, neither being obliged to wait for steamboats, or write to see whether hotels are full, they come hither by thousands, and those thousands in families, secure of accommodation on the beach, and food from the lake, to make a long holiday out of the occasion. There were near two thousand encamped on the island already, and more arriving every day.

As our boat came in, the captain had some rockets let off. This greatly excited the Indians, and their yells and wild cries resounded along the shore. Except for the momentary flash of the rockets, it was perfectly dark, and my sensations as I walked with a stranger to a strange hotel, through the midst of these shrieking savages, and heard the pants and snorts of the departing steamer, which carried away all my companions, were somewhat of the dismal sort; though it was pleasant, too, in the way that everything strange is; everything that breaks in upon the routine that so easily incrusts us.

I had reason to expect a room to myself at the hotel, but found none, and was obliged to take up my rest in the common parlor and eating room, a circumstance which insured my being an early riser.

With the first rosy streak, I was out among my Indian neighbors, whose lodges honeycombed the beautiful beach, that curved away in long, fair outline on either side the house. They were already on the alert, the children creeping out from beneath the blanket door of the lodge, the women pounding corn in their rude mortars, the young men playing on their pipes. I had been much amused, when the strain proper to the Winnebago courting flute was played to me on another instrument, at anyone fancying it a melody; but now, when I heard the notes in their true tone and time, I thought it not unworthy comparison, its graceful sequence, and the light flourish at the close, with the sweetest bird song; and this, like the bird song, is only practised to allure a mate. The Indian, become a citizen and a husband, no more thinks of playing the flute, than one of the "settled down" members of our society would of choosing the "purple light of love" as dye stuff for a surtout. [88]

Mackinac has been fully described by able pens, and I can only add my tribute to the exceeding beauty of the spot and its position. It is charming to be on an island so small that you can sail round it in an afternoon, yet large enough to admit of long, secluded walks through its gentle groves. You can go round it in your boat; or, on foot, you can tread its narrow beach, resting, at times, beneath the lofty walls of stone, richly wooded, which rise from it in various architectural forms. In this stone, caves are continually forming, from the action of the atmosphere; one of these is quite deep, and a rocky fragment left at its mouth, wreathed with little creeping plants, looks, as you sit within, like a ruined pillar.

The arched rock surprised me, much as I had heard of it, from the perfection of the arch. It is perfect, whether you look up through it from the lake, or down through it to the transparent waters. We both ascended and descended - no very easy matter - the steep and crumbling path, and rested at the summit, beneath the trees, and at the foot, upon the cool, mossy stones beside the lapsing wave. Nature has carefully decorated all this architecture with shrubs that take root within the crevices, and small creeping vines. These natural ruins may vie for beautiful effect with the remains of European grandeur, and have beside, a charm as of a playful mood in Nature.

The sugar loaf rock is a fragment in the same kind as the pine rock[89] we saw in Illinois. It has the same air of a helmet, as seen from an eminence at the side, which you descend by a long and steep path. The rock itself may be ascended by the bold and

106

agile: half-way up is a niche, to which those who are neither can climb by a ladder. A very handsome young officer and lady who were with us did so, and then, facing round, stood there side by side, looking in the niche, if not like saints or angels wrought by pious hands in stone, as romantically, if not as holily, worthy the gazer's eye.

The woods which adorn the central ridge of the island are very full in foliage, and in August, showed the tender green and plant leaf of June elsewhere. They are rich in beautiful mosses and the wild raspberry.

From Fort Holmes, the old fort, we had the most commanding view of the lake and straits, opposite shores, and fair islets. Mackinac itself is best seen from the water. Its peculiar shape is supposed to have been the origin of its name, Michilimackinac, which means the Great Turtle. One person whom I saw wished to establish another etymology, which he fancied to be more refined; but, I doubt not, this is the true one, both because the shape might suggest such a name, and the existence of an island of such form in this commanding position would seem a significant fact to the Indians. For Henry[90] gives the details of peculiar worship paid to the Great Turtle, and the oracles received from this extraordinary Apollo of the Indian Delphos.

It is crowned, most picturesquely, by the white fort, with its gay flag. From this, on one side, stretches the town. How pleasing a sight, after the raw, crude, staring assemblage of houses everywhere else to be met in this country, is an old French town, mellow in its coloring, and with the harmonious effect of a slow growth, which assimilates, naturally, with objects round it! The people in its streets, Indian , French, half-breeds, and others, walked with a leisure step, as of those who live a life of taste and inclination, rather than of the hard press of business, as in American towns elsewhere.

On the other side, along the fair, curving beach, below the white houses scattered on the declivity, clustered the Indian lodges, with their amber-brown matting so soft and bright of hue in the late afternoon sun. The first afternoon I was there, looking down from a near height, I felt that I never wished to see a more fascinating picture. It was an hour of the deepest serenity; bright blue and gold, with rich shadows. Every moment the sunlight fell more mellow. The Indians were grouped and scattered among the lodges; the women preparing food, in the kettle or frying pan, over the many small fires; the children, half naked, wild as little goblins, were playing both in and out of the water. Here and there lounged a young girl, with a baby at her back, whose bright eyes glanced, as if born into a world of courage and of joy, instead of ignominious servitude and slow decay. Some girls were cutting wood, a little way from me, talking and laughing in the low musical tone, so charming in the Indian women. Many bark canoes were upturned upon the beach, and, by that light, of almost the same amber as the lodges; others coming in, their square sails set, and with almost arrowy speed, though heavily laden with dusky forms, and all the apparatus of their household. Here and there a sail boat glided by, with a different but scarce less pleasing motion.

It was a scene of ideal loveliness, and these wild forms adorned it, as looking so at home in it. All seemed happy, and they were happy that day, for they had no fire water to madden them, as it was Sunday, and the shops were shut.

From my window, at the boarding house, my eye was constantly attracted by these picturesque groups. I was never tired of seeing the canoes come in, and the new arrivals set up their temporary dwellings. The women ran to set up the tent poles, and spread the mats on the ground. The men brought the chests, kettles etc. the mats were then laid on the outside, the cedar boughs strewed on the ground, the blanket hung up for a door, and all was completed in less than twenty minutes. Then they began to prepare the night meal, and to learn of their neighbors the news of the day.

The habit of preparing food out of doors gave all the gypsy charm and variety to their conduct. Continually I wanted Sir Walter Scott to have been there. If such romantic sketches were suggested to him, by the sight of a few gypsies, not a group near one of these fires but would have furnished him material for a separate canvas. I was so taken up with the spirit of the scene, that I could not follow out the stories suggested by these weather beaten, sullen, but eloquent figures.

They talked a great deal, and with much variety of gesture, so that I often had a good guess at the meaning of their discourse. I saw that whatever the Indian may be among the whites, he is anything but taciturn with his own people; and he often would declaim, or narrate at length. Indeed, it is obvious, if only from the fables taken from their stores by Mr. Schoolcraft, [91] that these tribes possess great power that way.

I liked very much to walk or sit among them. With the women I held much communication by signs. They are almost invariably coarse and ugly, with the exception of their eyes, with a peculiarly awkward gait, and forms bent by burdens. This gait, so different from the steady and noble step of the men, marks the inferior position they occupy. I had heard much eloquent contradiction of this. Mrs. Schoolcraft[92] had maintained to a friend, that they were in fact as nearly on a par with their husbands as the white woman with hers. "Although," said she, "on account of inevitable causes, the Indian woman is subjected to many hardships of a peculiar nature, yet her position, compared with that of the man, is higher and freer than that of the white woman. Why will people look only on one side? They either exalt the red man into a demigod, or degrade him into a beast. They say that he compels his wife to do all the drudgery, while he does nothing but hunt and amuse himself; forgetting that upon his activity and power of endurance as a hunter depends the support of his family; that this is labor of the most fatiguing kind, and that it is absolutely necessary that he should keep his frame unbent by burdens and unworn by toil, that he may be able to obtain the means of subsistence. I have witnessed scenes of conjugal and parental love in the Indian's wigwam, from which I have often, often thought the educated white man, proud of his superior civilization, might learn a useful lesson. When he returns from hunting, worn out with fatigue, having tasted nothing since dawn, his wife, if she is a good wife, will take off his moccasins and replace them with dry ones, and will prepare his game for their repast, while his children will climb upon him, and he will caress them with all the tenderness of a woman; and in the evening the Indian wigwam is the scene of the purest domestic pleasures. The father will relate, for the amusement of the wife and for the instruction of the children, all the events of the day's hunt, while they will treasure up every word that falls, and thus learn the theory of the art whose practice is to be the occupation of their lives.

Notwithstanding the homage paid to women, and the consequence allowed them in some cases, it is impossible to look upon the Indian women without feeling that they *do* occupy a lower place than women among the nations of European civilization. The habits of drudgery expressed in their form and gesture, the soft and wild but melancholy expression of their eye, reminded me of the tribe mentioned by MacKenzie,[93] where the women destroy their female children, whenever they have a good opportunity; and of the eloquent reproaches addressed by the Paraguay woman to her mother, that she had not, in the same way, saved her from the anguish and weariness of her lot. More weariness than anguish, no doubt, falls to the lot of most of these women. They inherit submission, and the minds of the generality accommodate themselves more or less to any posture. Perhaps they suffer less than their white sisters, who have more aspiration and refinement, with little power of self-sustenance. But their place is certainly lower, and their share of the human inheritance less.

Their decorum and delicacy are striking, and show that, when these are native to the mind, no habits of life make any difference. Their whole gesture is timid, yet self-possessed. They used to crowd round me, to inspect little things I had to show them, but never press near; on the contrary, would reprove and keep off the children. Anything they took from my hand was held with care, then shut or folded, and returned with an air of lady like precision. They would not stare, however curious they might be, but cast sidelong glances.

A locket that I wore was an object of untiring interest; they seemed to regard it as a talisman. My little sun shade was still more fascinating to them; apparently they had never before seen one. For an umbrella they entertained profound regard, probably looking upon it as the most luxurious superfluity a person can posses, and therefore a badge of great wealth. I used to see an old squaw, whose sullied skin and coarse, tanned locks told that she had braved sun and storm, without a doubt or care, for sixty years at least, sitting gravely at the door of her lodge, with an old green umbrella over her head, happy for hours together in the dignified shade. For her happiness pomp came not, as it so often does, too late; she received it with grateful enjoyment.

One day, as I was seated on one of the canoes, a woman came and sat beside me, with her baby in its cradle set up at her feet. She asked me by a gesture to let her take my sun shade, and then to show her how to open it. Then she put it into her baby's hand, and held it over its head, looking at me the while with a sweet mischievous laugh, as much as to say, "You carry a thing that is only fit for a baby." Her pantomime was very pretty. She, like the other women, had a glance, and shy, sweet expression in the eye; the men have a steady gaze.

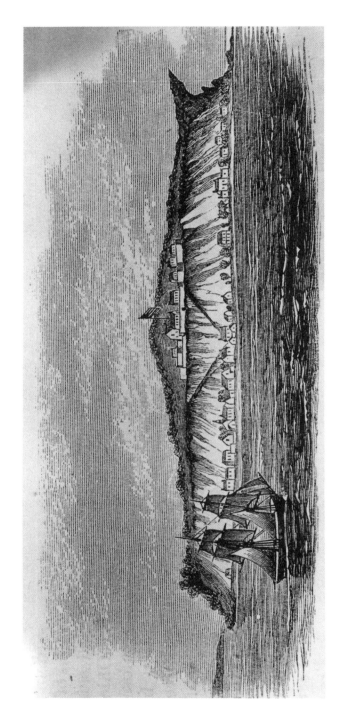

An early view of Mackinac from *Harper's Monthly*.

It is also evident that, as Mrs. Schoolcraft says, the women have great power at home. It can never be otherwise, men being dependent upon them for the comfort of their lives. Just so among ourselves wives who are neither esteemed nor loved by their husbands have great power over their conduct by the friction of every day, and over the formation of their opinions by the daily opportunities so close a relation affords of perverting testimony and instilling doubts. But these sentiments should not come in brief flashes, but burn as a steady flame; then there would be more women worthy to inspire them. This power is good for nothing, unless the woman be wise to use it aright. Has the Indian, has the white woman, as noble a feeling of life and its uses, as religious a self-respect, as worthy a field of thought and action, as man? If not, the white woman, the Indian woman, occupies a position inferior to that of man. It is not so much a question of power, as of privilege.

The men of these subjugated tribes, now accustomed to drunkenness and every way degraded, bear but a faint impress of the lost grandeur of the race. They are no longer strong, tall, or finely proportioned. Yet, as you see them stealing along a height, or striding boldly forward, they remind you of what was majestic in the red man.

On the shores of Lake Superior, it is said, if you visit them at home, you may still see a remnant of the noble blood. The Pillagers (Pilleurs),[94] a band celebrated by the old travellers, are still existent there.

"Still some, 'the eagles of their tribe,' may rush."

I have spoken of the hatred felt by the white man for the Indian: with white women it seems to amount to disgust, to loathing. How I could endure the dirt, the peculiar smell, of the Indians, and their dwellings, was a great marvel in the eyes of my lady acquaintance; indeed, I wonder why they did not quite give me up, as they certainly looked on me with great distaste for it. "Get you gone, you Indian dog," was the felt, if not the breathed, expression towards the hapless owners of the soil; - all their claims, all their sorrows quite forgot, in abhorrence of their dirt, their tawny skins, and the vices the whites have taught them.

A person who had seen them during great part of a life expressed his prejudices to me with such violence, that I was no longer surprised that the Indian children threw sticks at him, as he passed. A lady said: "Do what you will for them, they will be ungrateful. The savage cannot be washed out of them. Bring up an Indian child, and see if you can attach it to you." The next moment, she expressed, in the presence of one of those children whom she was bringing up, loathing at the odor left by one of her people, and one of the most respected, as he passed through the room. When the child is grown, she will be considered basely ungrateful not to love the lady, as she certainly will not; and this will be cited as an instance of the impossibility of attaching the Indian.

Whether the Indian could, by any efforts of love and intelligence from the white man, have been civilized and made a valuable ingredient in the new state, I will not say; but this we are sure of, the French Catholics, at least, did not harm them, nor disturb their minds merely to corrupt them. The French they loved. But the stern Presbyterian, with his dogmas and his task work, the city circle and the college, with their niggard concessions and unfeeling stare, have never tried the experiment. It has not been tried. Our people and our government have sinned alike against the first born of the soil, and if they are the fated agents of a new era, they have done nothing, - have invoked no god to keep them sinless while they do the best of fate.

Worst of all is it, when they invoke the holy power only to mask their iniquity; when the felon trader, who, all the week, has been besotting and degrading the Indian with rum mixed with red pepper, and damaged tobacco, kneels with him on Sunday before a common altar, to tell the rosary which recalls the thought of him crucified for love of suffering men, and to listen to sermons in praise of "purity"!!

"My savage friends," cries the old, fat priest, "you must, above all things, aim at *purity.*"

Oh! my heart swelled then I saw them in a Christian church. Better their own dog feasts and bloody rites than such mockery of that other faith.

"The dog," said an Indian, "was once a spirit; he has fallen for his sin, and was given by the Great Spirit, in this shape, to man, as his most intelligent companion. Therefore we sacrifice it in highest honor to our friends in this world, to our protecting geniuses in another."

There was religion in that thought. The white man sacrifices his own brother, and to Mammon, yet he turns in loathing from the dog feast.

"You say," said the Indian of the South to the missionary, "that Christianity is pleasing to God. How can that be? Those men at Savannah are Christians."

Yes! slave drivers and Indian traders are called Christians, and the Indian is to be deemed less like the Son of Mary than they! Wonderful is the deceit of man's heart!

Thus the missionary vainly attempts, by once or twice holding up the cross, to turn deer and tigers into lambs; vainly attempts to convince the red man that a heavenly mandate takes from him his broad lands. He bows his head, but does not at heart acquiesce. He cannot. It is not true; and if it were, the descent of blood through the same channels, for centuries, has formed habits of thought not so easily to be disturbed.

Amalgamation would afford the only true and profound means of civilization. But nature seems, like all else, to declare that this race is fated to perish. Those of mixed blood fade early, and are not generally a fine race. They lose what is best in either type, rather than enhance the value of each, by mingling. There are exceptions, one or two such I know of, but this, it is said, is the general rule.

A traveller observes, that the white settlers who live in the woods soon become sallow, lanky, and dejected; the atmosphere of the trees does not agree with Caucasian lungs; and it is, perhaps, in part an instinct of this which causes the hatred of the new settlers towards trees. The Indian breathed the atmosphere of the forests freely; he loved their shade. As they are effaced from the land, he fleets too; a part of the same manifestation, which cannot linger behind its proper era.

The Chippewas have lately petitioned the State of Michigan, that they may be admitted as citizens; but this would be vain, unless they could be admitted, as brothers, to the heart of the white man. And while the latter feels that conviction of superiority which enabled our Wisconsin friend to throw away the gun, and send the Indian to fetch it, he needs to be very good, and very wise, not to abuse his position. But the white man, as yet, is a half tamed pirate, and avails himself as much as ever of the maxim, "Might makes right." All that civilization does for the generality is to cover up this with a veil of subtle evasions and chicane, and here and there to rouse the individual mind to appeal to Heaven against it.

I have no hope of liberalizing the missionary, of

humanizing the sharks of trade, of infusing the conscientious drop into the flinty bosom of policy, of saving the Indian from immediate degradation and speedy death. The whole sermon may be preached from the text, "Needs be that offences must come, yet woe unto them by whom they come." Yet, ere they depart, I wish there might be some masterly attempt to reproduce, in art or literature, what is proper to them, a kind of beauty and grandeur which few of the every day crowd have hearts to feel, yet which ought to leave in the world its monuments, to inspire the thought of genius through all ages. Nothing in this kind has been done masterly; since it was Clevengers's[95] ambition, 't is pity he had not opportunity to try fully his powers. We hope some other mind may be bent upon it, ere too late. At present the only lively impress of their passage through the world is to be found in such books as Catlin's[96] and some stories told by the old travellers.

The conviction here livingly enforced of the superiority on the side of the white man, was thus expressed by the Indian orator at Mackinac while we were there. After the customary compliments about sun, dew, etc. "This," said he, "is the difference between the white and the red man; the white man looks to the future and paves the way for posterity. The red man never thought of this." This is a statement uncommonly refined for an Indian; but one of the gentlemen present, who understood the Chippewa, vouched for it as a literal rendering of his phrases; and he did indeed touch the vital point of difference. But the Indian, if he understands, cannot make use of his intelligence. The fate of his people is against it, and Pontiac and Philip have no more chance than Julian in the times of old.

The Indian is steady to that simple creed which forms the basis of all his mythology; that there is a God and a life beyond this; a right and wrong which each man can see, betwixt which each man should choose; that good brings with it its reward, and vice its punishment. His moral code, if not as refined as that of civilized nations is clear and noble in the stress laid upon truth and fidelity. And all unprejudiced observers bear testimony, that the Indians, until broken from their old anchorage by intercourse with the whites, who offer them, instead, a religion of which they furnish neither interpretation nor example, were singularly virtuous, if virtue be allowed to consist in a man's acting up to his own ideas of right.

I have not wished to write sentimentally about the

Indians, however moved by the thought of their wrongs and speedy extinction. I know that the Europeans who took possession of this country felt themselves justified by their superior civilization and religious ideas. Had they been truly civilized or Christianized, the conflicts which sprang from the collision of the two races might have been avoided; but this cannot be expected in movements made by masses of men. The mass has never yet been humanized though the age may develop a human thought. Since those conflicts and differences did arise, the hatred which sprang from terror and suffering, on the European side, has naturally warped the whites still further from justice.

The Indian, brandishing the scalps of his wife and friends, drinking their blood, and eating their hearts, is by him viewed as a fiend, though, at a distant day, he will no doubt be considered as having acted the Roman or Carthaginian part of heroic and patriotic self defence, according to the standard of right and motives prescribed by his religious faith and education. Looked at by his own standard, he is virtuous when he most injures his enemy, and the white, if he be really the superior in enlargement of thought, ought to cast aside his inherited prejudices enough to see this, to look on him in pity and brotherly goodwill, and do all he can to mitigate the doom of those who survive his past injuries.

In McKenney's[97] book is proposed a project for organizing the Indians under a patriarchal government; but it does not look feasible, even on paper. Could their own intelligent men be left to act unimpeded in their behalf, they would do far better for them than the white thinker, with all his general knowledge. But we dare not hope the designs of such will not always be frustrated by barbarous selfishness, as they were in Georgia. There was a chance of seeing what might have been done, now lost for ever.[98]

Yet let every man look to himself how far this blood shall be required at his hands. Let the missionary, instead of preaching to the Indian, preach to the trader who ruins him, of the dreadful account which will be demanded of the followers of Cain, in a sphere where the accents of purity and love come on the ear more decisively than in ours. Let every legislator take the subject to heart, and, if he cannot undo the effects of past sin, try for that clear view and right sense that may save us from sinning still more deeply. And let every man and every woman, in their

116

private dealings with the subjugated race, avoid all share in embittering, by insult or unfeeling prejudice, the captivity of Israel.

The drowning of the Ossoli family as drawn by a 19th century artist.

117

Buffalo to Detroit by Ship &
Detroit to Niles by Rail: 1850
by
Frederika Bremer

The building of the Michigan Central and Michigan Southern railroads, which slowly snaked their way from Detroit across southern Michigan in the 1830s and 1840s, would end the pioneer era for the communities they reached. In 1852 both railroads finally reached Chicago.

Frederika Bremer, a Swedish novelist and woman's rights reformer, arrived in Detroit in September 1850 and then took a train ride across the state to Niles, the end of the line at the time. Her description of Michigan is included to illustrate the vast changes a decade of progress had made.

Born in Finland in 1801, Bremer moved to Sweden when she was three. She began writing verse at the age of eight and as a teenager was deeply impressed with Johann Schiller's romantic lyrics and historical dramas. She publishd her first novel in 1828 and it and her succeeding books became very popular in Sweden and through translation into English even more so in England and America. By the 1850s Bremer had also become increasingly involved in the advancement and emancipation of woman and she devoted herself to that cause until her death in 1865.

Beginning in the Autumn of 1849 Bremer would spend nearly two years in America, traveling over much of the east, south and midwest. Upon her return to Europe she published her impressions of the country in a lengthy book, *The Homes of the New World* (Stuttgart, 1853), which was almost immediately translated into English. In the following exerpt, Bremer describes her impressions of Michigan in 1850.

Toward evening I went on board, *The Ocean,* a

magnificent three decked steam boat, which conveyed me across Lake Erie, frequently a very stormy and dangerous lake; its billows, however, now resembled naiads sporting in the sunshine. "Erie," says M. Bouchette, a French writer, describing this part of the country, "may be regarded as the great central reservoir from which canals extend on all sides, so that vessels from this point may go to every part of the country inland, from the Atlantic Ocean on the east and north to the countries and the sea of the south, and bring together the productions of every land and climate."[99] Emigrants of all nations cross Lake Erie on their way to the colonies west of those great inland seas. But to too many of them has Erie proved a grave. Not long since a vessel of emigrants, mostly Germans, was destroyed by fire on Lake Erie, and hundreds of these poor people found a grave in its waters. Among those who were taken up were seven or eight couples, locked in each other's arms. Death could not divide them. Love is stronger than death. The helmsman stood at the helm steering the vessel toward land till the flames burned his hands. The negligence of the captain is said to have been the cause of this misfortune. He too perished. Only between thirty and forty passengers were saved.[100]

For me, however, the sail across Lake Erie was like a sunbright festival, in that magnificent steamer where even a piano was heard in the crowded saloon, and where a polite and most agreeable captain took charge of me in the kindest manner. My good old pioneer related to me various incidents of his life, his religious conversion, his first love and his last, which was quite recent; the old gentleman declaring himself to be half in love with "that Yankee woman, Mrs. L.;" and I do not wonder at it. It convinced me that he had good taste. He declared himself to be "first and foremost a great ladies' man."[101]

At four o'clock in the afternoon - that is to say, of the day after we went on board, we reached Detroit, a city first founded by the French upon that narrow strait between the Lakes Erie and St. Clair, which separates Michigan from Canada. The shores, as seen from the vessel, appeared to be laid out in small farms consisting of regular allotments, surrounded by plantations. The land seemed to me low but fertile, undulating hill and valley. Detroit is, like Buffalo, a city where business life preponderates, yet still it looked to me pleasanter and more friendly than Buffalo. I saw at the hotel some tiresome catechisers, and also some very agreeable people, people whom one could talk well and frankly with, and whom one could like in all respects. Among these I remember, in particular, the Episcopal bishop of Michigan,[102] a frank, excellent, and intellectual man; and a mother and her daughters. I was able to exchange a few cordial words with them, words out of the earnest depths of life, and such always do me good. The people of Detroit were, for the rest, pleased with their city and their way of life there, pleased with themselves, and with each other. And this seems to me to be the case in most of the places that I have been to here in the west.

The following evening we were at Ann Arbor, a pretty little rural city. Here also I received visitors, and was examined as usual. My good old pioneer did not approve of traveling *incognito,* but insisted upon it that people should be known by people, and could not comprehend how any one could be tired, and need a cessation of introductions and questions. In Ann Arbor, also, the people were much pleased with themselves, their city, it situation, and way of life, The city derived its name from the circumstance that when the first settlers came to the place they consisted principally of one family, and while the woods were felled and the land plowed, the laborers had no other dwelling than a tent like shed of boughs and canvas, where the mother of the family, "Ann," prepared the food, and cared for the comfort of all. That was the domestic hearth; that was the calm haven where all the laborers found rest and refreshment under the protection of Mother Ann. Hence they called the tent Ann's Arbor or Bower, and the city, which by degrees sprung up around it, retained the name. And with its neat houses and gardens upon the green hills and slopes the little city looked, indeed, like a peaceful retreat from the unquiet of the world.

We remained over night at Ann Arbor. The following morning we set off by railroad and traveled directly across the State of Michigan. Through the whole distance I saw small farms, with their well built houses, surrounded by well cultivated land; fields of wheat and maize, and orchards full of apple and peach trees. In the wilder districts the fields were brilliant with some beautiful kind of violet and blue flowers, which the rapidity of our journey prevented me from examining more closely, and with tall sunflowers, the heads of which were as large as young trees. It was splendid and beautiful. My old pioneer told me that he never had seen any where such an affluence of magnificent flowers as in Michigan, especially in the olden times before the wilderness was broken up into fields. Michigan is one of the youngest states of the Union, but has a rich soil, particularly calculated for the growth of wheat, and is greatly on the increase.

The legislation is of the most liberal description, and it has abolished capital punishment in its penal code. Nevertheless, I heard of crime having been committed in this state which deserved death, or at least imprisonment for life, if any crime does deserve it. A young man of a respectable family in Detroit, during a hunt, had shot clandestinely and repeatedly at another young man, his best friend, merely to rob him of his pocket-book. He had been condemned for an attempt to murder, which he acknowledged, only to twenty years imprisonment. And in prison he was visited by young ladies, who went to teach him French and to play on the guitar! One of these traveled with me on the railroad. She spoke of the young prisoner's "agreeable demeanor!" There is a leniency toward crime and the criminal which is disgusting, and which proves a laxity of moral feeling.

The weather was glorious the whole day. The sun preceded us westward. We steered our course directly toward the sun; and the nearer it sank toward the earth, more brightly glowed the evening sky as with the most transcendent gold. The country, through the whole extent, was lowland, and monotonous. Here and there wound along a lovely little wooded stream. Here and there in the woods were small frame houses, and beside one and another of them wooden sheds, upon which a board was fastened, whereon might be read in white letters, half a yard, the word "Grocery." The cultivated districts were in all cases divided regularly, scattered over with farm houses resembling those of our better class of peasant farmers. The settlers in the West purchase allotments of from eighty to one hundred and sixty or two hundred acres, seldom less and seldom more. The land costs, in the first instance, what is called "government price," one dollar and a quarter per acre; and will, if well cultivated, produce abundant harvests within a few years. The farmers here work hard, live frugally, but well, and bring up strong, able families. The children, however, seldom follow the occupation of their fathers. They are sent to schools, and after that endeavor to raise themselves by political or public life. These small farms are the nurseries from which the Northwest States obtain there best officials and teachers, both male and female. A vigorous, pious, laborious race grows up here. I received much enlightenment on this subject from my good old pioneer, who, with his piety, his restless activity, his humanity, his great information, and his youthfully warm heart, even in advancing years, was a good type of the first cultivators of the wilderness in this country. He parted from me on the journey in order to reach his home in the little city of Niles.

In company with an agreeable gentleman, Mr. H., and his agreeable sister-in-law, I went on board the steamer which crosses Lake Michigan. The sun had now sunk; but the evening sky glowed with the brightest crimson above the sea-like lake. We departed amid its splendor and in the light of the new moon. The water was as a mirror.

Frederika Bremer

Detroit: 1812
by
Nancy Howard

And now for the wolverine women. Literary fame was not their forte, rather, they cast their lot with Michigan and helped carve homesteads out of the wilderness. But with hands more used to the ax, hoe, butter churn and scrub board, they picked up pens and wrote of their early life in Michigan. Little is known about most of these women beyond what has survived in their own narratives. And what those stories lack in polished literary style is more than made up for in sincerity and interest.

We begin with Nancy Howard's recollections of of Detroit in 1812. At the age of 83 Howard narrated her story to a Detroit *Free Press* reporter who visited her at her Port Huron home. The article appeared in the *Free Press* on August 29, 1889 and was reprinted in volume 14 of the *Michigan Pioneer Collections* published in 1889. Her husband, John, was one of the early merchants of Detroit and served as a constable there in 1829.

I was born August 31, 1806, at Fairfield, Pennsylvania. Shortly after, my father, Mr. Jonathan Hubbard, moved his family to Grand River, Ohio, where we lived until 1812, when he decided to move to Detroit for the purpose of trading. Packing our household effects into an open boat, together with mother and eight children, we left Painesville for the territory of Michigan. We were two whole weeks making the trip to Detroit, following as we did the Lake Erie shore, and stopping until morning wherever night overtook us. I was but five years old at the time, but remember the tedious trip very well.

We reached Detroit at last and landed on the shore at a point very near to the foot of what is now known as Randolph Street. What is now Atwater Street was then the river shore. No large sailing or steam vessels then piled the waters of the lakes and rivers, principally small sailing vessels and canoes. There was but one dock on the river front, that belonging to the government. There were no settlements back of the river, the primeval forests then being in their glory and inhabited by numerous Indians. The little hamlet or trading post was made up principally of French, there being a few English and American families, mostly traders. There was but one church, Ste. Anne's Catholic. The presiding priest was Father Richard.[103]

We had lived in Detroit but a few months when father rented a farm at Grosse Pointe, where we moved in time to put in fall crops. While we were a long distance from English neighbors, there being only one other family between the point and Detroit, yet we felt quite contented as our prospects were quite bright, until father was taken ill and died in the middle of the winter. His remains were laid to rest on the banks of Lake St. Clair. No language can express the anguish of that hour. A wife without a husband, and eight children without a father and so far from friends and home surely we could say we were strangers and in a strange land. After returning from the grave and the darkness had settled down so black and gloomy, we sat about the old fashioned fireplace in sadness and anguish. I could not bear it long, and going to my eldest brother I crowded in between his knees, looked him in the face, and said: "Edward, will you be a father to me?" The silence broke into tears, but in a moment he replied: "Yes, my dear sister, so far as I can."

Very soon after our severe trial the dreadful news came of war being declared with England,and the dear brother in whom we had placed so much reliance, volunteered for six months. He provided his own horse and was appointed to mounted sentinel duty between Detroit and Grosse Pointe, to guard the river shore.

Mother remained on the farm to secure what crops were possible. It was while we were there alone that we were one day surprised by the blood thirsty savages. I was in the yard, and, looking up onto the lake, I espied a canoe load of Indians coming near the shore. A squaw was coming up the road, and when she was opposite the house she beckoned, and at that moment they sprang on shore and ran up to the fence, leaped over it with the agility of deer and ran up to the house. We saw the whole proceeding from a window, and fully expected that our time had come. My eldest sister sprang to the door and her first impulse was to lock it and did so, but again turned the key and opening the door as they came up, in French she asked them to come in

A view of Detroit in 1815.

and get warm, as it was a cold day. They shouted at her and she turned and walked into the kitchen, where mother and the children were sitting around the fireplace. The Indians followed and surrounded the family. As they stood there in their war paint, with their tomahawks and scalping knives in readiness, they did present a most hideous spectacle. They discussed the situation between themselves to considerable length, not being certain that the family were English after what my sister had said to them in French. In a few minutes, however, my sister took up the youngest child and walked out of the back door, and mother and the rest of the family followed, going across the fields to the nearest French neighbor.

The Indians then most thoroughly plundered the house of nearly everything save my sister's clothing, which they knew by the size. The dishes they took down to the beach and broke them into pieces. They then went up the lake shore several miles and related the circumstances, saying that if we were not French they would come back that night and kill us, but they were assured that we were French. Notwithstanding this they seemed determined to kill us, and word was sent us to leave the house. This we did for several nights but came back during the day. Sometime after this a white man well known on the river came one day with the Indians and drove off a span of horses from our barn. My young brother went out and pleaded with the wretches, but to no purpose. After the harvesting was done mother moved the family back to Detroit and we were placed under the care of the garrison at the fort. Many were the days that I went to the store house to draw our rations.

But when Hull surrendered so ignominiously to the British[104] we were again left to the mercy of the Indians. When Proctor took command of the fort under Brock[105] he accepted the home of Col. Cass, that stood where the Biddle House[106] now stands. We lived just east, a block or so nearer the river. Proctor had a standing offer of five dollars for American scalps. I have seen as many as twelve Indians go into his yard at a time with their scalp trophies. They would form a circle about one of their number, who would beat the drum, and the others would dance and give the war whoop and push the trophies into the air on the sticks. Childlike I have often peeked through the fence and seen the cruel spectacle. Proctor did not remain long. After he had destroyed all the public buildings possible he went back to Canada. What few men remained after Hull had delivered over his handsome army had nearly all secured boats, and they went down the river by night to join the American army in Ohio and have it march up and again take possession of the Fort of Detroit. My oldest brother was one of the brave volunteers who started on this perilous journey. We never heard from him again. What fate overtook the courageous hearts we never learned.

Some little time intervened before the heartily welcomed American army came. During this time the few remaining families would gather into a house and the men would stand guard outside through the night with clubs, as they had no guns. I remember well the beautiful and joyful sight the army made when they finally came. There was great rejoicing then.

I lived in Detroit about a year after this, possibly more. The house that Hull and Proctor had occupied was turned into a hospital and so many died there. It was frightful, the number of deaths during that period. I used to see a great deal of it as I carried milk to the hospital. No boxes or coffins were used for burial. The corpses were wrapped up in a blanket and the ends tied up to a pole and two men carried the same to the old burying ground that was situated where the old First Baptist Church[107] was built. There they were buried as thick as they could lie.

It was during and previous to this time that the Indians used to bring their white prisoners captured down in the Ohio campaign to Detroit, where they used to sell them for tobacco, and whiskey, and money. If any of the older ones or children could not stand the journey they were summarily dispatched. Many were the instances where mothers and fathers have seen their own children brained for this reason. I remember of one young boy about sixteen or seventeen years of age, a bright fellow, that the Indians would not sell for any price. It seems they had lost a young brave about his age and size, and they captured the young lad to fill his place. They took him away up north and we never heard of him again.

When I was about eight years of age, my eldest sister married Josuha Townsend and they went to Ohio to live. I went with them and did not return to Detroit for some seven or eight years. Of course, the town had changed considerably, but it was slow of growth. I remember and knew quite well many of the old families whose names are familiar to all. In my 19th year I was married to John Howard, a young man who had but a short time before come from Ohio and established himself in the grocery business. We lived in Detroit until 1834, when we removed to

127

Port Huron, where we have since lived, Mr. Howard dying about two years ago. Several of our children were born in Detroit, and I have many fond recollections of the city, as well as some disagreeable ones, as I have related.

Flavius Littlejohn's *Legends of Michigan* contains this idealized depiction of a Chippewa chief named Ne-O-Me.

Mackinac Island &
Bois Blanc Island: 1814
by
Elizabeth Therese Baird

From the "City of the Straits" in 1812 we go to the Straits of Mackinac two years later. Elizabeth Therese Baird wrote up her childhood recollections of Mackinac Island and Indian customs for the Green Bay *Gazette* in 1882 with additional articles published in 1886-1887. These were later reprinted in the *Wisconsin Historical Collections.*

Born at Prairie du Chien, Wisconsin, on April 24, 1810, Baird was the daughter of Henry Munro Fisher, a prominent American Fur Company trader of Scotch ancestry. Her mother was Marienne Lasaliere, a daughter of Madame Therese Schindler. Madame Schindler's mother was Migisan, the daughter of an Ottawa chief. Lyman Draper, the great Wisconsin historian and collector who edited the *Wisconsin Historical Collections*, wrote that "Though Mrs. Baird's Indian inheritance, as she expresses it is not great, yet like the descendants of Pocahontas, 'she boasts of all she has!'

Beginning in 1814, Baird lived at Mackinac Island for ten years. At the age of 14 she married Henry S. Baird, a Green Bay attorney. She remained in Green Bay until her death in 1890.

The first of the excerpts from Baird's articles which follow deals with Mackinac Island and the second with sugar making on nearby Bois Blanc Island.

My earliest recollections of Mackinac, which date back to 1814, are perfectly delightful. All about the island was so fresh and fair. True, the houses were quaint and old; however, they were but few, not enough to mar the beauty, but rather to add to the charms of the little crescent shaped village.

How vividly I still see the clear, shining broad beach of white pebbles and stones, and clear blue water of the "Basin."

The houses were of one story, roofed with cedar bark, Some of the fishermen's residences were entirely covered with bark in the place of clap-boards. Every house had its garden enclosed with cedar pickets, about five feet in height, making a close enclosure. This was white-washed, as were also the dwelling houses, and the fort as well, giving the entire place more the appearance of a fortress than an ordinary village.

One street, if it may be called so, ran from one point of the crescent to the other, and as near the water's edge as the beach would permit, the pebbles forming a border between the water and road. The other street, for there are but two, is a short one, which runs back of the front street. A foot path in the middle of the street was all that was needed. Weeds grew luxuriantly on each side of the trail; those next to the enclosures were almost as high as the pickets. There were no vehicles of any description on the island in those early days, except dog trains or sleds in the winter. Hence, the weeds had it all their own way.

The natural curiosities of the island seemed more wonderful in those days, because reached with so much difficulty. The surroundings were wild, and no carriage road led up to them. A visit to the Arched Rock, and the Sugar Loaf, made a high holiday. Ascending the hills in the outset, to get the fine view that rewarded our exertions was grand, but it needed a good guide to reach and enjoy it. In returning we descended by the way of "Robinson's Folly," and so on down, reaching home by the beach. The whole island is a rock, covered with grass, cedar, juniper, and some pines. Among our favorite walks, was one to Fort Holmes, which is on the highest hill of the island.

Small fruits, such as the wild strawberry, raspberry, and gooseberry were abundant on the island; and the surrounding islands abounded in huckleberries, blackberries, and sand cherries. These were the sole varieties of fruit known to the writer in childhood.

Mackinac is a true summer home, but I loved it in the winter, with its mountains of ice. The isolation of the place was great - eight months of the year were passed in seclusion from the outside world; communication with it was impossible. But the other four months of the year made up for it all. About the middle of October navigation closed. How well I remember the quiet of the place. Once a month the mail came, when it didn't miss.

The religion of the inhabitants was Roman Catholic. There was no regular priest stationed there, but one came occasionally. We had no schools, and no amusements except private parties, and these were principally card parties. All ladies played whist and piquet. The other set had their balls. The children were happy in making houses in the snow drifts, and in sliding down hills, or coasting, as it is now called. In the autumn of 1823, the ice made very early, but owing to high winds and a strong current in the straits, the ice would break up over and over again, and was tossed to and fro, until it become piled up in clear, towering, blue masses. These immense blocks extended from island to island, block piled upon block to a great height, so that all that met the eye were beautiful mountains of ice, with gorges of exquisite light and shade. A beautiful sight, indeed, on a sunny day. As soon as the mass became sufficiently solid, the soldiers - for Mackinac had been a military post for years, held in turn by the French, British, and Americans - and the fishermen turned out and cut a road through the ice from one island to the other. This was necessary, as fire wood had to be procured from the opposite island. The fishermen also had to cut places for their nets.

A sleigh ride through that road way was novel and grand; and in a dog sled it was at times in a degree terrifying. On each side of a high wall of ice, nothing to be seen but the sky above; the road so winding that one seemed hemmed in by the high masses of ice, until a sharp turn brought him into the road again. With horse and cutter, which at a late date had been introduced on the island, it was a charming drive way.

Some seasons the lakes and basins would be clear of ice, except as great cakes of it would fill the shore; it was piled so high at times, as to exclude all sight of the water, except through occasional glacial openings. Other seasons the ice would be as smooth as possible. Spring always came late at Mackinac, and it used to be the custom to plant a May-pole on the frozen surface. Quoting from a friend's diary, we find: "1837, May 1st, May-pole put on the ice today. Monday, May 8th, May-pole renewed, and flags added to it. Ice in basin good."

Mackinac, or as the Indians formerly named it, Michilimackinac, "The Great Turtle," was, in those days, called the emporium of the West, a town of extensive commerce. All the fur traders went there to sell their furs, and buy their goods. Prior to the establishment of the American Fur Company by John Jacob Astor, the Hudson's Bay Company occupied the island in the

This view of Fort Mackinac appeared in Disturnell's 1875 guide to Mackinac Island.

same manner, as a depot. All the goods for this large trade came from Montreal in birch bark canoes, by way of Niagara Falls. All goods and canoes were carried past the rapids on the backs of the Indians. It made most exciting times when *Le Caneau du Nord* came, arriving sometimes as early as June, and bringing from Montreal merchants, and merchandise. As the canoes neared the town, there would come floating on the air, the far-famed Canadian boat song. How plainly I hear it now! Then the voyageur came in with furs, and then the Indians, and the little island seemed to overflow with human beings. These exciting, busy times would last from six weeks to two months, then would follow the quiet, uneventful, and to some, dreary days, yet to most, days that passed happily.

Bois Blanc Island

A visit to the sugar camp was a great treat to the young folks as well as to the old. In the days I write of, sugar was a scarce article, save in the Northwest, where maple sugar was largely manufactured. All who were able, possessed a sugar camp. My grandmother[108] had one on Bois Blanc Island, about five miles east of Mackinac. About the first of March, nearly half of the inhabitants of our town, as well as many from the garrison, would move to Bois Blanc to prepare for the work. Our camp was delightfully situated in the midst of a forest of maple, or a maple grove. A thousand or more trees claimed our care, and three men and two women were employed to do the work.

The "camp," as we specifically styled the building in which the sugar was made, and the sugar makers housed, - was made of poles or small trees, enclosed with sheets of cedar bark, and was about thirty feet long by eighteen feet wide. On each side was a platform, about eighteen inches high and four feet wide. One side was intended for beds, and each bed when not in use was rolled up nicely, wrapped in an Indian mat, then placed back against the wall; the bedroom then became a sitting room. The walls on the inside were covered with tarpaulin, also the floor. The women's bedding was placed at one end of the platform.. The platform on the opposite side served as a dining floor, one end of which was enclosed in cedar bark, forming a closet for the dishes and cooking utensils. The dishes consisted of some crockery, tin plates and cups, and wooden dishes and ladles. A wing was added at one end, for the men's bedroom.

At either end of the camp were doors, made large to admit heavy logs for the fire. The fireplace was midway between the two platforms, and extended to within six feet of the doors. At each corner of the fireplace were large posts, firmly planted in the ground and extending upwards about five feet or more. Large timbers were placed lengthwise on top of these posts, and across the timbers extended bars from which, by chains and hoops, were suspended large brass kettles, two on each bar. On the dining room side, half way up the wall, ran a pole, horizontally. This was to hold in place hemlock branches, which were brought in fresh every evening. The place between the fire and platforms was kept very neat by a thick, heavy broom, made of cedar branches, cut off evenly on the bottom, and with a long handle. These brooms are still used by semi-civilized Indians.

The hanging of the kettle was quite a test of skill, requiring three persons to perform the task. The fire had to be burning briskly when the hanging began. It was the duty of one person to hang the kettle properly; of the second, to pour in immediately a small quantity of sap to keep the vessel from burning; of the third, to fill it with the sap. The peak of the roof was left open to allow the smoke to escape, and at night to let in the stars, as was my childish fancy. In early morning, the birds would arouse us to listen to their songs and catch a sight of the waning stars. Blue jays were especially numerous, and so tame that one could fairly enjoy them. Other birds would in turn sing and whistle, as the stars disappeared and the day dawned. An owl made its abiding place in a tree near by, sentinel like, and ever uttered its *coo-coo-coo-hoo*, as the Indian had named its utterance. The sound of the whip-poor-will was a harbinger of spring, and a warning that time to cease sugar making had arrived.

Now for the work: All the utensils used in making sugar were of that daintiest of material, birch bark. The *casseau* to set at the tree, to catch the sap, was a birch bark dish, holding from one to two gallons. The pails for carrying the sap were of the same material, and held from three to four gallons. The men placed a *gauje* or yoke on their shoulders, then a bucket would be suspended on each side. The women seldom used this yoke, but assisted the men in carrying the buckets, doing so in the usual manner. The mocock, in which the sugar was packed, was also of birch bark and held from thirty to eighty pounds. The bark was gathered in the summer at Bark Point. The name was afterward done into French as "Point aux Encorces," meaning "bark point." The sailors now miscall it, "Point au Barques." [109]

The *gouttiere* or spout, which was made of basswood, had to be cleaned each spring, before it was placed in the tree; the birch bark for the *casseau* was cleaned by taking off a layer of the inner bark and then washing it. The buckets were made by sewing the seams with *bast* (which is taken from the inner bark of basswood), then gummed over with pine pitch. They also were carefully washed and dried before use. As a matter of course, the larger vessels to receive the sap were barrels made of oak. No pine was ever used about the camp, as that would impart a disagreeable taste. The strainers were made of a particular kind of flannel, of very coarse thread and not wooly, brought especially for this purpose by the merchants. I remember well, the cleaning of these. After they had been used, they were put into a tub of very hot water and washed (without soap); or pounded, rather, with a *battoir* or beetle, then rinsed in many waters.

By this time the sap must be boiling. It takes over twenty-four hours to make the sap into syrup, and the boiling is usually begun in the morning. The fire is kept bright all day and night. Two women are detailed to watch the kettles closely, for when the sap boils down nearly to syrup, it is liable to bubble over at any moment. The women therefore stand by with a branch of hemlock in hand; as soon the liquid threatens to boil over, they dip the branch in quickly, and, it being cool, the syrup is settled for a while. When at this stage, it requires closest watching. When the sap has boiled down about one half, the women have to transfer the contents of one kettle to another, as the kettles must be kept full for fear of scorching the top of the kettle, which would spoil all. As fast as a kettle is emptied it will be filled with water and set aside, awaiting the general cleaning. The kettles require the utmost care, being scoured as soon as possible each time emptied, keeping one woman employed nearly all of the time. Sand and water are the cleansing agents used.

All this time, if the weather favors the running of the sap, it is brought as fast as possible and the boiling goes on. At this period, my grandmother would send me my little barrel full of the syrup. This miniature barrel I still have in my possession. The barrel bears the date 1815, and is now dark and polished with age, and is a rare memento of those halcyon days. It holds less than a pint, and was made by an Ottawa Indian, out of a solid piece of wood, sides and ends all one, the interior being ingeniously burned out through the bung hole. The receipt of this was the signal that the time had come when I too might visit the camp.

When made, the syrup is placed in barrels, awaiting the time when it can be made into sugar of various kinds, the modus operandi thus: a very bright brass kettle is placed over a slow fire (it cannot be done at boiling time, as then a brisk fire is required), this kettle containing about three gallons of syrup, if it is to be made into cakes; if into *cassonade*, or granulated sugar, two gallons of syrup are used. For the sugar cakes, a board of basswood is prepared, about five or six inches wide, with moulds gouged in, in form of bears, diamonds, crosses, rabbits, turtles, spheres, etc. When the sugar is cooked to a certain degree, it is poured into these moulds. For the granulated sugar, the stirring is continued for a longer time, this being done with a long paddle which looks like a mushstick. This sugar has to be put into the mocock while warm, as it will not pack well if cold. This work is especially difficult; only a little can be made at a time, and it was always done under my grandmother's immediate supervision.

The sugar gum, or wax, is also made separately. Large wooden bowls, or birch bark *casseaus*, are filled with snow, and when the syrup is of the right consistence it is poured upon the snow in thin sheets. When cooled it is put into thin birch bark, made into a neat package, and tied with bast. The syrup made for table use is boiled very thick, which prevents its souring. For summer use, it is put into jugs and buried in the ground two or three feet deep, where it will keep a year, more or less.

The trip to Bois Blanc I made in my dog sled. Francois Lacroix (the son of a slave), whom my grandmother reared, was my companion. The ride over the ice, across the lake, was a delightful one; and the drive through the woods (which were notably clear of underbrush), to the camp, about a mile from the shore, was equally charming.

The pleasures of the camp were varied. In out-of-door amusement, I found delight in playing about great trees that had been uprooted in some wind storm. Frequently, each season, near the close of sugar making, parties of ladies and gentlemen would come over from Mackinac, bent on a merry time, which they never failed to secure.

One time, a party of five ladies and five gentlemen were invited to the camp. Each lady brought a frying pan in which to cook and turn *les crepes* or pancakes, which was to be the special feature and fun of the occasion. All due preparation was made for using the frying pan. We were notified that no girl was fitted to be married until she could turn a *crepe*. Naturally, all were desirous to try their skill in that direction, whether matrimonially inclined, or not. The gentlemen of the party tried their hand at it, as well as the ladies. It may not be amiss here to explain what to turn the *crepe* meant; when the cake was cooked on one side, it was dexterously tossed in the air and expected to land, the other side up, back in the pan. Never did I see objects miss so widely the mark aimed at. It seemed indeed that the *crepes* were influenced by the glee of the party; they turned and flew everywhere, but where wanted. Many fell into the fire, as if the turner had so intended. Some went to the ground, and one even found its way to the platform, over the head of the turner. One gentleman (Henry S. Baird)[110] came up to Mrs. John Dousman, and holding out his nice fur cap, said, "Now turn your cake, and I will catch it." Mrs. Dousman was an adept at turning, and before the challenger had time to withdraw his cap, with a toss she deftly turned the cake and landed it fairly into the cap. You may imagine the sport all this afforded. In due time, a nice dinner was prepared. We had partridges roasted on sticks before the fire; rabbit and stuffed squirrel, cooked French fashion; and finally had as many *crepes*, with syrup, as we desired. Every one departed with a bark of wax and sugar cakes.

The Wreck of the
Walk-in-the-Water: 1821
by
Mary A. Witherell Palmer

Much of what we know about the famous steamship, the *Walk-in-the-Water*, the first such vessel to ply the waters of lakes Erie, Huron and Michigan, comes from the following letter written by Mary A. Witherell Palmer some years before her death in 1874. Originally solicited by the Buffalo Historical Society, the letter was reprinted in the *Michigan Pioneer Collections* in 1884.

Mrs. Palmer was born in 1795, the daughter of James Witherell, a prominent judge in Michigan Territory beginning in 1810. She married Thomas Palmer in 1821. Of the seven children she bore, only one, Thomas W. Palmer, was alive in 1881. Her son achieved a notable political career himself, representing Michigan in the Senate in 1883-1889, serving as Minister to Spain 1889-1891 and as president of the World's Columbian Exposition of 1893.

In 1881 he wrote of his mother: "All that a son would like to say of his mother I can say of her. She was a woman of superior understanding and high ideals. She was a woman lenient toward others, but incorruptible in her judgement of herself. She was an ardent politician although not obtrusive or masculine. She loved her country, but she wanted her country to be right, and desired that its policy should be determined by highest moral impulses."

The first steamboat built on the Upper Lakes was named the *Walk-in-the-Water*, not only from its appropriateness, but from a chief of the Wyandotte Indians, who lived with his band about twelve mile below Detroit River. His Indian name was Mier, and signified a turtle, and his Totem, or signature, was the figure of a turtle.

The boat has been so often described that it is needless to repeat it.[111] She was built at Black Rock,[112] which place continued for some time to be her most eastern port and the terminus of her route; Buffalo at that time having no pier or dock to accommodate her.

She was hauled up the rapids by sixteen yoke of oxen, aided by her engine. She made her trial trip in August, 1818.[113] I was passenger on her first regular trip, as well as her last. She left Buffalo on her first regular trip, as near as I can recollect, on Wednesday morning, September 1st, 1818. She carried at that time considerable freight and a large number of passengers, among whom was the Earl of Selkirk, Lady Selkirk, and two children; Colonel Dixon, the British Indian Agent for the Northwest, Colonel Jno. Anderson, U.S. Engineer, his wife and wife's sister, Miss. Taylor; Colonel Leavenworth, U.S.A., wife and daughter, Colonel James Watson of Washington city, Major Abraham Edwards, who subsequently lived in Detroit and afterwards removed to Kalamazoo, Michigan, where he died about two years ago.[114] She reached Detroit at about 9 o'clock on Monday morning, September 5th, 1818, and as she ushered in a new era in the navigation of the Upper Lakes, her arrival was hailed with delight, and announced by the firing of one gun, which custom was continued for many years.[115] Captain Job Fish was, I think, the commander at that time.

It so happened that on my return from New York, in company with my husband, Mr. Thomas Palmer,[116] and his sister, now Mrs. Catherine Hickman of this city, we arrived in Buffalo just in time to take passage on her last trip. She lay at the pier on the middle ground. We went on board in a yawl. The boat immediately got under way at 4 p.m., the last day of October, 1821, and steamed up the lake. Before we reached Point Abino the wind came on to blow a gale. Captain Rogers,[117] her commander at that time, made every effort to get behind the Point (Abino), but the wind was too strong ahead. It rained incessantly. The night was very dark, and to add to the danger of the situation, the boat began to leak badly. About eight o'clock, the captain, finding it impossible to proceed farther, put about and started for Buffalo.

The sailing master (Miller) proposed running the boat into the Niagara River and anchoring, but the captain said it was so dark that she might strike the pier in the attempt, and in such a case no human power could save a soul on board. The boat was run to within a few miles of the pier, as the Captain supposed, no light from the lighthouse being visible, although as was afterwards learned, it had been kept brightly burning. Three anchors were dropped, one with a chain and two with hempen cables. The boat plunged heavily at her anchorage. This, I think, was about 10 o'clock in the evening. The leak continued to increase. The whole power of the engine was applied to the pumps. The boat dragged her anchors. The night was one of terrible suspense. It was the impression of the greater number on board that we should never see the morning.

The water gained gradually in spite of every exertion, and it became evident, as the night wore on, that the bark must founder or be run on shore, which the captain concluded, either from the sound of the breakers or from calculations of distances and courses, could not be far off. Most of the passengers were calm. One instance of coolness I remember. A Mr. Thurston, when requested to go on deck and prepare for the worst, replied: "No, I have great confidence in Captain Rogers; he promised to land me in Cleveland, and I know he will do it," wrapped his cloak around him and lay down on a settee.

About half past four in the morning the captain sent down for all the passengers to come on deck. He had decided, although ignorant of the exact location, to permit the boat to go on shore. We could see no lights. The chain cable was slipped, and the two hempen ones cut. Drifting before the gale, the *Walk-in-the-Water*, in about half an hour, grazed the beach. The next swell let her down with a crash of crockery and of glass, the third left her farther up the shore, fixed immovable in the sand. The swells made a clean breach over her. some of the ladies were in their night clothes, and all were repeatedly drenched.

When daylight came, a sailor succeeded in getting ashore in a small boat, with one end of a hawser, which he tied to a tree, the other end being tied on board. By the aid of the hawser, all the passengers were taken ashore in the small boat. I was handed down by the captain to a sailor in the small boat, who placed me on a seat. My husband was not so fortunate. A swell carried the yawl ahead just as he jumped, and he went into the water shoulder deep.

We found ourselves about a mile above the lighthouse, in dismal plight, but thankful for the preservation of our lives. In company with a Mr. Cahoon, who was the engineer of the steamer, I ran to the lighthouse. After the lapse of so long a time, it seems to me that I almost flew along the beach, my exhilaration was so great.

The lighthouse keeper anticipating wrecks or disasters (I think signal guns had been fired during the night on board the *Walk-in-the-Water*) had a rousing fire in his huge fireplace, by which we remained until carriages came down for us from Buffalo. The citizens had supposed it impossible that the boat could live through the night, and when, at break of day, she was descried upon the beach, their efforts were directed to the care of the passengers and crew. All that could be done for our comfort was done. We were taken to the Landen House, a two story frame building, then the principal hotel at Buffalo. It stood on the brow of the hill as we went up town from the creek. We returned to Detroit by wagon through Canada, a trip occupying two weeks.

The day after we got back to Buffalo, Captain Rogers called upon us. In the course of conversation he told me that his assurance of safety during the storm was anything but heartfelt; that during the gale he had secured the boat's papers on his person, thinking that should the boat and he be lost, his body would be washed ashore and the papers recovered.

Among the passengers now remember were Major or Jed. Hunt, Lieutenant McKenzie, U.S.A., Jno. Hale, Esq., then a merchant of Canadaigua, afterwards merchant of this place, Jason Thurston, Esq., of Michigan, Rev. Mr. Hart, a missionary to Michigan and wife, John S. Hudson and wife, and a Miss Osborn, who were on their way to Fort Gratiot to establish a mission for the Indians. Mr. and Mrs. Salsmer, of Ohio, Mr. Palmer and myself, and Mr. Palmer's sister, now Mrs. Catherine Hickman, of this city.

A young gentleman of Buffalo, by name of J.D. Matthies, went down the beach where the wreck lay, and, being an amateur artist, took sketches of it in two different positions, painted them and sent them to me at this place. They are now deposited among the archives of the Michigan Historical Society.

The deck of the *Walk-in-the-Water* was like that of sailing vessels of the present day. The cabins were beneath the main deck, the after part partitioned off for ladies. The rest was devoted to gentlemen and answered for lodging, dining, and baggage room. The mast ran down through the gentlemen's cabin, and that part in the cabin was set in octagon with small mirrors. In visiting the wreck, a few days after the disaster, I remember that it lay broadside on shore. I could almost walk around it dry shoed; the sand had been deposited around it such an extent, the oakum had worked out of the seams in the deck for yards in a place, and the panel work had become disjointed in many places.

Captain Rogers, I believe afterwards engaged in business in New York City, but I have heard nothing concerning him for many years.

The above recital agrees with my husband's recollections, and is substantially correct, although there may be some slight inaccuracies.

One of many 19th century illustrations of the *Walk-in-the-Water*.

Ann Arbor: 1823
by
Sarah Bryan

When Elizabeth Ellet was collecting material for her *Pioneer Women of the West,* published in 1852, she realized that "a vast store might be yielded from the records of private families, and the still vivid recollections of individuals who had passed through the experiences of frontier and forest life, and it was not yet too late to save from oblivion much that would be the more interesting and valuable, as the memory of those primitive times receded into the past." Among those who Ellet solicited for information on pioneer women was Miss Mary H. Clark of Ann Arbor. Clark, who with her sisters ran a famous private school for girls in Ann Arbor from 1839 - 1875, provided her with several Michigan recollections including the following two exerpts describing early Washtenaw County pioneers. Sarah Bryan's unpleasant experiences testify to the genuine hardship suffered by pioneer women. Harriet Noble's recollections demonstrate the strength and resourcefulness of women working in harness with their husbands. Her final paragaph is a poignant statement undoubtedly often felt by these women but rarely committed to print.

We left Geneseo October 7th, 1823, for our new home, arrived in Detroit in ten days; put up at the Widow Hubbard's, who kept a sort of boarding house, and deposited our goods in the cellar till my husband could go out to the "Grove"[118] (as the settlement was then called) and procure a team to move us through. He returned in three days with a man, two yoke of oxen, and a wagon, which we found was not sufficient to contain all our goods and the family. This consisted of five children, besides myself and husband. Fortunately for us, however, we found a young man who was going out with but half a load, and persuaded him to take the remainder of ours. After a wearisome and almost indescribable journey of four days through thick woods, my husband cutting the road before us with an axe, we came the night of October 23rd, to the beautiful Huron shore. We had the privilege of staying in a log cabin till we could build one of our own, which we moved into the last day of December. Eight weeks after this, February 27th, 1824, Alpha was born; we called him Alpha Washtenaw, the latter name being given in honor of the county, and the former on account of his being the first white child born in the county. Allen and Rumsay, [119] the first settlers of Ann Arbor, agreed to mark the auspicious event by presenting the infant with a lot of land at the county seat.

It was amusing that first fall and winter to hear the corn mills in operation every morning before daylight. There were but two in the settlement, made by burning a hole in the top of a sound oak stump, large enough to hold a peck or more. After scraping the coal clean from the stump, one end of a stick, some six feet long and eight inches in diameter, was rounded, and it was suspended from a spring pole so that the rounded end would clear the stump when hanging loosely. A hole was bored through this pestle and a stick driven through projecting on each side for handles, and the mill was finished. One man would pound a peck of dry corn in half an hour so that half of it would pass through a sieve for bread; the coarser part being either ground again or boiled for hominy. Very little bread of any other kind was used in the settlement for the first two years.

But as regards my own experience, the autumn of 1824 was the most trying. Thus far we had encountered few more inconveniences than we anticipated in the wilderness, and I was prepared for them, prepared to bear all without a murmur. In October Mr. Bryan accepted an offer to finish a building at Maumee City, [120] and shipped his tools at Detroit, where he had been doing an eight months' job. He came home and stayed a few days to provide some wood, and told me if he was likely to be more than three weeks absent, he would return at the end of that time and put up more provisions, as our small stock would be exhausted. No person had then attempted to penetrate the forest from our place to Monroe, but rather than go round by Brownstown, [121] he determined to take the risk of finding his way through the woods alone. My heart sank within me to think of what would be my fate and that of my six children, if any evil should befall him alone in the forest; I however summoned my fortitude and resolved not to be faint hearted.

An attack of illness followed. The three weeks passed; a

good supply of potatoes was nearly all the provisions we had left, and I began to look with great anxiety for my husband. A felon on my right hand deprived me entirely of the use of it for more than three weeks. With the pain, fatigue, and want of sleep I was ready to despair, but for my children's sake I kept up my resolution; still no tidings came from Mr. Bryan, and my fears for his safety became more and more painful. Two months passed, and brought cold December for me and my little ones, but brought no news from him whose duty it was to provide for us. My sufferings became extreme. I tried to get some one to go in search of him, and ascertain at least if he ever got through the woods alive, but I had no money even to bear expenses, and all told me they 'guessed' he was safe and would soon return. How myself and babes were to live meanwhile I knew not. We had eaten nothing but potatoes for several weeks; the neighbors were nearly as destitute and had nothing to lend, even if I could have borrowed when I could not expect to pay again. For a temporary change in diet from potatoes alone, I ventured to borrow a few ears of corn, promising to pay if Mr. Bryan ever returned; this I shelled and boiled to jelly, which we relished very much while it lasted.

It was now the 23rd of December; I had been all day trying to induce some one to go to Maumee for tidings, and had succeeded in obtaining a promise from a young man that he would go in two or three days if I would get a horse. Alas! horses were as scarce as bread, and I knew it would be impossible to procure one. I returned home and stood in our log cabin door, thinking what to do next, when my husband rode up, and put an end to my fears. He had written several letters, which were delayed in Detroit, and never reached me. Finding wages high, and the roads very bad, he had concluded to remain, supposing I was well provided for. Our sufferings for five or six years after this were even greater, if possible, than before, but it would take a volume to describe them.

The earliest known view of Ann Arbor (1852).

Ann Arbor & Dexter: 1824
by
Harriet L. Noble

My husband was seized with the mania, and accordingly made preparation to start in January with his brother. They took the Ohio route, and were nearly a month in getting through; coming by way of Monroe, and thence to Ypsilanti and Ann Arbor. Mr. John Allen and Walter Rumsey[122] with his wife and two men had been there some four or five weeks, had built a small house, moved into it the day my husband and his brother arrived, and were just preparing their first meal, which the newcomers had the pleasure of partaking. They spent a few days here, located a farm a little above the town on the river Huron, and returned through Canada. They had been so much pleased with the country, that they immediately commenced preparing to emigrate; and as near as I can recollect, we started about the 20th of September, 1824, for Michigan. We travelled from our house in Geneva to Buffalo in wagons. The roads were bad, and we were obliged to wait in Buffalo four days for a boat, as the steamboat *Michigan* was the only one on the lake. After waiting so long we found she had put into Erie for repairs, and had no prospect of being able to run again for sometime. The next step was to take passage in a schooner, which was considered a terrible undertaking for so dangerous a voyage as it was then thought to be. At length we went on board the *Prudence,* of Cleveland, Capt. Johnson. A more inconvenient little bark could not well be imagined. We were seven days on Lake Erie, and so entirely prostrated with seasickness, as scarcely to be able to attend to the wants of our little ones. I had a little girl of three years, and a babe some months old, and Sister Noble had six children one an infant. It was a tedious voyage; the lake was very rough most of the time, and I thought if we were only on land again, I should be satisfied, if it was a wilderness. I could not then realize what it would be to live without a comfortable house through the winter, but sad experience afterwards taught me a lesson not to be forgotten.

We came into the Detroit River; it was beautiful then as now; on the Canada side, in particular, you will scarce perceive any change. As we approached Detroit, the 'Cantonment' with the American flag floating on its walls, was decidedly the most interesting of any part of the town; for a city it was certainly the most filthy, irregular place I had ever seen; the streets were filled with Indians and low French, and at that time I could not tell the difference between them. We spent two days in making preparations for going out to Ann Arbor, and during that time I never saw a genteelly-dressed person in the streets. There were no carriages; the most wealthy families rode in French carts, sitting on the bottom upon some kind of mat; and the streets were so muddy these were the only vehicles convenient for getting about. I said to myself, 'if this be a western city, give me a home in the woods.' I think it was on the 3rd of October we started from Detroit, with a pair of oxen and a wagon, a few articles for cooking, and such necessaries as we could not do without. It was necessary that they should be few as possible, for our families were a full load for this mode of travelling. After travelling all day we found ourselves but ten miles from Detroit (at what is now Dearborn); here we spent the night at a kind of tavern, the only one west of the city. Our lodging was the floor, and the other entertainment was to match. The next day we set out as early as possible, in hopes to get through the woods before dark, but night found us about half way through, and there remained no other resource but to camp out, and make ourselves contented. The men built a large fire and prepared our supper. My sister and myself could assist but little, so fatigued were we with walking and carrying our infants. There were fifteen in our company. Two gentlemen going to Ypsilanti had travelled with us from Buffalo; the rest were our own families. We were all pretty cheerful until we began to think of lying down for the night. The men did not seem to dread it, however, and were soon fast asleep, but sleep was not for me in such a wilderness. I could think of nothing but wild beasts, or something as bad; so that I had the pleasure of watching while the others slept. It seemed a long, long night, and never in my life did I feel more grateful for the blessing of returning day. We started again as early as possible, all who could walk moving on a little in advance of the wagon; the small children were the only ones who thought of riding. Every few rods it would take two or three men to pry the wagon out of the mud, while whose who walked were obliged to force their way over fallen timber, brush, etc. Thus passed the day; at night we found ourselves on the plains, three miles from Ypsilanti. My feet were so swollen I could walk no further. We got into the wagon and rode as far as Woodruff's Grove,[123] a little below Ypsilanti. There were some four or five families at this place. The next day we left for Ann Arbor. We were delighted with the country before us; it was beautiful in its natural state; and I have sometimes thought that cultivation has marred its loveliness. Where Ypsilanti now stands, there was but one building - an old trading house on the west side of the river; the situation was fine - there were scattering oaks and no brushwood. Here we met a large number of Indians and one old squaw followed us some distance with her papoose, determined to swap babies. At last she gave it up, and for one I felt relieved.

We passed two log houses between this and Ann Arbor. About the middle of the afternoon we found ourselves at our journey's end, but what prospect? There were some six or seven log huts occupied by as many inmates as could be crowded into them. It was too much to think of asking strangers to give us a place to stay in even for one night under such circumstances. Mr. John Allen himself made us the offer of sharing with him the comfort of a shelter from storm, if not from cold. His house was large for a log one, but quite unfinished; there was a ground floor and a small piece above. When we got our things stored in this place, we found the number sheltered to be twenty-one women and children, and fourteen men. There were but two bedsteads in the house, and those who could not occupy these, slept on feather beds upon the floor. When the children were put in bed you could not set a foot down without stepping on a foot or hand; the consequence was we had music most of the time.

We cooked our meals in the open air, there being no fire in the house but a small box-stove. The fall winds were not very favorable to such business; we would frequently find our clothes on fire, but fortunately we did not often get burned. When one meal was over, however, we dreaded preparing the next. We lived in this way until our husbands got a log house raised and the roof on; this took them about six weeks, at the end of which time we went into it, without door, floor, chimney, or anything but logs and roof. There were no means of getting boards for a floor, as everything must be brought from Detroit, and we could not think of drawing lumber over such a road. The only alternative was to split slabs of oak with an axe. My husband was not a mechanic, but he managed to make a floor in this way that kept us from the ground. I was most anxious for a door, as the wolves would come about in the evening and sometimes stay all night and keep up a serenade that would almost chill the blood in my veins. Of all noises I think the howling of wolves and the yell of Indians the most fearful; at least it appeared so to me then when I was not able to close the door against them. I had the greatest terror of Indians; for I had never seen any before I came to Michigan but Oneidas,[124] and they were different, being partially civilized.

We had our house comfortable as such a rude building could be, by the first of February. It was a mild winter; there was snow enough to cover the ground only four days, a fortunate circumstance for us. We enjoyed uninterrupted health, but in the spring the ague with its accompaniments gave us a call, and by the middle of August there were but four out of fourteen who could call themselves well. We then fancied we were too near the river for health. We sold out and bought again ten miles west of Ann Arbor, a place which suited us better; and just a year from the day we came to Ann Arbor, moved out of it to Dexter. There was one house here, Judge Dexter's;[125] he was building a saw mill, and had a number of men at work at the time; besides these there was not a white family west of Ann Arbor in Michigan territory. Our log house was just raised, forming only the square log pen. Of course it did not look very inviting but it was our home, and we must make the best of it. I helped to raise the rafters and put on the roof, but it was the last of November before our roof was completed. We were obliged to wait for the mill to run in order to get boards for making it. The doorway I had no means of closing except by hanging up a blanket, and frequently when I would raise it to step out, there would be two or three of our dusky neighbors peeping in to see what was there. It would always give me such a start, I could not suppress a scream, to which they would reply with "Ugh!" and a hearty laugh. They knew I was afraid, and liked to torment me. Sometimes they would throng the house and stay two or three hours. If I was alone they would help themselves to what they liked. The only way in which I could restrain them at all, was to threaten that I would tell Cass; he was governor of the territory, and they stood in great fear of him. At last we got a door. The next thing wanted was a chimney; winter was close at hand and the stone was not drawn. I said to my husband, "I think I can drive the oxen and draw the stones, while you dig them from the ground and load them." He thought I could not, but consented to let me try. He loaded them on a kind of sled; I drove to the house, rolled them off, and drove back for another load. I succeeded so well that we got enough in this way to build our chimney. My husband and myself were four days building it. I suppose most of my lady friends would think a woman quite out of "her legitimate sphere" in turning mason, but I was not at all particular what kind of labor I performed, so we were only comfortable and provided with the necessaries of life. Many times I had been obliged take my children, put on their cloaks, and sit on the south side of the house in the sun to keep them warm; anything was preferable to smoke. When we had a chimney and floor, and a door to close up our little log cabin, I have often thought it the most comfortable little place that could possibly be built in so new a country; and but for the want of provisions of almost every kind, we should have enjoyed it much. The roads had been so bad all the fall that we had waited until this time, and I think it was December when my husband went to Detroit for supplies. Fifteen days were consumed in going and coming. We had been without flour for three weeks or more, and it was hard to manage with young children thus. After being without bread three or four days, my little boy, two years old, looked me in the face and said, "Ma, why don't you make bread; don't you like it? I do." His innocent complaint brought forth the first tears I had shed in Michigan on account of any privations I had to suffer, and they were about the last. I am not of a desponding disposition, nor often low spirited, and having left New York to make Michigan my home, I had no idea of going back, or being very unhappy. Yet the want of society, of church privileges, and in fact almost every thing that makes life desirable, would often make me sad in spite of all effort to the contrary. I had no ladies' society for one year after coming to Dexter, except that of sister Noble and a Mrs. Taylor, and was more lonely than either of them, my family being so small.

The winter passed rather gloomily, but when spring came, every thing looked delightful. We thought our hardships nearly at an end, when early in the summer my husband was taken with the ague. He had not been sick at all the first year; of course he must be acclimated. He had never suffered from ague or fever of any kind before, and it was a severe trial for him, with so much to do and no help to be had. He would break the ague and work for a few days, when it would return. In this way he made his garden, planted his corn, and thought he was quite well. About August he harvested his wheat and cut his hay, but could get no help to draw it, and was again taken with ague. I had it myself, and both my children. Sometimes we would all be ill at a time. Mr Noble and I had it every other day. He was almost discouraged, and said he should have to sell his cattle or let them starve. I said to him, "tomorrow we shall neither of us have the ague, and I believe I can load and stack the hay, if my strength permits." As soon as breakfast was over, I prepared to go into the meadow, where I loaded and stacked seven loads that day. The next day my husband had the ague more severely than common, but not so me; the exercise broke the chills, and I was able to assist him whenever he was well enough, until our hay was all secured. In the fall we had several added to our circle. We were more healthy then, and began to flatter ourselves that we could live very comfortably through the winter of 1826; but we were not destined to enjoy that blessing, for in November my husband had his left hand blown to pieces by the accidental discharge of a gun, which confined him to the house until April. The hay I had stacked during the summer I had to feed out to the cattle with my own hands in the winter, and often cut the wood for three days at a time. The logs which I alone rolled in, would surprise anyone who has never been put to the test of necessity, which compels people to do what under other circumstances they would not have thought possible. This third winter in Michigan was decidedly the hardest I had yet encountered. In the spring, Mr. Noble could go out by carrying his hand in a sling. He commenced ploughing to prepare for planting his corn. Being weak from his wound, the ague returned again, but he worked every day until his corn was planted. He then went to New York, came back in July, and brought a nephew with him, who relieved me from helping him in the work out of doors. Although I was obliged to stack the hay this third fall, I believe it was the last labor of the kind I ever performed. At this time we began to have quite a little society; we were fortunate in having good neighbors, and for some years were almost like one family, our interests being the same, and envy, jealousy, and all bitter feelings unknown among us. We cannot speak so favorably of the present time.

When I look back upon my life, and see the ups and downs, the hardships and privations I have been called upon to endure, I feel no wish to be young again. I was in the prime of life when I came to Michigan only twenty-one, and my husband was thirty-three. Neither of us knew the reality of hardship. Could we have known what it was to be pioneers in a new country, we should never have had the courage to come; but I am satisfied that with all the disadvantages of raising a family in a new country, there is a consolation in that our children are prepared to brave the ills of life, I believe, far better than they would have been had we never left New York.

The *Michigan* carried thousands of immigrants across often stormy Lake Erie.

Marine City: 1826
by
Emily Ward

Emily Ward, the sister of Eber Brock Ward, who became a millionaire through shipping, lumbering and iron manufacturing, settled at Yankee Point, now Marine City, at the age of 12 in 1822. Four years later she experienced the events as narrated in the following excerpt. In 1827 the Ward family moved back to Conneaut, Ohio, where they lived until 1831. At that time her father, Eber Ward, was appointed lighthouse keeper on Bois Blanc Island. She assisted her father with his duties there and in his absence during a storm she singlehandedly rescued the valuable lamps and reflectors just before the lighthouse tower toppled into the surf.

In 1845 the Wards moved back to Marine City where she spent the succeeding 22 years. She never married, but following the death of her two sisters she raised their ten children. She devoted her life to caring for orphans, ultimately raising 29 men and women, many of whom became and rich and successful.

Ward moved to Detroit in 1867 where she lived until her death in 1891. "Aunt Emily" was dearly beloved by the many she had helped get a start in life. Six hundred people paid her their respects at a reception held to celebrate her 80th birthday. Frances Hurlbut, one of the "little girls" she had raised, produced a volume of recollections Ward had earlier told the children. Published as *Grandmother's Stories* (Cambridge, 1889), it was presented to Ward as a birthday present. The following narrative is included in that publication.

It was in the early summer of 1826, for I was seventeen years old when this little happened, said grandma in response to some questions of the children.

It was training day, as it was called, and every man and boy who was well enough and old enough to carry a gun had to go to the county seat to be trained in military movements. [126]

That morning father and Eber[127] and every man and boy in the settlement, except a poor lame shoemaker, had gone to Port Huron, twenty miles away, to the training, and the women and children were left alone. But no one thought anything of it, for the country was at peace, and though there were Indians around they were friendly, and we had nothing to fear from them.

It was bright and lovely morning when we went down the river bank[128] to see father and Eber off. The river shone like a mirror, and reflected the trees that overhung its banks so clearly that they looked like twin trees growing into its shining depths. The robins were singing their loudest, and everything was so fresh and beautiful and peaceful that I lingered a long time dreaming over it. But the cares of a housekeeper drove me home after a while, and I went into the house to do my morning work.

I had put the house to rights, and had just finished baking my bread, when the door suddenly opened, and in poured a great number of Indians in full war paint and dress, muskets in their hands and knives and tomahawks in their belts. They paid no more attention to me than if I had been a block of wood, but went to the cupboard, and took the bread and cake and everything eatable. They drank some vinegar there was in a barrel in the corner, and then began looking around after something in particular, but which they didn't find; finally, one old fellow looked at me and said, "Whiskey?" I shook my head, and told him we hadn't any. He started to open the door into the room where the whiskey barrel was, but I stepped ahead of him quick, put my hand through the door handle, looked him right in the eye, and told him that he could not go in there.

When they first came in I seized the broom, as it was the only weapon left in the house, and a woman's weapon at that, said grandma, smiling; and when some of the young men tried to pull me away from the door I hung on tight with one hand, and struck right and left with the broom handle as hard as I could strike, hitting an Indian at every blow.

I knew I might as well die fighting as any other way, and that if I couldn't keep them from the whiskey barrel they would get drunk, and then kill every woman and child in the place. After

155

a little some of the young men made motions as if to strike me; but this old fellow, who seemed to be their chief, said in Indian "Leave her to me. I'll put her to sleep."

I knew what he meant, for I could understand Indian some, but I made up my mind that I'd not let go of that door as long as I had life to hold it.

Then the old Indian made as if to strike me with a stick, but I didn't flinch, and kept on looking him right in the eye. Then he threw it down on the floor, and said, "pick it up!"

I knew that if I stooped he would strike me on the back of the head, and that I would die without making any outcry; so I shook my head and would not pick it up.

In the mean time I could hear Sallie screaming and crying in the yard, for the young Indians were amusing themselves beating her with long, slender whips, for no other purpose than the fun of hearing her scream. But just at that moment she put her head in at the door, and I shouted to her, "Sallie, run quick, and tell the men!"

Now I knew that there were no men around but the lame old shoemaker, but I said it for a double purpose: one to get Sallie away, and the other that the old Indian, who understood a little English, might think there were a good many men around, and so go away for fear of them.

Sallie ran quick as a flash, and the old fellow, who had understood what I said, as I expected he would, left me, and began talking in a low tone with some of the older Indians. They seemed to come to some sudden decision, for he gave a word of command, and they all left the house as abruptly as they had entered it, went down the bank, got into their boats, pushed off into the river, and were half-way across before Sallie got back with the news "that the shoemaker was afraid and would not come."

"Oh, grandma! weren't you afraid?" said the children.

No; though I knew they might kill me, I didn't seem to have any fear. I remember I thought I might just as well be killed then as after they got drunk. But after they were gone I was so weak and trembled so I could not stand up. I had to sit down, and I shook like a leaf in the wind for hours after. It took me several days to get over the nervous depression that followed.

"Oh, grandma, I think you were awfully brave," said Golden-Hair.

"No, it was not bravery," replied grandma thoughtfully. "I was afraid they would get the whiskey, and then kill everybody."

"What made them go away so quick?" inquired one of the mammas.

"You see," said grandma, "these Indians were warriors from the Saginaw tribe, who were very fierce and warlike; and they were then on their way to Detroit to try and release from prison their chief, old Kishkawko, who had a year before killed a man in the streets of Detroit. Just in pure wantonness, without the least provocation, he had thrown a tomahawk at a white man who was walking peacefully along, and struck him down. He had been arrested, tried, and condemned to be hanged."

The Indians thought it an overwhelming disgrace "to be hung like dogs," as they said, and they determined, if they could not release him, to give him poison. I suppose the reason they went, when I told Sallie to run after the men, was that, going for the purpose they were, they did not wish anything to defeat that purpose. They were afraid that if the men came there would be a fight, and they would be delayed and perhaps stopped altogether.

"It was luck," said one of the aunties, "that they did not know there was but one man in the place."

"Yes, indeed!" cried the children.

"What became of Kishkawko?" asked one of the mammas.

He took poison the morning he was to be hanged. They found the white man's government too strong for them to rescue him, so they gave him the poison. [129]

157

The great immigrants highway, the Erie Canal, is shown here at Lockport, New York.

Cass County: 1829
by
Catherine Calkins Brunson

Among the first land to be taken up by the homesteaders who flocked to Michigan Territory in the 1820s were the numerous small prairies scattered across the southern two tiers of counties. The soil was extremely fertile and did not require the laborious chopping down of trees prior to cultivation.

Catherine Calkins Brunson wrote the following account of her experiences as a Michigan prairie pioneer for the St. Joseph County Pioneer Reunion held on June 10, 1896.

My father, Caleb Calkins, and family emigrated from Caledonia Springs, New York, to Baldwin's Prairie,[130] Cass County, Michigan, in the fall of 1828. Our journey nearly all the way was through a wilderness country, and we arrived at Solomon Hartman's on the bank of the St. Joseph River on the 1st of January, 1829, where we were delayed ten days before we could ford the river at Mottville.

When we arrived at Mr. Baldwin's, our destination, we found him in bed a mass of bruises and his life hanging in the balance. We learned he had some trouble with the Indians a short time before. The Indians claimed that Baldwin had been cheating them with poor watered whisky, and that they could drink a pint of it and never phase them. Baldwin told them that he would furnish the whisky for nothing if they thought he was cheating them. So Baldwin gave them a pint of his best. One of then took the pint of whisky and turned it down his rat-hole of a throat without stopping to taste. Soon there was a dead Indian around there . This angered his brother Indians, who said that Baldwin had played a rascally and murderous trick on them, and they came at him with clubs and pounded him to a pulp and left him for dead. Baldwin, being a man of strong vitality, came to, but was all winter in recovering. The nearest doctor was Loomis[131] of White Pigeon, eleven miles away. Joel Baldwin, a boy about 14 years old, attempted to find an axe or something to help defend his father, but failed to find anything, as the Indians had secured everything.

Joel mounted a horse and put him down to best speed to their nearest neighbor, Nathan Odell, near Mottville, for assistance. Here assistance was procured and Dr. Loomis of White Pigeon sent for. Young Baldwin just then began to realize that a single shirt was a thin protection for the cold, wintry December night.

The Shave Head band buried their dead brother Indian in a log pen four feet square and six feet in height, standing upright securely tied to the logs with his gun and ammunition by his side, facing the rising sun. They then roofed this holy of holies over with logs six or height inches in diameter. This receptacle of the dead was erected on a knoll about fifty rods from Baldwin's house and fifteen rods north of the Chicago Road. It remained for many years and until the forest fires consumed it.

For this Indian depredation Baldwin received over a thousand dollars from the Unites States government, it being deducted from this band's annuities. So the Indians lost one of their band and a thousand dollars all on account of a pint of whisky which went done one Indian's thirsty throat.

One side of Mr. Baldwin's room was splashed all over with blood where the Indians attacked and clubbed him. We remained with him the balance of the winter and until we built a house of our own about sixty rods away. Quaker Baldwin was a good friend to our family in sickness and misfortunes, of which we had many, as our house burned down and we had two deaths in our family the first few years.

Every family had their dead to bury as best they could. My father, being a carpenter, made the coffins, Sometimes he had to cut packing boxes and often wagon boxes, as no lumber was made here then. The pioneer log cabins were floored with slabs split from logs and hewn down.

Once when my father was sick my mother and her little son went to Sage's Mill, now Adamsville. On their way they passed Chief Shave Head and his band of about 200, who were camped near the Chicago Road. Chief Shave Head was quite old and black, six feet tall and as straight as an arrow, with not a vestige of hair on his head; a mere skeleton on account of his age, and altogether he was a frightful looking specimen of humanity. In passing the Indian camp on their way home from the mill the old chief came out and stopped them and demanded the grist. They tried to compromise with him, but no compromise would do, as his people were hungry. When he attempted to take the grist out of the wagon the oxen got a smell of the old chief and ran for dear life like wild buffaloes. The hind wheel of the wagon ran over and knocked old Shave Head flat upon the ground, and he did not attempt to get up and follow them, and they were soon out of sight and hearing of the camp. In the melee two Indian boys had climbed into the wagon and were eating the boy's lunch; but they didn't seem to care what happened, as they were hungry. So Shave Head lost the grist and children too. After the oxen slackened their speed they unloaded the Indian children and sent them back.

After the mail stages began to run on the Chicago Road, Chief Shave Head established himself as a toll gate at Mud Run, about three and a half miles west of Mottville. Here he made everybody pay tribute for passing through his domain. Savery,[132] the stage agent at White Pigeon went over to Mud Run, where he found the old chief, who demanded toll. Savery got off the stage, took the chief's gun from him, fired it off and rammed the muzzle down into the mud. Then he got his horsewhip and licked the chief down on the dead run out of sight, and he was never seen as road agent at that point afterward.

The Indian burying ground was located between the south forks of Shave Head Lake on a mound of ten or twelve feet elevation. Here they buried most of their dead. Their sarcophagi were made by cutting off logs six or eight feet long and by splitting off a slab from the upper side. After cutting sufficient space in the log to hide the body the slab was replaced, and if they did a good job this casket would be air tight. Four stakes were driven into the ground, caps were placed on cross ways and wedged down on these stakes so that nothing could disturb their dead, In one of these sarcophagi there was not sufficient depth to receive the feet. They had to cut a cavity in the cover or slab to receive the toes, as it was traditional among the tribe that none should be maimed, as it was expected of all Indians to be good runners on their arrival at the Indian paradise, the happy hunting ground, where game would be plentiful and where Indians would never tire. The log pen receptacle of the dead where the whisky Indian was buried remained undisturbed, as it was understood by the white people that if anyone disturbed this Indian they would serve him as they did Baldwin.

161

The burial ground at Shave Head Lake has been torn up by vandal relic hunters, everything taken out of these wooden sarcophagi; nothing remained in them but a red pasty clay mould. The bones were strewn all around the grounds. There was one large skull and jaw bones, the teeth of which had cavities and much decay. This would indicate that the Indians must have suffered with toothache some day.

A 19th century Michigan Indian woman.

Jackson: 1830
by
Mary G. DeLand

Mary G. DeLand, the cousin of Horace Blackman, Jackson's pioneer settler, narrated her recollections of early life at that community to Electa Sheldon. Sheldon, author of the first selection in this book, edited DeLand's narrative and published it in the *Michigan Pioneer Collections* (Vol. 5, 1884).

In an epic poem about Jackson's history composed by Dr. J.A. Robinson and read by him at the Semi-Centennial Celebration of the County in 1879 appears the following tribute to DeLand:

"Old Squire DeLand, the Justice, gave the news,
And Mother DeLand gave poor children shoes;
She never was found lying in the lurch,
When work was needed for the village church;"

In June, 1829, my uncle, Lemuel Blackman, of Tompkins, Broome County, N.Y., accompanied by his son Horace, came to Michigan "to look land," as the phrase went.

The interior of the state was then an almost unbroken wilderness. Ann Arbor, then a mere hamlet, being the most western settlement in the state. [133]

My resolute uncle and cousin pushed on beyond; but they had gone only a few miles when uncle was taken sick, and was obliged to return to Ann Arbor. Cousin Horace, undaunted by this misfortune, procured the services of an Indian guide and kept on till he reached Grand River at Jackson. Jackson County was the most western county then in market, and Horace, after some time spent in exploring it, selected the place which he thought would probably be the site of the county seat, as the future residence of his father's family, and located a large tract of land on the west side of Grand River. This was the first location of land in Jackson County.

After the land was located Uncle Blackman returned home, and soon after Russell, an older brother joined Horace at Jackson, where he was living in a rude shanty. The brothers, with the assistance of two men from Ann Arbor, immediately commenced building a log house about 20 x 30 feet, and succeeded in getting the roof on in time for Horace to go east before the close of navigation.

About this time, in the fall of 1829, Dr. Benjamin H. Packard of Ann Arbor, came on to Jackson with a party of friends - "land-seekers," from the State of New York. They reached the east bank of Grand River early in the evening and spent the night in a kind of shanty made of bushes by "Potato Bronson."134 There were seven of them: Isaiah W. Bennett, John Daniels, Samuel Roberts, James D. Cleland, Capt. Alexander B. Laverty, Moses Allen, and Dr. Packard. They ranged over the county, up and down the river and finally I.W. Bennett selected the water power where the first saw mill was afterward built, and Dr. Packard located the land. The doctor also located a tract of land on the west side of the river, adjoining the Blackman tract. In the winter Dr. Packard went to Detroit and secured the appointment of three commissioners, who came to Jackson and stuck the stake for the courthouse, on Dr. Packard's land, where the Central Union Schoolhouse now stands.

The doctor brought the commissioners from Ann Arbor in a wagon. When he returned he made a map of the would be city and took it to the register's office, and also sent out a glowing hand bill written to Gideon Wilcoxen, proposing to set off ten acres for the future capitol of the state. But the map was stolen, and through Detroit influence a new set of commissioners: Chauncy Goodrich, Henry Rumsey, and John Allen were sent out in June, who removed the stake to where the court house now stands, and a later day the state prison, instead of the state capitol was given to Jackson.

After Horace Blackman left for the east, Russell left the half built house stand as it was, without door or window, and bent all his energies to secure the route of the territorial road through the prospective city. He labored assiduously six weeks to effect this object and finally succeeded. He was engaged most of the winter in assisting Jonathan F. Stratton to survey the road to Jackson, and from thence to Kalamazoo. While Russell was absent on this road business, Mr. Linus Gillett, with his wife and two children, arrived in Jackson. It was mid-winter, and they had no place of shelter till they cut a hole in Uncle Blackman's half finished house large enough to answer for a door. They took off their wagon box, laid it across the sleepers, and Mrs. Gillett made a bed in it for herself and children, while the men were building a fire on the ground where would some day be the fireplace. After supper the men rolled themselves in their blankets, laid down on the ground between the sleepers for their nights rest. Mrs. Gillett was the first white women in Jackson County. With such additions to their comfort as Mr. Gillett could make, he and his family remained in the Blackman house till spring, in the meantime boarding Mr. Wickham and Hiram Thompson, who were employed by I.W. Bennett and Wm. R. Thompson to build a house and the much needed saw mill. They began to build the house in February or March, and as soon as the logs could be rolled up and a roof put on, with slabs split out of large logs for the lower floor and rails for the upper floor, they opened it as a hotel.

Bennett & Thompson's hotel was the first in Jackson, and was used for that purpose many years.

Mr. Gillett built a house and moved his family out of Uncle Blackman's house into his own in April, and Mr. Josephus Case and family came in March and lived in a rude shanty built on the spot where Bascom's Hotel was afterward erected.

Our company, consisting of Uncle Blackman's family of eleven and our own family of four reached Jackson May 27, 1830. We crossed Grand River on the flats a little below Trail Street, the teams fording the stream, and the men, women, and children crossing on a fallen tree which served us for a footbridge for a long time afterwards.

"Rather a small stream for such a grand name," I remarked as we crossed the river.

"We are only a few miles from its source," was the reply; "Grand River rises in Jackson County."

"Well, Cousin Mary, here we are in Jackson," said Horace, as we emerged from the thicket along the margin of the river.

"This Jackson! This low valley beside such a paltry stream the site of a future city! Why didn't they select some place high and dry?" I thought, as we walked on towards a rude log house without a door, windows, floor, or chimney, built where the Blackman family residence now stands. But likes or dislikes made no difference - all must give place to right down hard work in making this pioneer house as comfortable as possible. Mr. Case had brought a load of boards for us from Ann Arbor, and these were laid down for a floor, but they did not cover more than half the room. One board was reserved for a table, which was made by running one end through between the logs, and placing the other end on a barrel. The fire for cooking was done out of doors, and a blanket supplied the want of a door. The first night we made our beds on the floor, but next day we made a decided improvement by filling our straw ticks with marsh hay, and making two "Michigan bedsteads" in this wise: Two holes were bored in a log forming the side of the house, into which were driven poles of the required length; the other end of these poles was fastened to short pieces of wood which served as posts, and into these posts was fastened a larger pole which formed the bed rail opposite the log; a rude lacing of bed cord across these poles and the bedstead was complete.

This was the second day of our residence in Jackson; and you will doubtless suppose that, with all these improvements, we were ready to receive the company; and so it proved. The first day we had been so much fatigued that we had taken supper very early, and laid us down to sleep before dark. So it was the second evening; we had taken supper, and were already thinking of retiring to rest, when a man and boy, who were looking land, claimed our hospitality, which in a new country is never refused. We hastened to prepare their supper of pork and potatoes, and a cup of tea. When all was ready we found to our dismay that we had no candles. Not one in the crowd had thought of them when we were making our purchases in Ann Arbor, and not needing them we had not missed them the first night. It was getting quite dark in the house - what would we do? In our perplexity we applied to Cousin Russell. "Don't look so anxious," said he, laughing; "I'll make a candle in a minute." He went to the pork barrel, cut a long strip of fat pork, coiled it up in a tin cup, and set fire to the end, and to our great joy it burned. Delighted with the success of the experiment, I ran out to the fire to bring in the supper, when, hitting my toe against a little stump, I fell full length at the very feet of Messrs. Hiram Thompson and I.W. Bennett, two of our neighbors who had come to make us a friendly call. You may imagine my mortification at such an unusual introduction, though I joined heartily in the laugh which my mishap occasioned.

The following night we had three guests; and for two months not a day passed without more or less company. Sometimes as many as fifteen men would come for supper, and then camp down on the floor to sleep. It made a great deal of hard work for us, but we could not say them nay.

A pioneer matron narrates her life story.

A week or two after our arrival, additional supplies of food and another load of boards were brought from Ann Arbor. Half of the chamber floor was laid, more "Michigan bedsteads" were made, and curtains of blankets and quilts partioned off the chamber into bedrooms. By this arrangement a larger space on the floor below could be used by travelers. Our family remained with Uncle Blackman's about two months, when Mr. DeLand[135] bought eight village lots on Blackstone Street, between Clinton and Luther, on which was an unfinished log house built by Prussia & Mills. There was neither floor, chimney, nor window, and the door was rudely constructed of small pieces of boards. But two months' experience in pioneer life had made us familiar with all sorts of inconveniences, and there was a novelty in this manner of living that suited the dash of romance in my character. When we had been in our new house two weeks, Mr. DeLand split out basswood slabs and laid a lower floor. At one end of the room a place was left for a chimney, and there I did my cooking, hanging the kettles on a crane fastened to a post driven in the ground. The floor was perhaps two feet from the ground, and that portion nearest the fireplace served the family for seats when they wished to "gather 'round the domestic hearth." In a few weeks we were the owner of a glass window - a great luxury.

By this time there were seven houses in the village, occupied by Messrs. Gillett, Case, Blackman, Chapman, Major D. Mills, DeLand, and Bennett & Thompson's hotel.

Mr. Mills' was the first frame house in Jackson; the clapboards, shingle, and all the other boards were split out by his own hand.

Emigrants now began to pour into the country. A few families settled at Sandstone,[136] six mile beyond us, and here and there a family east of us. Most of the settlers came supplied with a year's provisions, except flour, which was all brought from Ann Arbor. It was the Jackson custom to send a team for a load of flour, and then divide it in the neighborhood according to the size of the families, each family bearing its proportion of the expenses and paying a share of the purchase money.

The great event of our first year's residence in Michigan, was the celebration of the Fourth of July, It was determined that this first general celebration of our nation's birthday should be a time "long to be remembered." A public meeting was called, and a committee of arrangements chosen, to select speakers, and make all necessary arrangements for the great event. The committee consisted of Hiram Thompson, Anson Brown, and Wm. R. DeLand, and a better committee could not have been selected. Invitations were sent to all the settlers in the county, and to many friends in Ann Arbor and Dixborough.[137] Expectation was on tiptoe; and the liberality and ingenuity of the inhabitants of our village were taxed to the utmost. It was a busy time for the ladies, grave consultations were held concerning the table and its adornments; all were united and happy in doing their utmost to make the affair a success. The eventful day at length dawned, ushered in by volleys of musketry, and other appropriate rejoicings. About 10 o'clock the inhabitants of Jackson County, with five gentlemen from Ann Arbor, and two ladies from Dixborough, Mrs. Dix and Miss Frances Trask, afterwards wife of Wm. R. Thompson, of Ann Arbor and Texas, assembled in a grove on the east side of Jackson Street, a little south of Franklin Street, where a platform had been erected for the officers of the day, and seats for the audience. The assembly was called to order by I.W. Bennett, president of the day, and the divine blessing was invoked by Capt. John Durand. The Declaration of Independence was read by George Mayo, of Massachusetts; oration was delivered by Hon. Gideon Wilcoxen, of Ann Arbor, followed by a short and appropriate speech by the president of the day. After the oration a procession was formed, which marched to the Pubic square under the escort of the military commanded by Capt. Laverty; Horace Blackman of Jackson, and Edward Clark of Ann Arbor, acting as marshals of the day. A bowery had been built on the square, where the new Baptist church now stands, and a large table spread with the finest damask of the village housewife, and loaded with choice viands of the new settlement, awaited the guests.

When we remember that all supplies came from Ann Arbor, and even some of the crockery in use that day was borrowed there, I may be permitted to name the various dishes which composed that feast. We had roast veal and venison, baked pork and beans, for the first course; the second course consisted of apple and pumpkin pies, nice Indian baked puddings and a great variety of cake, tea, coffee, brandy, wine, and whisky were also abundant.

Eighty persons were seated at tables, twelve of whom were ladies. After the cloth was removed, Anson Brown, Esq., gave a toast to the ladies, which was received with "three times three" hearty cheers. The ladies then retired and enjoyed a fine ramble in the woods, while the gentlemen drank patriotic toasts. After each toast Capt. Laverty's musketry fired a salute.

The entire day passed away very pleasantly, and the next morning the intrepid ladies from Dixborough mounted their horses and, escorted by the gallant gentlemen from Ann Arbor, returned to their homes. The borrowed crockery reached Ann Arbor without accident, and the Jacksonians resumed their usual employments.

Sometime in September we were able to enjoy the luxury of a chamber floor, and a ladder to ascend to the chamber. Our house was also chinked, as the weather was getting cool.

Scarcely had we made these additions to our comfort, when a man named Daniel Hogan arrived in the village with a small supply of goods. There were no houses to rent, not a vacant room; and what could the poor man do, till he could build a shelter for himself and family. He applied to us for the privilege of remaining with us a few weeks, and we could not deny him. Our own family consisted of four persons, Mr. Hogan's of three; and a week or two later my sister with one child came to spend the winter with me, her husband being absent from home, nine persons in all, besides the occasional addition of two or three workmen who were building Mr. Hogan's house; and the frequent claims of our hospitality made by emigrants. Then the traffic with the Indians was quite lucrative, and Mr. Hogan;s goods must, of course be displayed. Just think of three families and a store of goods in a house 16 x 18 feet.

Fortunately we all enjoyed excellent health; indeed there were but two cases of sickness in the village that season. Hiram Thompson and George B. Cooper were both very ill, and we were obliged to send forty miles, to Ann Arbor, for a physician. Dr. Benjamin H. Packard was the physician called, and his was the first professional visit in Jackson County, and the only one that year.

Late in fall we had a chimney built; the fireplace was rudely constructed of stones, with a rough stone hearth, and the chimney was finished out with sticks plastered with clay. The outside of the house between the logs was also plastered, or mudded, as it was termed. We then considered ourselves prepared for winter; and as our little colony was considerably enlarged we anticipated no small degree of enjoyment.

We did pass a very pleasant winter in the enjoyment of good health, united among ourselves, and with plenty of leisure to enjoy each other's society. Our various privations, and the numberless inventions which necessity originated, gave zest and variety to our everyday life. True, we were rather thickly settled at our house, as Mr. Hogan was disappointed about getting his house finished, and remained with us till spring; however, that did not prevent my giving a party about mid-winter, on the arrival of Mr. and Mrs. Perrine, from Ann Arbor. Mr. Perrine had spent a few of the previous weeks in Jackson, and improved the first fall of snow to give all the Jackson ladies a sleigh ride. We now felt it incumbent on us to reciprocate his kindness, by polite attentions to his wife. Besides, Mrs. Perrine was a distinguished poetess, and for her own sake we wished to treat her with consideration.

There were no very marked distinctions in society then, so the whole town was invited. As our house was not very spacious, we took down two bedsteads, and set them out of doors, and arranged benches against the wall for seats. I then rejoiced in the possession of four chairs, recently purchased. We set a long table in the center of the room, and having procured supplies from Ann Arbor expressly for the occasion, we had quite a sumptuous feast.

I recollect the surprise and gratification expressed by Mr. Perrine during supper, that forty miles in the wilderness, they were permitted to enjoy such good company, and such a bountiful supply of good cheer. The evening was pleasantly spent, quite to my satisfaction.

There were several similar parties during the winter, which we thought greatly assisted the flight of time.

At the beginning of that winter Miss Silence D. Blackman, now Mrs. John T. Durand, opened the first school in the county, consisting of eight scholars.

The first death in the county, was that of the oldest son of Wm. R. Thompson, who was killed by the fall of a tree, in the autumn of 1830.

There were a great many Indians in Jackson County during the first few years, small bands belonging to the Ottawa, Chippewa, and Potawatomi tribes. They were never ugly, but sometimes afforded us no little amusement by their inquisitiveness and consequent blunders. I recollect one day, soon after our arrival, I was washing, and a number of Indians came to the door near which I stood. A squaw pointed to my soft soap and asked it if was *cis-po-quet.* I did not know the meaning of the word, but nodded my head at a venture. She immediately put her finger into the dish, and twisting it around, took up as much as possible, supposing it to be honey, which the Indians call *cis-po-quet.* You may be sure the delicious mouthful was speedily ejected, while her contortions of countenance and expressions of disgust called forth peals of laughter even from her habitually grave companions. The poor squaw was very angry, but by signs I told her I did not understand her questions, and taking some of the soap, I rubbed it on my clothes. This seemed to satisfy her, and she joined in the laugh at her blunder.

But my story is getting too long, though the half has not been told. I think all the pioneers who are still living will agree with me that there is a charm to those early memories; a tenderness felt toward those pioneer friends which no later associations have ever called forth.

OLD HOME BUILT IN 1833

The many Michigan county histories published in the 1880s often contain views of the pioneer's first primitive shanties like this 1833 home.

Grand Blanc & Saginaw: 1831
by
Azubah L. Jewett

Another pioneer lady who like "Aunt Emily" "extended innumerable kindnesses to those who, "as young men in the wilderness, were laying foundations for the business which made many of them fortunes and built these cities" was Mrs. Azubah L. Jewett.
Born Azubah Miller in Hartland, Vermont, in 1806, she was a descendant of the original Puritan settlers of New England. She related the story of her immigration to Grand Blanc in 1831 in the following narrative written for the *Michigan Pioneer Collections* at the request of her brother, Judge Albert Miller of Bay City. As she mentions in her story she married Eleazer Jewett that fall and moved to her new home in Saginaw. Her husband figures prominently in the pioneer annals of Saginaw. He served as the county's second probate judge. The Jewetts built a hotel in Saginaw which they continued to operate until 1858. They then moved to a farm near the Saginaw County ghost town of Kochville. She died in Saginaw in 1889 at the age of 84.

I was a school teacher, had kept a large school at Hartland, Vermont, 1830 and 1831. At the finishing of my school, the last of March, found myself in very poor health, a violent cough, and every indication of consumption[138] which was so prevalent in that climate. Each one of my friends recommended the physician I should employ; but I had never known any one to recover from all the medical skill that could be obtained, and was bound to take a different course from those that were almost daily falling victims to the fatal disease. I had only to mention that change of climate might benefit my health. My mother, then a widow over fifty years of age, readily complied with my wish, and Michigan was the place designated as we had friends located there. My mother sold her property and got ready for the long and tedious journey the first of May, 1831. We came over the Green Mountains with horse teams; when we arrived at Whitehall where we had to wait three days for the Northern Canal to be ready for the boats, two days took us to the Erie Canal, then one of the wonders of the world.

Three weeks from the time we started from Vermont we arrived in Buffalo, waited one day for a steamboat; took passage on the *Ohio*; were three days and three nights on Lake Erie; the wind was blowing fearfully all the while, I made up my mind that I had better have stayed in Vermont and taken my chances there than to be cast away on Lake Erie. But few of the five hundred passengers that were on the boat expected to see land. At last we reached Detroit, where we stayed one day, and were met there by my brother who had previously gone to Michigan. Teams were hired to take us to our place of destination. Grand Blanc was where our friends had settled at that time. The roads were passable five miles out from Detroit; after going that distance we put up at Young's Hotel and stayed over Sunday on May 28, 1831. For amusement I went one mile through a dense forest with Mr. Young's family to visit some English people that had made a clearing that far from neighbors or a road. A few rods aside from the path that led to the place a man had been found a few days previous in a sitting posture by the side of a tree, dead. He was a stranger, the tree was marked, a stake driven by the side of it, and a white flag attached to it. Several carriages were driven out from Detroit that day loaded with people, to visit the spot where the dead man had been found.

Monday morning we left Mr. Young's for Grand Blanc; we found the roads almost impassible, the mud was so deep one span of horses could not draw the wagon through; would often take two and sometimes a yoke of oxen besides. The worst part of the road was between Detroit and Pontiac. A few miles from there we went by a trail where there had been no roads made and got along passably well.

We arrived at Stony Run [139] the third day of June. We were very cordially received at the residence of Mr. Ewing and wife who had left Vermont two years before. We remained with them till my brother could build a log house two miles from any other residence. The inhabitants were few and far between at that time. All that had previously located in that vicinity made it a special business to visit every stranger that moved into the place. Even the very few people that lived in Saginaw were interested in every new inhabitant that was located on the trail between that place and Pontiac. They had often had to take lodging in the open air on the ground when going to and from Detroit before the people began to move into the place. Seldom one person would travel alone, but they would go in groups; four or five was all that could leave Saginaw at one time in those days. In the month of August I was visiting a former acquaintance from Vermont that lived ten miles from Flint River - one day at eleven o'clock four men rode up; they were Messrs. Gardner, Ephraim Williams, Col. Stannard, and Mr. Jewett, from Saginaw. They soon made their wishes known; they had camped out two nights, their provisions were exhausted and they had no breakfast; they were on their way to Detroit. On seeing me a stranger in the wilderness, many questions were asked, and also some observations made. There was one of the party that took a little more interest in my welfare than the rest; and on their return from Detroit made it manifest by informing me of his native place and the circumstances that brought him to Saginaw. In the conversation it was revealed that his native place was but a few miles from my own, and he was acquainted with many of my friends; my brothers were under the same tutor that he was while in preparation for school teaching. It was Mr. Eleazer Jewett; his former home was in New Hampshire. He had been in Saginaw five years, most of the time in the employ of the American Fur Company; had a home at Green Point at the head of Saginaw River, had built a block house and lived by himself. But suffice it to say we were not long forming an acquaintance, and subsequently a wedding day was appointed which was October 22, 1831, at which time the wedding took place. Now I will give a brief description of my wedding trip and show the contrast between that time and the present.

There was a wagon road as far as Flint River, and I had the benefit of a ride the first ten miles, and put up at the residence of Mr John Todd to wait for a boat to take us to Saginaw; but not for a steamboat, we were entirely off from that line. But we waited for the men that came from Saginaw to row the boat, to cut down a big pine tree on the bank of the river and make one, that was far superior to any that could be obtained at this place. It took five days to get the boat finished in good style, every one was well satisfied with their work, and all seemed to rejoice that I was going to have so nice and safe a conveyance.

The night before I took passage in the new boat, there was an arrival from Saginaw. It was Mr. Gardner Williams and his wife, on horseback, with a Frenchman leading a pony loaded with a tent, blankets, and cooking utensils. They were conveyed across the river long after dark; they were on their way to Pontiac. That was the third day after they left home. The first day they got as far as Cass River, and were paddled across in a small Indian canoe. The horses had to swim. They made a fire by means of a flint and steel, pitched their tent, had their supper, and took their lodging under the canopy of the heavens. The next day they went as far as Pine Run, and had the same fare as the night previous.

When they arrived at Mr. Todd's they fared somewhat better. Mrs. Williams and I occupied the only spare bed, and the gentlemen had the privilege of spreading their own blankets on the floor; but the Frenchman that escorted Mr. Williams, and the men that were going to row the new boat down the river, had to pitch their tent on the outside; the house was so small there was no room for them.

The next morning when we were about to separate, I was congratulated on account of the superior facilities I was to have on my bridal trip, it being considered preferable to riding on horseback. There had been heavy rains and there was standing water in some places; it was not safe to ride through it, and the guide would have to go a long way around to chop away the fallen limbs so the horses could pass, and after much delay they got on the right trail again. After the description given of the horseback ride, I was quite delighted with my prospects. Every one spoke very cheerfully about it too. On account of the high water the boat would glide smoothly down the river. In due time the boat was ready; I, of course, had the best seat; it was made of blankets nicely folded. Everything was just right, all seemed cheerful and happy. There were three men besides my husband, and I began to think there was considerably novelty in such a trip.

We had not gone far before I heard some talk of driftwood, and soon had a full understanding of it. The boat would often shove on to trees that had fallen into the river, and it would take hours to get it released, and get started again; the men would frequently have to get out into the water up to their waists and lift with their whole strength to remove the boat. This was a common occurrence for three days, and then we came to a place where the river was filled up entirely. We had to unload the boat and get the Indians to draw it a long distance on the land, past the obstruction, and launch it into the stream again.

The Indians had anticipated the arrival, and prepared themselves for the delightful task; they had previously assisted in the same performance, but this time it was the heaviest boat they had ever encountered, therefore the more excitement. The night was very dark when we passed from Flint River to the Shiawassee, and the novelty of my wedding trip began to wear off somewhat after sleeping on the ground four nights, and only a tent for a shelter. But I was frequently cheered, and told that it was only four miles to the mouth of Cass River, then we would soon be in the Saginaw River.

The Flint, Cass, Shiawassee, and the Titibawassee all unite in one stream, that forms the Saginaw River; at this place was my future home, a fine block house situated on the bank of the river at the head of navigation at Green Point. Several of Mr. Jewett's friends came as far as the mouth of the Flint River to meet us, and all concluded it would be better to pass our own home and go two miles farther and stay at a public house kept by Col. Stannard; we were kindly received by all; we received some bridal calls that were novel in the extreme. There were a few half French people here that were partially civilized, and all anxious to see the bride. They would stand and wait for a door to be opened, and if they could get one view, would go away quite satisfied.

In three days I was conveyed to my home, in a canoe, that was the only way of riding; no roads had yet been made in the place. My home looked very pleasant to me after the little excitement I had, riding in the new boat down the river.

I soon became accustomed to the new life I had undertaken; and was bound to cast aside every obstacle that might mar my happiness, and succeeded in everything except the fear of the Indians. I had formerly read so much of their wickedness and murder, in the time of the war, that whenever I saw a group of them with tomahawks in their belts, it would send a pang to my heart that I could not overcome; notwithstanding I was so frequently told of their innocence. In time I got accustomed to their habits, and learned to speak their language, it lessened my fears somewhat, but I never got to admire the race. There were very few people in Saginaw at that time; all lived in block houses;

the timber had been taken from the fort for building dwellings, but a part of it was standing yet. [140] Every one was cheerful and happy, not a murmur was expressed at the privations we were all subjected to, but we all made the best of it.

Pontiac was the nearest post office and no mail carrier; it was only by particular favor that we got our mail brought to us. Sometimes it would be many weeks without an opportunity of sending or receiving our letters. There were no roads here, all the way we could ride, was on the river in a canoe. Some weeks would often pass that I would not see a female friend.

I was necessarily brought in contact with many things that the young ladies of the present day would hardly think they could endure, and it is but expected of them.

Mr. Jewett, was the only surveyor in the place, and business often called him from home for days at a time; I could seldom get any one to stay with me. I was subject to many annoyances from the Indians, who had been praised to me so frequently for their innocence. They would come and steal corn from the crib, and rob the garden, and hen roost; but they would do it only when they knew I was alone.

At a late hour one night when I was alone, there was a call from the opposite side of the river. Some man wanted to come across. I informed him that there was no one to set him over. He said then he would lie down and die; he had been riding all day and could go no farther. I had never paddled a canoe across the river yet; the night was very dark, but I concluded to make the attempt to set him over. Put a candle at my window for a guide to come back, took a canoe, and succeeded in reaching the opposite shore, by often calling to know where to land. Found Mr. Phineas Braley there; he was hardly able to get into the canoe. He had been taken with ague and fever on the way; he got in and led his horse by the side of the little boat, and I paddled them across at the hour of midnight. A good many strangers came from the east in 1831 to purchase land. I would often have the benefit of entertaining them.

Among our guests were Doctor Little and Mr. Hermon Ladd, from Avon, state of New York. They admired the country very much, bought a large quantity of land, and designed settling all their children in Saginaw.

They praised me for my bravery and the sumptuous fare I had given them, and said many encouraging things about the future prospects of the country; among the rest they said to me: "You many live to see a steamboat come up this river; it is not impossible." They never expected to themselves, but were in hopes their children would. It did not prove a very extravagant idea when they imagined that I would live to see a steamboat come up the river.

I have seen very many; and I have seen all the improvements, from a wilderness to the present. I was one of twenty-six inhabitants that lived in Saginaw, no other person here now that has been in the place as many years as myself; am now in my seventy-eighth year, living with my only daughter, the first white child born in Saginaw. She is the wife of Doctor N.D. Lee. My Husband has been dead seven years.

A typical settler's homestead in the Michigan woods.

Kalamazoo County &
Allegan County: 1833-1838
by
Arvilla Smith

Arvilla Smith suffered almost unbelievable
hardships as the wife of a missionary to the Ottawa.
Born in St. Albans, Vermont, in 1808, she married
George Nelson Smith when she was 22. The
following excerpt from the narrative she wrote for the
Grand Traverse Herald in 1892 covers her life
beginning in 1833 and for the following five years.
She subsequently established with the Rev. Smith
the Old Wing Mission to the Ottawa in Allegan
County's Fillmore Township. With the arrival of the
Rev. Albertus Van Raalte's colony of Hollanders in
1847, who made life intolerable for the local Ottawa,
the Smith's relocated their mission to Waukazooville,
now part of Northport, in the Leelanau Peninsula in
1849. At the Old Wing Mission Arvilla left the graves
of five of her children.

At her new home in the wilderness on the
shore of Grand Traverse Bay she again found herself
a pioneer and additional hardships and suffering
followed. The Rev. Smith died in 1881, leaving her
destitute. Nevertheless, this strong woman survived
another 14 years "retaining her facilities in a
remarkable degree up to the time of her last illness."
She died at her daughters' home in Northport at the
age of 87.

Mr. Smith[141] had an earnest call to join a colony of
Congregationalists, coming to settle on Gull Prairie, Michigan
(now Richland), with the expectations of preaching to them after
their settlement was perfected, but they never came.

The idea once taking effect, he purposed coming,
although opposing forces were met on every side, but his will
was law.

We left St. Albans, Vermont, in May, 1833, crossing Lake

Champlain by a steamer, took the Northern and Western canal to Buffalo, crossing Lake Erie to Detroit and made the trip in two weeks, Mr. Smith having but a sixpence in his pocket. Fortunately, we met an old neighbor of mine and he took us to the only hotel, a log cabin kept by a Frenchman. He found a teamster to take us through to Gull Prairie, he becoming security for the expenses amounting to $20.00. This was a journey, not to be forgotten. After a week's torture in a lumber wagon, prying wheels out of mud holes, eating poor fare on boxes, exposed to rain, sleeping on shanty floors, we at last reached our destination, and what was our consternation to find Gull Prairie a typical hospital, groans resounding in every quarter, from bilious fever,[142] typhoid fever and ague, [143] and not a house or even a room could be obtained. We found a home with a Presbyterian minister. He heard of our arrival, and rushed to secure our services, for his wife and children were down with the fever and ague and he was putting up a barn, and could get no help. We remained with them through the summer and in the fall rented a room that had been used as a an office. It was convenient and roomy with a large brick fire place, and added to these comforts, a Christian family were our nearest neighbors and they were to me father, mother brother, and sister.

Mr. Smith was appointed agent to distribute bibles in Kalamazoo County at $14.00 a month. We escaped the ravages of those terrible diseases that winter, but when spring came they visited us without mercy. My sister Jane, who came with us from Vermont and was teaching school a few miles from us, was brought home on a bed, being stricken with bilious fever, and I had been confined some days with fever. In the midst of this my second son was born and died in a few hours.

The next year was a perilous one. Mr. Smith preached where he could get hearers, but the people were too poor to render him any help and I was compelled to support myself and little son by taking all kinds of sewing, often sewing all night and the next day having an attack of ague. Mr Smith received a call to preach in Plainfield [144] and Otsego alternately, with the prospects of getting support from the Home Missionary Society, then in its infancy. We removed to Plainfield in the month of August of 1835, but not a shelter could we find. A frame of a house had been erected and we might occupy it if Mr. smith would enclose it. He boarded it up with green lumber just from the mill, but not a door, window, chimney or stove could be found. Mornings my bedding would be so wet that I would have to hang it out to dry. I had to bring water a quarter of a mile with my baby in my arms. Mr. Smith, at this time, was distributing bibles throughout Allegan County, and when I could get anything to cook, I had to make a fire out doors. We occupied this house from August till October and the owner then urged us to leave. A subscription was circulated and enough money raised to buy us an acre of ground, lumber was given, and a general turnout to raise a small frame house. The frame was raised but it was not enclosed till late in November as the green lumber had to be drawn fifteen miles over rough roads.

Now another trial of life and death for my little feeble, sickly children. We must season another dwelling, with no door, window, or chimney, no stove, only a fire made against the green lumber wall where a place had been left floorless. Both children were soon taken with pneumonia and I watched three weeks, night and day, with no expectation or hope that either would live. My little Mary, now Mrs. M.J. Wolfe, was reduced to a mere skeleton, and as she would lie in her cradle, I would have to put my ear to her mouth to know if she still breathed. We lived in that damp, desolate house until the lst of December and then, failing to find brick, Mr. Smith put up a stick chimney. A clay hearth was beaten down, one door and window put in, but starvation drove me into anguish and tears. When one meal was eaten nothing remained for the next.

The Home Missionary Society was limited in its means, the farmers were poor and helpless, and the location of our house, at two cross roads greatly travelled, brought us many hungry wayfarers to feed and shelter. All the merchants and land seekers from abroad laid siege to our hospitality. Many amusing incidents occurred to brighten our gloomy life, yet they were attended with the delicate sensitiveness peculiar to womankind. I had no means of hanging a kettle over the fire and only stones for andirons. My cooking utensils consisted of a tea kettle, a three quart kettle and a frying pan. How often I was thrown into an abyss of consternation by six or seven calling for dinner or for quarters for the night. One little incident will serve as a sample of many that I could relate.

We had eaten the last of everything but potatoes and flour when two gentlemen came to stay all night on their way to New York. They had walked from Allegan and were hungry and tired. One was Judge Littlejohn[145] and the other a brother minister. My attic was my closet for prayer. I poured out my soul to God for help, put on my potatoes and the tea kettle and a knock came at the door. I opened it and there stood a neighbor with a large piece of fresh beef. He said, "I was tired but somehow I felt I must come."

It was a direful year for us. Mr. Smith had been wholly absorbed in having organized a Congregational association. He had been absent some days when about ten o'clock one forenoon, he came with six gentlemen, four ministers and two delegates. They were to have dinner and all go on to Marshall to organize. What was I to do! A little flour, potatoes and a small piece of butter, my kettle not large enough to boil my potatoes! I washed and dried them and spread them on the clean hot hearth, covered them with hot embers. Water was all I had to make my cakes with, so I pounded and kneaded the dough until it cracked, and rolled it into thin pieces and served it as I did the potatoes. I sent my little boy George to a neighbor's for milk, and made a milk gravey. This dinner was eaten with a merry good will, jokes and witty humor filled the air as is always the case when a company of ministers meet together. When they declared it the best dinner they had eaten I felt more than repaid.

The next year matters brightened. Our little home was to us a paradise. The little log church was getting too small for the increasing congregation and a new building was the talk. Our prayer meetings were well attended and we had an interesting society of well educated and intelligent people.

The Home Missionary Society sent $100.00 for the year and pledged the same amount for the coming year. Mr. Smith had been holding council with the Allegan County Indians as Agemaoninna,146 the chief of the Ottawas, had been making a strong appeal for a missionary and teacher. His appeals were reaching the hearts of men from all parts of Michigan. A union called the Western Michigan Society for the Benefit of the Indians pledged to erect a building and support a teacher and missionary, and a bitter cup I had to drink when the sad news reached me of his appointment! My children! What was their future? Tears and pleadings were nothing. That was his life work and in 1837 we left our little home and moved to Allegan. I drank the bitter cup, but the dregs remained. Thus closed our labors with the Home Missionary Society...

We arrived at Allegan August of 1837; this was to be a stepping stone to the colonization of the Indians and a spot was

Allegan as it appeared in 1840.

selected and surveyed. Mr. Smith gathered all the scattered Indian children together and taught them through the winter, preaching occasionally for the Presbyterian minister in Allegan who was in feeble health.

My fears began to be realized. The new society could not raise funds, every man finding empty pockets. There was no alternative. I opened our home to boarders, with a third babe in arms. Aside from this, my little boy was again dangerously ill with pneumonia. Our house was very cold, the winter unusually severe and we were all thinly clad. Flour was fifteen dollars a barrel and this had to be chopped from the barrel then rolled; it being put up when too hot and packed. Meat was scarce and expensive. We had a good cow, but she wandered off in the woods and was never found.

Mr. Smith was seldom at home when spring came. He was surveying the locality at North Black River (now Holland) from there to Ionia to purchase for the Indians; later, a trip up north shore as far as the Straits of Mackinac, taking in Cross Village, L'Arbre Croche and Little Traverse. This was at the request and in company with the chief, who wanted to see all his people and get them to colonize. They were all Roman Catholics at the north. The chief was firmly determined to get his young people to join him in his change of religion, and away from the priests "whose works were only evil." They were to be absent north but three weeks, and the time lengthened into six before the party returned. I was again alone without food. In the midst of my trouble, I received an invitation to visit cousins[147] living at the mouth of the Kalamazoo some fifty miles down the river. I boarded the first canoe, a log dugout, propelled by an Indian and his wife. I had my three children with me and the day was sickening with its heat. We reached our destination by night, the fifty miles being easily covered by the monotonous paddling of these two silent workers. I remained three weeks, but was compelled to return with my sister who had closed her school there and expected to open a school in Allegan. We found two of the laziest specimens of natives who were going to sell cranberries at Allegan. We started in a birch bark canoe heavily loaded with twenty bushels of cranberries, two lazy Indians, my sister, and my three children. After a long tedious day we reached the half-way house late at night, and presented ourselves tired and cramped, the three children bitten and swollen from mosquitoes. The atmosphere the entire distance was fairly alive with mosquitoes. We took an early start the next morning, and what was our surprise to find on entering the canoe, that our entire lunch, left there over night, had found its way into the recesses of the cadaverous mouthed Augustus and Prickett.[148] We spent the entire day suffering all the former tortures and added one inflicted upon us.

When within six miles of Allegan the canoe was abandoned, and a three mile land cut walked. My sister carried my little girl, and George, hungry and weak, trudged the distance bravely. Our home was reached, but only emptiness greeted us. A kind neighbor, seeing our arrival, brought bread and fish. We feasted once more.

In September of 1838, Mr. Smith decided suddenly to move on to the Black River. At two o'clock one afternoon, he came in and said he had launched his boat, a log canoe, and wished to load up for the Black River.

The suddenness was overwhelming, but we started, friends lining the shore entreating us to remain.

The river was treacherous with snags, and several times we just escaped upsetting. We had covered twelve miles by nine o'clock, and our night was spent with Mr. West, a kind Christian family. Mr. Smith complained of feeling badly the next morning, but insisted on starting. A few miles of paddling brought on a chill and he was unable to work. My little boy steered and I paddled fifteen miles, Mr. Smith lying ill in the boat.

The journey finally ended. Our new home was on the Black River, three miles from its mouth, at what was known as Superior.[149] This was only to be a temporary one, however, while Mr. Smith was up the lake clearing a spot to locate his people.

My days of suffering began with this. I remained in Superior two months, but this was only a respite before my plunge into the woods as an Indian missionary's wife. [150]

Richland & Grand Rapids: 1833
by
Marion Louise Hinsdill Withey

It took a special kind of person to become a pioneer. Those content with their situation stayed back East. But those willing to risk all for the chance of bettering their lot traveled west. If their first attempt at selected a homestead proved unsatisfactory it was not uncommon for pioneers to sell out and try again in another part of Michigan or further west. Such was the case with Myron Hinsdill. He first brought his wife and four little daughters from Vermont to Richland in 1833. But the following year he came under the spell of the Grand River country and moved once again to the little settlement couched at the Grand Rapids. His daughter, Marion, who was six-years-old in 1833, tells of the family's experiences in the following article.

Marion Louise Hinsdill married Solomon L. Withey in 1845. Her husband served as a district judge for western Michigan in the 1860s. Mrs. Withey was very active in the foundation of religious, philanthropic and educational institution in Grand Rapids including the Park Congregational Church, the public library and the Ladies' Literary Club. She wrote her recollections to be read at the Pioneer Society meeting held in Grand Rapids in January, 1913, but she died the previous November. Prior to her death she claimed the distinction of being the oldest continuous resident of the city.

In the spring of 1833, my father, Myron Hinsdill, came form Hinesburg, Vermont, to Richland, then called Gull Prairie. This journey was made through the Erie Canal, by boat from Buffalo to Detroit, from there on by teams, one of which father brought with him. Most of the towns on the way were mere stopping places. The vision of Ann Arbor, Michigan, as it was then, still lingers in my memory. Mother used to tell the story of our stop there. The landlord came out to assist us. As he took down four little girls one after the other, he turned to father and in some emphatic words inquired what he had come with them to this country for.

We were warmly welcomed to our new home by the family of Elder Knappen[151] whom my parents had known in Vermont. They had come to Michigan but a short time before us and were sufficiently settled so that we could remain with them until some place could be provided for us. Father at once set about building a log barn for his horses. When it was up and roofed mother proposed that we should move into it ourselves and relieve the Knappens. Accordingly a floor was laid, a stick chimney built, and we took possession with two pieces of furniture brought with us, a small, light stand with leaves and a sideboard and bureau together. I still have this and it is a useful article of furniture. I don't remember where we got our bedsteads but father went down to the southern part of the state and obtained six wooden chairs and a small rocking chair, which I still cherish among my household goods.

In this primitive way my parents, who had left a fine old homestead in the east, commenced life in Michigan. A young woman who came with us to assist mother, very soon accepted an offer of marriage from a man who was probably in want of a housekeeper and mother, a frail, delicate woman, was left to struggle with small children, housework, fever and ague.

How that house did leak every time it rained. We had to cover the beds with tin pans and dishes to catch the water. As warm weather came on we did most of our work out of doors. One incident I well remember. Mother had prepared the bread ready to bake in a tin oven before the fire out of doors, and had gone to bed with an attack of the ague, leaving my older sister and myself to attend the baking. Child like we were interested in our play, and so forgot the fire entirely. Imagine our consternation when we saw two great hogs walk off with poor mother's bread.

The contest with fever and ague was fearful, and ague usually had the best of it. At one time when our distress was the greatest a cousin of father's, Stephen Hinsdill, came to us and remained some time to assist in taking care of us. We were all sick at once. Dr. Deming was our physician. [152]

The music of the wolves at night was quite common when I was a girl. There were other exciting times also. One time during this first summer in Michigan we had a narrow escape. A violent whirlwind passed over that region and blew a large tree, which stood in front, down on the house, crushing in the front part. Mother saw it coming and gathered us into the back part, near the one window, from which we were taken out, unhurt but badly frightened.

A Mr. and Mrs. Baker riding through the woods during the same storm were killed by a falling tree. A baby sister of mine who died that november was buried by their side. I have been told that these graves have an enclosure near the center of the present cemetery at Richland. We were living at that time in a house owned by Deacon Gray, [153] near the center of the prairie. Of this winter I remember little except our going to meeting on an ox sled. I don't know why we did this as my father had horses.

The next spring my uncle, Mitchel Hinsdill, came with his family to Richland. My father and this brother located on adjoining farms just south of the prairie. My father had five acres cleared and wheat sown when my uncle arrived. They both commenced to build on their farms and located their homes not far apart. Uncle's house was finished first, or as nearly finished as houses were in those days. Here one of my brothers, Chester B. Hinsdill, was born. Before cold weather our own house was ready and we moved into it, although it was not plastered. We used blankets for inside doors for a time and a carpenter's bench was a part of the furniture. My mother's mother, a woman over seventy, came and spent the winter with us. It was a comfort to mother but poor grandmother was greatly tried at the hardships mother had to endure. She was mostly troubled that the little girls must be brought up in such a wild place.

Our evenings were enlivened by visits from our neighbors who often came several miles for that purpose. Hickory nuts, of which the woods yielded an abundance, were our usual refreshments. My father often read aloud for our entertainment. I have a vivid remembrance of his reading Cooper's "Leather Stocking Tales." The evening he read the scene of the shooting of the panther over Charlotte's head, Mr. Foster Gilkie was with us. He seems to be almost before me, as I recall him with his emphatic "hum! hum!"

During that winter father once went to a point south of our home where some large sycamores grew. Mother and some of us children went along, I presume for a visit. We came home in the bright moonlight, riding inside the tree as it lay length wise on

189

the sled. These trees were used for smoke houses, corn cribs, etc. Several large specimens were standing not far from Kalamazoo a few years ago.

During the winter father also made a trip on horseback to the Grand River country as it was then styled. Here the spring before, his cousin Hiram Hinsdill, of Bennington, Vermont, had gone with his family. Father must have been captivated by the scenery. The fine, rapid river and high hills seemed to him like his old home in New England. He fancied it would be more healthy, and was quite ready for a change. Accordingly he let his farm, soon after selling it, and the first of May or the first of June, removed to Grand Rapids.

We made this journey through the woods, following blazed trees, as there was no sign of a road. We were several days on the way. One evening as we were stopping for the night in a log house without a floor or roof, the first stage, George Coggshells' family passed us, bound for the same haven. Temporarily we stayed with Hiram Hinsdill's family. Father purchased of him the frame of the old National Hotel, and proceeded to finish it.[154] While this was being done, a part of the summer we lived in a new barn near by and as soon as a few rooms were done we moved in. This summer of 1836, on pleasant Sundays we used to cross the river to attend services at Mr. Slater's Mission chapel where he preached in the afternoon in English.[155] Occasionally he came over to the East Side and preached in a house built by a Mr. Lincoln. [156]

This summer Miss. Page, [157] afterward the wife of Judge Bacon, of Monroe, at the importunity of several families who had small children, opened a school in a new barn. This building, located a little to the rear of what is now the Morton House,[158] was built of boards set up endwise while the boards of the floor were laid down without matching. The school committee was not vexed with the matter of ventilation. It was here that I had my first struggles with *Webster's Spelling Book.*

One of the memorable events of that year was the Indian payment in October on the west side of the Grand River. The Indians were gathered there some two or three weeks waiting for the specie to come. It was great amusement for the white people to go and visit the camp and my father took us children.

Everything about the place seemed curious to us, including the savages themselves. Their campfires and wigwams; the men decked out with paint on their faces, feathers

Grand Rapids' Prospect Hill in 1833.

in their headgear, and with strings of tin cut in round pieces or with beads around their necks; the squaws, many of them with fine broadcloth blankets, handsomely embroidered leggings to match, and pretty moccasins; all this quite fascinated us. These varicolored figures, together with the lovely autumn landscape, made a picture well calculated to live in the memory.

This annual payment was kept up for twenty years and from fifteen hundred to two thousand Indians assembled in that place every year. Many of them we came to know personally and we looked forward to their coming. Some of the squaws were skilled with the needle and their petticoats were often embroidered with narrow ribbon and beads a quarter of a yard deep. Their bead and porcupine quill work was often a marvel of ingenuity and most neatly done. It is a great pity that more of the really fine specimens of their work have not been preserved.

Indians were a familiar sight but I do not remember having any serious fear of them or any apprehension of trouble with them. A seat by the fire when they were chick-es-sol (cold), or a generous supper when they were buck-a-tab (hungry), generally insured us the most friendly relation with them.

The summer of 1836 seems a long one to my recollection. The arrival of so many strangers; the rapid changes; the hurry of people to get some place to live before cold weather; the peculiar ways in which people did live; the feverish excitement of speculation; so many events crowded into the space of a few months, make those months seem now, like so many years.

To recall the state of things, I extract from a letter dated April 2, 1836, from my father to a brother-in-law:

"I have applied for fine lots of pine land up Grand River but there is such a press business at the land office, one cannot know under six or eight days whether he can get it or not, and if two men asked for the same land, the same day, they must agree which shall have it, as it is set up at auction. There have been four or five hundred people at Bronson[159] for a week past, all waiting to get land; if I get the pine land it will cost about $2.25 per acre, and a great bargain at that. If land buyers increase as we have reason to expect, when navigation opens there will not be a good lot in the territory at Congress prices, and then I see no reason why land will not be worth $10.00 per acre."

That this came to pass we now know. The resort of the early pioneers to every device to supply food and the other commonest necessities of life, was only equaled by their ingenuity for entertainment. During the winter months debating societies, singing schools and masquerade parties were in order. Conspicuous among these were the meetings of the Grand Rapids Lyceum. This society was organized in a room over the old yellow warehouse,[160] used as an office by Dr. Charles Shepard. Its moving spirits were C.H. Taylor, Noble H. Finney, William A. Richmond, W.G. Henry, George Martin, Simeon Johnson and others who came a little later.

Its public meetings were held in the dining room of the old National, my father's house, which was the place for all kinds of assemblages. Here was brought out the latent intellectual force and forensic ability of that little coterie of young men, that years after was conspicuous on the platform, the stump and at the bar. The women of that time were no whit behind the men and all womanly graces, intelligence, refinement of manners and accomplishments of head and heart were there. A long search might be made in vain to find finer examples of noble womanhood than were present at every social gathering in that old hotel dining room.

The Lyceum was maintained for many years and thus was started a valuable library. Some of the books are still doing service in our present public library.

My brother, Henry M. Hinsdill, was born in March, 1837. He was the second white child born here, Napoleon Godfrey who preceded him by a few weeks having claim to the first place. In August of that year an uncle, Truman Kellogg, moved his family here. They made the journey around the lakes and up the river. He had previously purchased a farm east of the town on Lake Avenue, his house standing where the Paddock House now is. Having a decided taste for horticulture, he took great care to get and set out choice orchards of peach, plum and apple trees. He also planted some fine varieties of grapes and all the small fruits. He gave quite a large plot of ground to the morus multi colus shrub, and embarked in the manufacture of silk. For several years he raised the cocoons and wound the silk. The family still possess many specimens of this, the earliest of Grand Rapids manufacturing products. At Belding, Michigan, there is now one of the finest silk factories in the country.

This uncle of mine, although one of the quietest of men, was an avowed abolitionist, subscribing to the abolition newspapers and quietly advocating their opinions. In his correspondence he used as a letterhead the figure of a negro kneeling and lifting manacled hands to heaven in supplication. The engraving was done by a colored man. Some of the letters from a brother in the South, containing pleas to discontinue the use of this paper for letters sent to that place as they were positively dangerous, are curious evidences of the public sentiment of that time.

To show that the higher interests of religion and eduction were not neglected I quote from a letter of father's dated February 25, 1837: "We have two schools in our house, one instructed by my sister (Aunt Mary Walker) who came out here last fall; the other by Mr. Smith, who was educated in your village. We have had from eight to ten boarders all winter, on the temperance plan in full, and have most of the good custom. Strangers from almost all parts of the Union visit our place and are much pleased. property has advanced one third or more since you were here; so much, I think people are crazy. Society has improved very much. A Presbyterian church was formed last October with twenty-two members and ten added since, and we have as talented society of young men as can be found in your state. Provision is very high, flour $15.00 a barrel; oats, $1.00; potatoes, $1.25; pork, $14.00 per hundred; butter 37 1/2 cents; and other things in proportion, board $4.50 per week; cash plenty; most of it paid out for land. I have had more silver and gold in my house this winter than a pair of horses could draw."

This is a good picture of the time. The church spoken of was soon changed to the Congregational polity, that element largely predominating. It is now the First Congregational Church of Grand Rapids. I remember distinctly the scene of the organization: the little company as they stood up to assent to the articles of faith, and afterwards to celebrate the Lord's Supper, with the bread on a common plate, a pitcher and tumblers for tankard and cups. So true were these early settlers to their convictions of faith and training, that the same roof frequently sheltered the family, the church, the school, and Sunday school. They were, however, very liberal to others; any preacher who could lead a Christian service was warmly welcomed.

The night before New Year's of 1838, we were treated to a new diversion. A company of French and Indian half breeds, masked and dressed in most grotesque and fantastic costumes, with horns and every hideous instrument of noise, rushed through the houses of the settlers, howling and dancing.

Everything the houses afforded in the way of refreshments was brought forth. The noisy hideous visitors threw it on the floor and stamped it down, to the ruin of house and furniture and to the great alarm of housekeepers. So disgusting was the performance and so general the disapprobation that it was never repeated. What it meant and where it originated, no one has ever seemed to know.

In February of 1838, great alarm was felt at the damming up of the ice below the town. One evening just in the midst of a spirited debate at the Lyceum, there came the cry that the water was rising. Everyone started to the rescue. An anxious night was followed by an exciting day. At mid-day, the ice began to move in a vast body while the water rushed back on the little settlement, to the great danger of several families who lived on the bank of the river. The Almy and Page families were taken from the upper windows of their houses in boats. Their houses were situated a little north of where Sweet's Hotel[161] now is. I remember Mrs. Almy's terror as she was brought to our house.

The spring of 1838 was marked by an event of interest to my own family. This was the marriage of my Aunt Mary Hinsdill to Mr. C.I. Walker. During the summer my father's mother paid us a visit. Father spent most of his time that summer looking and surveying land, and early in November he was taken down with a fever. He died on the 17th, at the age of thirty-nine, a victim to the exposures and hardships of a new country. His remains were interred in the Fulton Street Cemetery, then just purchased but not platted.

In recalling this bit of family history connected with the early settlement of our state, and bringing to mind the names of many contemporary with my parents, I am reminded of the precious material of which our foundations were built. If truth, integrity, intelligence, and heroism are traits of nobility, truly the pioneers of our fair peninsulas were a right royal race.

Allegan County: ca. 1835
by
Mrs. J.V.Rogers

The following selection has been included because it documents an interesting incident in pioneer life in Allegan County and because it represents another genre of narrative writing. Mrs. J.V. Rogers, a daughter of the pioneers who figure in the story, read the piece at a reunion of Allegan County pioneers held at Otsego on August 20, 1879.

This sketch dates back to the time when Michigan was almost an entire wilderness. It was when the howl of the wolf, the growl of the bear, and the scream of the lynx made night in those dim dark woods most terrible. The peril, the suffering, the privations, the hardships endured by the earlier settlers of Michigan are overlooked, and seldom brought into account by those of the present generation. As we pass through, a well-tilled farming country, and behold the barns filled, the fields of grain, the orchards bending with their burden of ripe fruit, we reflect not that the hand that planted those trees is palsied, and that strangers pluck and eat the fruit; that he who hewed that farm from out the desert wilderness, even as the sculptor artist hews the marble, piece by piece, so tree by tree, acre by acre, he wrought out this beauty, and has left to posterity the life work of his hands; for most of the first pioneers of Michigan have passed away, gone over to the other country.

In the privations and perils of pioneer life, woman plays no small part. It is true the sinews of her arm have not strength sufficient to fall the trees, or hold the plow as it first breaks the rooted, sodded soil, but in very many ways her active mind and ready sympathy find employment, and the woman who willingly consents to such a life is not one to fail in the hour of danger. Weighed down by the gloom of measureless and unknown forest, haunted by the fear of wild beasts, it must have been a loneliness of life hard indeed to be borne, and to one of a sensitive nature, used to the refinements of good society, it must have been almost revolting; and yet hundreds of that very class did come willingly, banishing themselves from society, stifling the pleadings of their own hearts, holding their very natures in subjection for the good of those that were to come.

Ere Michigan was admitted into the Union a family came from the State of New York and settled in one of the heaviest timbered sections of the territory. The man was strong and large, in the prime of life, one who could wield the ax as an experienced swordsman does his sword, with a masterly hand. The wife and mother was a small, delicate woman, but possessing a strong will and a great deal of energy, two very essential qualities to the woman who is to make her home in a new country, and it was to work out from that wilderness a home, that these people had left friends and society and come far away into the forest alone. Several other families with the same purpose in view had just settled in that locality, but their homes were from two to three and even five miles apart. In the desire for society they had met, exchanged words of welcome, and become friends and neighbors. Spring had come; the warm sunshine had brought the bright green foliage to the trees; from the maple they had made sugar enough for the season's supply and now the long warm days warned the woodsman that the time was nigh when the seed must be in the ground if he would raise corn and potatoes for the next winter's supply, and without which they must surely suffer. Every hand had been busy, and they had delayed sending the only team in the place for supplies until most of them were nearly out of food. Twenty-five miles was the nearest station where supplies could be obtained, and twenty-five miles was a long journey without a road and no guide but the marks on the trees. Three days had passed, and three more must elapse before the wagon would return. Fortunately a neighbor called, and learning their circumstances, told them he thought he had flour enough for both families, at least he would divide it with them, and the husband started between three and four o'clock in the afternoon to get it. As he left the house the wife warningly remarked: "Don't talk too long, for the road is but a foot path seldom traveled, and the marks on the trees will not serve you in the dark;" but he forgot the warning. It was very pleasant to tell their plans and talk over their work, and besides, it did not seem so near night in the little opening where the house stood, but when he passed into woods the marks on the trees were no longer visible. He took the direction that he thought was toward home, but after having traveled three times the distance there, he knew he was lost. The wife at home had done up the chores for the night, the cow had been securely fastened in the stable to protect her from the wild beasts, the night wood was piled in the corner, a bright fire kindled on the hearth, and the wife and her three little boys were sitting in its warm glow waiting for the father to come. The moments seemed hours to that anxious woman. The two smallest children had fallen asleep, with no supper but a cup of warm milk, but the eldest, a bright boy of seven, waited with her. The clock struck ten; the sound startled every nerve like electricity. She stirred the fire, threw on a fresh stick, and then went to the door to listen. Away to the southwest in the windfall she hear a lone wolf calling to its companions; and then far away, it seemed almost miles in distance to her excited ear, she heard a human voice, and she knew it was the voice of her husband calling for help. She tried to answer, but her voice for the moment failed her, and she turned to her little ones with pale cheeks and trembling lips, saying, "father is lost in the woods; the wolves are banding themselves together, and I am powerless to help him," At that moment her eyes fell on the bundle of torch wood that hung by the fireplace. Quickly she pulled out a handful, lighted it, and ascended to the loft, chiding herself that she had not thought of it before. She thrust her head and arms out of the little square window that served to light the low chamber, and with torch brightly burning, called many times, but no answer. Her voice would sound far away, and then echo bring it back again as though it meant to mock her. What must be done? She called to the little one, "bring up the whole bundle of torch wood; my voice fails to reach him; there is no hope now but in the light." Stick after stick was added to the flames until her hands could hold no more. They hissed and crackled and then ascended high into the air. But what if his face should be turned from the light and he be blindly going into the miry swamp, the swamp that she knew was the grand crossing way for wild beasts going from the windfall to the creek. She must call again, if but the faintest sound of her voice, he would turn his head in that direction and see the light, and with all the strength she had she did call. There was a faint sound came back, but was it his voice or the echo of her own? Once more; this time it seemed nearer, but she might be deceived. She added more fuel to the torch, and called once more. This time the answer came full and clear. He had seen the light. She tried to answer back, but emotions prevented, and tears rained down those tender cheeks the flames were scorching, for the torch wood contained heat as well as light. But she held those blazing fagots firmly, the small white hands were burned to blisters, the soft brown hair on her brow and temples was scorched and crisp; but she faltered not until she saw him emerge from the woods into the little clearing, and she knew he was saved. At the same moment she heard, not the howl of one lone wolf calling, but of the whole pack in concert. They were already on his track, but the light held by that noble woman cheated those wild beasts of their prey, brought the father back to his children, the husband to his wife, and the lost tired man to home and rest.

An Allegan County pioneer shanty and ox team from the 1830s.

Jackson County: 1835
by
Lory Wilbur

Lory Wilbur recorded her recollections of life in Jackson Township in the form of a letter to the Michigan Pioneer Society in 1880. She did not wax eloquent but told her story in a simple straightforward manner. Despite the final poignant statement about her failing health she would survive another ten years before her death in Rives at the age of 98.

We started from Byron, Genesee County, New York, the first Monday in November, 1835. We came to Detroit, stayed there over night. Mr. True[162] bought a yoke of oxen, hitched them on his wagon; he brought a new wagon with us; he loaded some things and loaded in the children, six in number, and started. We were five days coming from Detroit. We moved in with Mr. Town;[163] they had four children, we six, only one room and a bedroom; we stayed there six weeks. Mr. True built a log house and we moved into it. The next he had to go to Dexter to buy flour. He took his oxen, went to Detroit, after our goods; he was gone ten days. In March he went back to Byron to get money to buy a breaking up team; he got back in May with three yoke of oxen and three cows; he had to buy a breaking up plow; he got ready to break the ground; it was late; he broke a piece of ground, planted it to potatoes the 15th of June, then he went to breaking for wheat.

He raised over a hundred bushel of potatoes on what he broke in one day. The price of potatoes that fall was $1.00 a bushel. You see that would buy eighty acres of land at government price.

The Indians were very plenty. While Mr. True was gone after his cattle they used to come quite often. They came one day to borrow an ax; I dare not refuse them; they wanted to cut a bee tree; they brought the ax back; brought a piece of honey between a couple of chips; they always appeared very friendly. We had a pair of twin boys born the next November after we came here. The Indians would come in very often. One day they wanted to see them; I dare not refuse them. They came one day when I was gone to Mr. Prescott's[164] there was a ham bone hanging side of the house; they wanted the children to give it to them; they told them they must ask me; they came to Mr. Prescott's; I could not understand a word; they would slap themselves; I did not know what they wanted. Mrs. Prescott asked me if I had a ham hanging up. I told her I had a ham and a ham that was almost used up hanging at the side of the house; they told her they wanted the ham that was almost used up. I told her they might have it; they came and told the children I said they might have it; they gave it to them. Now if they had been dishonest they would have got the whole one. Mr. True bought a two-year old heifer and butchered her, hung the liver close to the outside of the back door; the wolves came and carried it off. We had seven pigs in a board pen between the house and road. The wolves came about ten minutes after the light was blown out. We heard a pig squeal and he jumped out bed and went to the pen. One pig was gone; all they could find of the pig was a piece of liver about as large as a peach stone; they could not see or hear anything of the wolves but their tracks. They tracked them up the road; they found several tracks. After that Mr. True shut his pigs in a box nights. I was very homesick when we first came here. After we began to raise something to live on I became contented. We always had plenty to eat. We were scant for clothes in a new country. Mr. True died September 13, 1862.

I knew a good many that saw hard times when they first came here. Mrs. Prescott said she had only a pound and a half of sugar the first year she lived in Michigan I took my little boy, went into the woods and made sugar myself while Mr. True was gone after his cattle. I am over eighty years old and my hand trembles. I was at the pioneer meeting last year and enjoyed it very much; my memory is good; I am sensible I am failing, and the probability is I never shall write much more. My name is Wilbur now; I married after Mr. True died. Mr. Wilbur is my present husband.

Eaton County: 1836
by
Margaret Lafever

It was not Indian attacks, wild animals or falling trees which proved the biggest danger to Michigan pioneers. It was the bite of the anopheles mosquito which transmitted malaria or "ague" as it was then called. Few pioneers escaped a bout with the intermittent fever, chills and shakes characterized by the disease. They developed numerous theories to explain the prevalence of the ague, ranging from rotting vegetation produced when settlers cut trees, that the disease was buried in the soil and released through plowing or that it came from stagnant swamp water from which emanated a "miasma," unhealthy to breathe. No one suspected that it actually resulted from the swarms of mosquitoes breeding in that swamp water.

While the ague made pioneer life miserable it rarely proved fatal by itself. Yet, many, weakened by its debilitating effects, succumbed to more virulent diseases. Worse yet were the remedies routinely practiced by the horseback doctors who treated their patients according to whatever medical school of thought they adhered. Some bled their patients copiously, others applied irritating poultices, while many practioners doled out massive doses of calomel, a poisonous mercury compound. As the following sad narrative by Margaret Lafever concerning her family's experiences among the Irish pioneers of Eaton County demonstrates these early medical practitioners were often more deadly than the disease.

Mr. McQueen[165] came to my father in the town of Murray, Orleans County, N.Y. and in glowing terms gave a description of Michigan. This was in 1836. My father got the western fever and sold his nice farm, for the man said there was plenty of good land near his place that could be had of the government, for the asking. He and his family had been neighbors of ours in "York State" and my mother gave her consent to come. So after I had been duly christened and could stand the sunlight a little, my mother and father took their six children, and started for Michigan. We had two covered wagons, well stocked with provisions, bedding, clothing and cooking utensils also mother's little linen spinning wheel, which she said had once belonged to her mother, and which she would not trust to come with the other goods later on. We had two strong teams of horses, one cow and a nanny goat, the latter to supply us with milk at all times of day. Father was advised to buy a large quantity of dry goods, boots and shoes and provisions and ship them across the lake on a line boat, as the freighters were called. He did so and that was the last he ever saw of them. From Detroit to Dexter and thence to Eaton Rapids there were trees, with a chip taken out, every little ways. Two men had gone through and blazed a road to Ionia. The Charlotte Road was called the Dexter Road for many years.

After three weeks hard work, traveling through dense forests and fording most of the streams, the family arrived at Eaton Rapids worn out and homesick. We occupied the wagons until the shanty was built, which did not take long for kind neighbors soon came to our assistance. The custom was, if any one heard the sound of wood chopping in a new direction, Mrs. McQueen would blow loud and long on her horn and all of the neighbors would come to her to learn where the sound of chopping came from. Then with axes on their shoulders the men would go to the newcomers assistance, clear a patch of ground, and build two shanties, one for the people and one equally as strong for the beasts, for bears and wolves came at night, the latter in large droves. One night the first week of our sojourn wolves were fighting on top or our shanty and two fell down the stick chimney. Father and my brother despatched them with axes.

Father found there was no government land and so had to buy of the man who deceived him. His wife was a noble woman and she and mother could not part again so we settled down and soon had all we could do with ague. Some of the poor sick people were at the starving point when one cold winter day father and brother went to the north lot to get wood and try and get a deer, but came back in a short time bringing on the sleigh an Indian sick and nearly frozen. The children were badly frightened to see him for the white men in authority had given all Indians notice to leave the country. Some of them who had large families felt very badly and strange to say, thought it was not just to rob them of their land. I shall never be able to see why God permitted these poor peaceable Indians to be driven like wild beasts from their homes. The soldiers came from Detroit and took most of them but a few managed to stay around the country.[166] I only heard of one Indian that was bad and one of our citizens saw him fall from his canoe into the Duck Lake.

The Indian father brought home was named Jack and he seemed nearly dead. When my mother had tried all remedies without his reviving, she thought he was dying and taking her rosary and kneeling by his side, began to repeat the prayer for the dying. Soon Jack opened his eyes and reached a feeble hand, took the crucifix and kissed it (an image of Christ was on the cross.) Mother then prayed for the restoration of the living, Jack joining in a feeble voice. He proved to be a Canadian half-breed and a Catholic. A bond of friendship sprang up between Jack and the family and he proved a great blessing to the poor white people some of whom were near the starving point. Jack brought down with his gun plenty of game and distributed it among the families that were needy. He also took medicines that he had made of roots and herbs, to those who were ill and they were many. He taught our boys and men to make traps to catch game, for ammunition was too expensive to be had at all times. All this was repeated to me as I grew up old enough to understand. The first I remember of Jack was one day when he made whistles for brother and me out of bass wood and popple[167] boughs. One night my mother and brother thought they heard a woman screaming down near the creek. They hastened in that direction in the pitchy darkness when a hand was laid upon them and in silence they waited. Soon the screams were heard again and with the report of Jack's gun a large panther fell nearly at their feet. Jack had understood the screams and saved their lives. He taught the boys how to make splint brooms out of hickory saplings. The waste splints were treasured for kindling as we started fires with flint and steel and punk, by striking the flint on steel and having a piece of punk under to catch the sparks it would soon be all on fire, then the splinters would be added and then the wood. I have known mothers to send a mile to us to get coals to start their fires, not having flint and punk. We always kept ours. Out by a stump was a place made with stones in a hollow of the ground where we kept coals covered with ashes, which we usually made our fires from.

While in the small shanty that was our home for nearly two years, all the new arrivals came to us and how the shanty held them at night is a wonder to me as I think of it. One man tried to claim relationship with mother but she told him "no you are not even Irish." "Well" said he. "my wife's cousin married an Irishman." All the neighbors were good in those days and when sorrow, sickness and death came, all were ready to render assistance and comfort them in their affliction.

McQueen told father, who was suffering with ague, that he would go to Detroit and get the goods for him, taking his son and father's two teams. Father gave him the receipts for the goods and after a long three weeks had passed he came back and said that he had lost the receipts and that the goods had not yet arrived in Detroit. After waiting a time father went to Detroit and was shown the records where a man claiming to be him took the goods away. It was a great loss to us.

Mother tanned and made our shoes of deer skin, made large and lined with coon fur in the winter. Each child had to knit so many rounds on the plain part of their stockings every evening, mother putting in the heels and narrowing off the toes. She had to knit for the store both linen and wool. Father built a new house nearer to the road. It was of split logs and was large with good chamber room and board partitions. Mother began to hope to have all the comforts of home as she had them in "York State," but ague followed my father.

A doctor at last came to settle in the village. I will give a brief history of the first three. Dr. Sumner[168] was tall and nice and very dignified. He would enter a house, hear the patient's story of shaking and suffering in perfect silence. Then he would say, "yes, I see, all run down, very weak, bilious, debilitated. We must draw off all the bad blood and give you a chance to make new and get strong again, give me a bowl and a bandage." They were brought and the poor victims gave up poor thin blood that was merely keeping the heart beating. The charge for a visit was a dollar, and fifty cents extra for bleeding. So every one in the house, who were ailing, sometimes a whole large family had to be bled. The doctor forgot his lance one day and so took his jack knife and sharpened it on his boot leg and bled all the family of Mr. Reagan. When he came to little Susan the hurt and fright were so great that she died in his arms. He came to our house but mother would not let him touch one of her children. Father was growing worse and tried the doctor's remedy, in fifteen minutes he was dead. Another doctor came who said that was no way to do, he never bled his patients, he wound them in a wet sheet. A promising young man, one of the very best, Sumner Hamlin, was wrapped in cold, wet sheets and died. Yet another doctor came and he sent a man and team down to Grand Ledge to get a load of hemlock bark which he would steep strong and give them hemlock sweats when they were so weak that they died from the heat and exhaustion. You may ask did these doctors get rich. Oh, no, they got the shakes, took some of their own medicine and soon died. They lie in our cemetery among the unknown dead that were removed form the old burial ground.

Now about our preachers. One day Mrs. Benjamin Knight with Mrs. Conklin in her wagon came through our neighborhood and stopped at every house. Mrs. Conklin went in and invited every family to meet at her home on such a date to hold religious services and bring the children, sure. Enough responded to the call to more than three times fill her house so we all went out and sat on the grass in the yard. Mrs. Conklin read some from the Bible, prayed and preached. All sang and I think it must have been the best as well as the first religious service held in Eaton Rapids. Meetings and a Sabbath school were organized by this brave woman. In one short year they met to show the respect and love they bore her and then followed with the sorrow stricken husband and placed her in her grave, dust to dust but the spirit to God who gave it. On her tombstone this meeting is recorded. You may read it, but uncover your head for her ashes and her memory are sacred to every old pioneer. She was only twenty-one years old when she died.

Amos Spicer's family and brother and Samuel Hamlin and family with Benjamin Knight and family were here when we came. Ed Knight was the first white child born in this town and the second in the county, the first being a Mrs. Rogers who resides in Bellevue.

A skein of thread cost five cents for cotton, ten for linen. It would measure three yards. Mother with her little wheel spun flax into thread and colored it with walnut shucks and supplied people for mile around, for women only used cotton on baby clothes and making their husband's dickies, a front piece like a shirt bosom tied in place with a string around the neck and waist and worn under the vest on their marriage day and on other grand occasions. No white shirts were then worn. When a man died they had a shroud without any back for bleached cotton was from fifty cents to one dollar a yard, calico fifty and colors that would fade. It did not wear either, so our mother got unbleached cotton, the coarse kind, for thirty-five cents and colored it with sassafras and butternut bark, a sort of brown, for our summer dresses. We got sheep and mother made our dresses of wool in winter, paying Mrs. Morse for weaving by spinning for her and giving her linen thread. She never received money for her thread but Indians would come and exchange fur for it. White folks would bring a calf or pig or some hens and exchange for linen cloth or thread. Mother had brought some flax seed with her and had sown it near the marsh the first year we came. Our boys wore tow cloth in summer and our bed ticks and bags and towels were made of linen. Mother worked hard. Many times after our father passed away I have wakened wrapped in a blanket in a fence corner with mother and the boys near by gathering and piling stones to get the field ready on time for the fall wheat, so by moonlight they piled them for mother had to have the daylight for her spinning.

The first pigs we owned mother got by exchanging a new black silk dress with Mrs. Leader. The dress was made before she had thought of moving to Michigan. She had no use for it, but did have for the pigs. You who would like to hear more of the pioneers., come some pleasant day and go with me to the cemetery and I will tell you of Mr. Hamlin and his good wife, how cheerful they were although sickness and sorrow came and how much they did for others. Also of the Gallerys[169] and Spicers and Winns,[170] liberal hearted good people, and of Mr. and Mrs. Knight whose many acts of kindness it would take years to tell. It lives in the memory of all the old settlers. Many more I might mention but will close.

Sorrowful memories come to me of my mother's struggles to keep her six children together. Five years to a day after we lost our father just as spring came with a warm gladdening breeze and robins were chirping around our door the worst stroke came to us poor children. Our mother passed to the great beyond. Our home was broken up and we were scattered never more to meet under one roof.

The William Nowlin homestead at Dearborn in 1836.

Clinton County: 1836
by
Harriet Munro Longyear

Not all pioneer women suffered the pain and sorrow described by Margaret Lafever. Harriet Munro Longyear, for example, remembered her pioneer experiences, which began in Clinton County in 1836, with great pleasure when she wrote the following article for the Michigan Pioneer Society in 1915. She was 89 years old at that time.

Her husband, John W. Longyear, also left his mark on the state's history. He immigrated to Ingham County from New York in 1844, became a lawyer and set up a practice in the new community of Lansing in 1847. When he married Harriet two years later she joined him in Lansing. Longyear represented Michigan in Congress from 1863-1867. He died in 1875.

Mrs. Longyear's father, who had brought his family of twelve children to Michigan in 1836, spent the last 13 years of his life, following the death of his wife in 1870, with several of his daughters who lived in Lansing. A veteran of the War of 1812, Munro died at Harriet's home at the age of 92 in 1883.

My father, Jesse Munro, was a native of Rutland County, Vermont. When twenty-one years of age, he decided to seek his fortune in the West. New York State at that time was considered far west, as it was a good deal of a wilderness. There were no railroads, no canals; he walked and carried his belongings on his back save when occasionally he secured a ride on a farmer's wagon. On arriving at Buffalo, he decided to enlist in the Army of 1812. He served on sentry duty at Black Rock until the close of the war, only a few months later.

He purchased land five miles east of Buffalo City on the Batavia Road and lived there until 1836. He then sold his property and came further west to find a place to settle with his family. He and my mother together with my mother's brother, Hiram Parker, traveled through Illinois, Indiana, and Wisconsin without finding anything that pleased them. Then they decided to look through Michigan, the one state they had no idea of settling in when they left home.

They had seen "Michiganders," as they were called, returning to the state of New York. Their sallow complexion and the tales they told of shaking with the fever and ague made my father think that Michigan was no place for him. Nevertheless they decided to see for themselves, and give Michigan a look. Much to their surprise they found the state satisfactory. They liked the beautiful forests with their magnificent trees. My father was captivated at first sight, arguing that land which supported such a growth of trees would raise anything planted. So he located land in Clinton County.[171] There were the black walnut, butternut, hickory, black cherry, bird's-eye maple, curled maple, sugar maple, silver leaf maple, beech, basswood, sycamore, ironwood, white, black and burr oaks; many being three and four feet in diameter, and the tulip tree, with its beautiful foliage and lovely blossoms.

Our New York State home sold in 1836 for $10,000. We came from Buffalo to Detroit on the steamer *Robert Fulton*. The family consisted of my father and mother, five daughters, and two sons. There were three hired men; two were sent with the stock through Ohio; one accompanied the family.

Detroit was very disappointing to the older members of the family - a very uninteresting town, as I remember it. The buildings were low and very unpretentious, right down in the mud; a small old French town!

The men with the stock arrived after having been delayed by bad roads. There were three horses, a yoke of young oxen and two cows. The workmen applied themselves to loading up the goods, and making ready for the journey. The first day out from Detroit we went only ten miles. The road was simply terrible. There were places where there were half a dozen tracks where different travelers had endeavored to get around the deep mud holes, but each one seemed equally bad. The wagon wheels would sink below the hubs and one team was powerless to draw the load. There was little travel through the country as inhabitants were far apart. Wherever there was an inhabitant we found hospitality. We were never obliged to go further for accommodations. We were asked to share with them what they had. One place I remember where there was a large log house with very wide doors. After supper the doors were thrown open, the two being on opposite sides of the house; a yoke of oxen then drew a log ten feet long and three feet in diameter through one door and rolled it into the fireplace for a back log. Another log two feet through was drawn in and placed on top of the first one for a back stick; a third one of similar size by the same process was placed on large stones in place of andirons for a forestick; smaller split wood was then piled upon these logs and then there was a fire to last for twenty-four hours, with a few additions of small sticks during the next day.

At another place where we were entertained over night there was no floor to the house. The family lived on the bare earth. It was worn smooth and hard. At this place they were building a new log house and the men all spent the night in this new structure where they had a fire, but no beds. The workmen spent the night in entertaining their guests by howling like wolves, so there was very little sleep for any one. In the morning the man of the house apologized for his workmen. Said he had kept them on wolf soup so long they had partaken of the nature of the animal. We were inclined to believe him, because their imitation was very good, as we learned the following winter in our new home.

We finally arrived at what was then called by everybody, Scott's[172] now Dewitt. There we found good accommodations. They were prepared to take care of travelers, having a double log house, provided with appetizing food. At this place my father left the family while he with his three men went on to build a log house. Another regular stopping place was owned by Mr. and Mrs. Niles,[173] who had been there long enough to be known and who were always ready to help new settlers. My father stopped with them and procured provisions. He was obliged to make a road from the Niles settlement to his land, about six miles. They went to work with a will and felled the trees and trimmed them ready to put together for a habitation. They soon had the logs put in place and a cover over them. The roofing consisted of logs hollowed out like a trough, laid side by side, edges close together, trough side up. Then another row, reversed, covered the edges of the first. This made a rain and snow proof roof. The lumber used in making the doors and window casings was from the boxing of the furniture.

There were no saw mills in the country. Floors were made of the logs split into slabs and adzed off. Smooth boulders were used in making the back and jams to the ample fireplace. A stick chimney finished and topped it out. A settler who lived one mile west of us, having heard strange noises made an investigation. He found my father with a house nearly ready for occupancy. He said, "What are you going to do with such a house? Are you intending to keep hotel?" My father answered, "When you see my family, you will see it is not any too large." This family proved to be desirable acquaintances; there were five sons well educated and companionable.

After three weeks time father came for us. The rains had raised the Looking-glass River so that it could not be forded. We were all taken across the river in an Indian canoe. A pole was used instead of a paddle. We enjoyed the drive through the woods. It was night when we arrived at the Niles settlement, but there was a large living room and a blazing wood fire which gave brightness to the scene and a welcome for the new comers such as is only known to those who settle in a new country. There we met Mr. and Mrs. Beers[174] who had come the week before from Connecticut. They were building a house. We became warm friends notwithstanding we were five miles from each other. We visited and continued the acquaintance during their lives. There is now a daughter living in Lansing, Mrs. Anna Smith; two grandson, Guerdon and Charles Smith, survivors of our pioneer friends.

The journey was ended the following day. We were home. Each one found something interesting. The little brook that ran near the house gave us great pleasure. The new house was warm and comfortable. It was now November; a light snow fell soon after we arrived. Father spent the winter in going to and from Detroit and Dexter for supplies, taking ten days or two weeks each trip. There was no fruit except dried fruits. Portland, five miles, west was a small village. There was one store, that kept a few groceries and a stock of domestic goods, Indian maple sugar, etc.

The inhabitants were eastern people delightful to know. Two young men called, and came in a "new country" sleigh. It was made of ironwood poles, the bark taken off only from the underside of the runners. This was the first sleigh of its kind I had ever seen. I was greatly amused. Lyons, ten miles from Portland was a larger and more flourishing town. We joined in the festivities of both places. All were neighbors.

As there were few children near us Mr. Shaff, our neighbor, suggested that his son teach the winter school and my older sister teach the summer school. His suggestion was carried into effect. He provided a room in his house until more scholars came into the neighborhood. The state road commissioners came through surveying the State Road, which passed by our door. That was most cheering to us. Father with his men built a bridge at his own expense across the Looking-glass River, one mile east from us. This bridge remained there many years for the good of the public.

The winters were severe, deep snow, and feed for the stock very scarce. In the spring the soft maple tees were chopped down for the animals when the buds were full and red. They would trim out a large tree top in a short time and run to the next one when that fell. They subsisted on buds until vegetation became plentiful. Then they were free to roam where they please, baring the swamps where vegetation was alluring. Our new milch cow ventured too far and was lost in the mire. That was a real tragedy, so much was depending upon the milk for the family. Bravery and self control were called into action. Each one bearing his or her share of sympathy for our mother who knew better than we younger ones what it cost to go without milk.

The sugar maple trees were tapped and maple syrup and sugar was plentiful. Several hundred pounds of sugar were made, which relieved one of the wants of a new country. Fish were plentiful, the men catching with dip nets hundreds a night. All surplus was put into half barrels and salted for future use. Wild onions grew along the banks of our brook. In the fall wild plums, crab apples and frost grapes were plentiful. Honey was found in trees. In the beautiful forests of Michigan there was not only honey but also bees wax, which furnished us with wax candles.

One day when the men were building the house, they neglected to replenish the fire after their midday meal. When they stopped work for the night and came to prepare their supper the fire was out. Numerous efforts to kindle it were made with flint and steel without results; there was no dry kindling; everything fresh and damp. The only alternative was to go to Mr. Niles' for supper and breakfast, six miles. Returning in the morning, one man carried by hand a firebrand, swinging it to keep it burning. There were no matches at that time.

Our discomforts and deprivations were many but all were overcome by cheerfulness and heroic perseverance. Mother was always cheerful. Reptiles and insects there were, but I will leave them to your imagination to picture. Indians were friendly and always hungry. Their liking for white man's bread was simply appalling. We bought venison from them whenever they brought it to us. We had no reason to fear them. They were always sober and peaceable.

Thousands of immigrant families jolted across Michigan in wagons like this.

Kalamazoo County &
St. Joseph County:1836
by
Ruth Hoppin

**While many pioneer women remembered
fearing the Indians they encountered, by the 1830s
those fears were practically ungrounded. An
occasional episode, however, served to keep some
in dread of the Indians. Ruth Hoppin, who in later life
became a prominent St. Joseph County educator,
recalled, in a paper she read at a Pioneer Society
meeting in Centreville in 1893, her pioneer
experiences including one of the few genuine
incidents in which an Indian murdered a settler.**

I was but three years old when my father moved to this
state in 1836. Many things which are distinct recollections would
have been forgotten had they not been told over many times by
parents and elder brothers and sisters. Our first sojourn was in
the northern part of the county in the Edwin H. Lothrop[175]
neighborhood. Our house was near the Buckhorn Tavern, then
owned by M. Bebee. After his death the place was purchased by
D. Parsons, who occupied the old inn as a private residence for a
while, but who later built the house now standing on the old site.
A sort of village was started there with nearly a dozen houses
within half a mile of each other. The spring run had been
dammed and buildings erected for a tannery and carding mill.
Too late, it was found that the stream did not afford sufficient
water power. The tannery later became a distillery and the
carding mill a dwelling house. The tavern was then the important
building. The rush of immigration made it profitable to its owner.
Its sign was a deer's horn fastened to the top of an upright
tamarack pole. This buckhorn named the inn, the neighborhood,
and the road leading from Prairie Ronde to Three Rivers. The
immigrant heard Buckhorn hundreds of miles away. The inn was
a good representative of the stopping places of pioneer times; a
two story frame house by the side of a well worn sandy road. Two
large rooms fronted on the road. The one outside door led to the

barroom. The house was destitute of paint and plaster. Bed quilts and blankets helped to piece out the partitions where the rough boards and studding failed. The barroom, which was also the sitting room, had little furniture, splint bottomed chairs and the bar with its sparkling bottles and glasses being the principal. The great brick fireplace with its log fires were needed even to keep out the autumn cold, for the building was a shell, merely clapboarded. The other front room contained many beds. When these were filled the immigrant might take from his covered wagon his own beds and spread them on the floor. Running back, was another room with a huge fireplace. This room was the kitchen and dining room. Such houses as the Buckhorn were a day's journey apart, so the movers came at night, went on in the morning and were not often seen during the day.

Long after pioneer times the old house stood there, unfinished, forlorn, a sort of monument to a brief period in our state, when land speculation ran wild, and all the world was coming to Michigan; then, the rush quitted this road and went by other routes to states further west. What had promised to be a village was left without an inhabitant, save the one family which occupied the old inn. But before the place became quite forsaken the distillery had its day. What could a child of five years remember about a distillery? Well, I recall impressions received from my parents who detested the whole thing. I recall the pigpens with all their squeals and odors. I remember seeing some of the employees and other low characters who will be hangers on at such places, and I had good reasons to remember the Indians who so frequently passed our door on their way between the Reservation in Park Township and the baleful place, where they went for firewater. A paper could be filled with the story of dreads and frights caused by our Indian neighbor. Drunken Indians often called at our house asking for food; for they were always hungry, wanting to rest, and sometimes wanting to fight. One of the latter proclivity, my father picked up on the trail one bitter cold night and brought him on his load of wood to our house. The savage came into the living room with his whiskey jug, his gun, and his dog. He drove the children away from the fire; he insisted on pulling fingers with my fourteen-year-old brother who had a felon on his right hand, and he wanted to pull the sore finger. My mother, seeing that the whiskey jug would make him no better, slipped that article out of doors and emptied its contents into the snow, the gun, too, was put where he could not get it. The dog, he called back to the best place as often as it was called away from the fireplace. He was eager to fight, so the older members of the family who sat up with him had a night of it; but managed to avoid any serious encounter. They got him sober, mended his gun, fed him and his dog, and by sunrise started him toward the Reservation happy and singing. I have a vivid recollection of how glad the little ones were when on coming down to breakfast we found the terror gone. I say terror, for not a month before a neighbor, Mr. Wisner, had been killed at his own fireside by an Indian. Had Mr. Wisner, like my father, been a temperate man, the tragedy would not have occurred. The Indian owed Mr. Wisner a grudge, but only manifested the spirit of revenge when under the influence of liquor. This time he got his victim "to drink too much" and the result was death to the white man. I never shall forget the outcry of voices, when that brave, fifteen-year-old lad, James Wisner roused us with the cry, "Help! Help!! the Indian has killed my father and I left him trying to kill the rest of the family." Then there was the hurry of dressing, harnessing and driving rapidly away to save the endangered wife and little ones. How relieved we felt when at daylight a horseman returned, with the word that no others had been killed, although some had been badly hurt. My father and brother did the last duties in dressing the murdered man for the grave. A day later the remains were brought to our house and the funeral was held.[176] No wonder such a history made cowards of children. Ever after have I experienced a terror in hearing or reading of Indian atrocities, which I attribute to this early fright. I was well grown before I ceased to have frightful dreams of being pursued, caught and even being scalped by Indians. When, a year or two later, the tribe moved to the Indian Territory, though my parents believed that in this deportation a great wrong was done the red man yet I, selfish child, was very thankful to see them go.[177] No more would I have to meet them on my way to school! How often on such occasions have I run, like a frightened deer into the woods or fields. Once, it was my mother coming to meet me, but I knew neither her person nor her voice. A drunken Indian had passed that way one hour before and I saw in every stump and bush a savage. When these people came to our house, the first thing they asked for was whiskey, next they always asked for bread, flour and salt pork. This latter they liked cut in slices one half inch thick and laid raw between two thick pieces of bread. This they would bite through as easily

217

as we could the bread alone. It seemed wonderful to us children that they always refused my mother's good berry and pumpkin pie. They brought us in return, berries in baskets or mocoes, (mococks) and maple sugar. More often they brought us fish and venison. Once they brought young turkeys. The mocock was a round box like a bandbox, but made of bark sewed together with thread of bark or twigs.

We had a chance to see how they treated boys, so that when they grew up they became straight, finely formed men. I have seen the baby lashed to a straight board tied down from head to heel. We thought the papooses were pretty and their mothers, too, seemed so happy when the whites admired their little ones. The Indian woman was a devoted mother and patiently carried her child on her back, no matter how long or how difficult the way. I remember seeing a family coming through the trackless snow a foot deep. The long legged, strong father had nothing to carry, the short dumpy mother had her baby strapped to her back, her blanket drawn over her own head as well as that of the papoose. When they entered the house she was pretty well tired out, her lord was not tired at all. But it was not all selfishness that caused the red man to refuse to carry such burdens. It was his duty as warrior and hunter to keep himself straight. If there were horses, the squaws always rode, when not enough ponies to go around, it was the men who walked. These people loved their own and sincerely mourned their dead. I have known them to go long distances to lay their friends in some favored Indian burying ground. It is a shame that the whites have not preserved some of these aboriginal cemeteries which today we would deem interesting memorials of a vanished race.

There are those here today who recall the interesting character of the squaw whose husband killed Mr. Wisner. She was a pure Indian, and her virtues were of savage origin and native growth, as she had not been instructed by civilized people. The devotion to her husband could not be excelled, her efforts to keep him from committing the crime ought to have saved the life of the victim. She did all she could to warn the endangered man, and when the Indian sprang upon him, fought for the enemy of her race. Not until she saw that the Indian was likely to be killed did she cease to help Mr. Wisner; but with true wifely instinct, when she saw one of the two must die, determined that that one should not be her husband. In the trial at Kalamazoo, much sympathy was shown her, and many thought that in this sad affair this uninstructed sister from the wigwam experienced the keenest sorrow and was the truest mourner.

A story had gone out that the Indian had killed the papoose. She felt that such a report would lessen his chances in the trial, and she took great pains to dispute the statement by removing her baby from under the blanket on her back and showing it to the white people as she passed. Mr. Lothrop who was taking her in his cutter to the trial was quite patient in the detentions caused by these frequent exhibitions of the papoose. The story of the Indian killing his own child was not without foundation, for a boy had mysteriously disappeared from the family two or three years before. The whites had suspected foul play, but the disappearance was never investigated. It all came out at the time of the Wisner murder. That morning when his captors brought the Indian bound down in the sleigh to the cabin where his victim lay dead, my mother went out to the sleigh to see him. His face was badly mangled; for they had a desperate fight in capturing him; he did not want to be taken alive for he believed that they would, as the squaw had told him, burn him alive. My mother bound up his wounds and tried to alleviate his sufferings. Seeing her kindness he said. "Good squaw, good squaw, you tell white man to kill me quick; no burn me, but kill me quick." She tried to make him understand that he would not be tortured but would have a fair trial. But she could not convince him; then he tried to anger her, so if possible she would through vengeance, set the men on to kill him quick. He said, "Me very bad Indian, you kill me quick, me very bad, me kill papoose, put him under ice in swamp." What became of his wife we never knew, probably she went with the rest of her tribe to their lands beyond the Mississippi. The Indian, after a fair trial, was condemned to be hung, but the sentence was delayed on account of the law pending in our legislature in Detroit. That law abolished capital punishment, and our Indian was the first to receive the sentence for life imprisonment. He lived but four years. He was quite heartbroken, and docile, and became a sincere Christian.

What pioneer does not recall the Buckhorn Road as it wound through the forest from Prairie Ronde to Three Rivers? When my father came to Michigan, the only houses on this road between Three Rivers and the Buckhorn Tavern, were those of Joseph Sterling, Grant Brown, Abram Schoonmaker, and Reuben Bristol, now the Woodward place. Around each of these

Pioneers declared war on the forest and wastefully burned it to clear the land.

houses were a few acres of clearing, all the rest of the way was an unbroken forest. The pole bridge on this road which crossed the great marsh just below the outlet of Goose Lake was another landmark known all over the country. The Indian trail from the Marantette agency at Notawasippi [178] struck the main road just below the pole bridge. This trail passed over the Kellogg farm in Park Township and crossed the Portage by the White Man's Bridge about a mile below the Portage lake. The trial was in places a foot deep and packed so hard that it was along time before anything would grow on it. Years after the red man had left the country this trail could be traced in my sister's dooryard.

The earliest pioneer found Michigan healthy, but later so much ground was ploughed up and the malarial gases set free, that the country became very sickly. [179] Our family came at the worst time. My father shook with the ague every day for eighteen months; there were ten all down at once, my mother, the only one able to administer the cup of cold water and care for the sick.

Crops went back into the ground, animals suffered for food, and if the people had not been too sick to need much to eat they, too, must have gone hungry. The pale, sallow bloated faces of that period were the rule; there were no healthy faces except of persons just arrived. "The doctor came with a free good will, and portioned out his calomel." [180]

He came every day, he purged, he bled, he blistered, he puked, he salivated his patient, he never cured him. He forbade the nurse to give the patient any water or any milk. The doctor's bill was something that no sane physician would present today, not so much for a single visit, but the visits had seemed endless. The subject of sickness brings us to that of death and the grave. How many pioneers lay sleeping in nameless graves we shall never know, for too often the avaricious land owner in a few years plowed over the few acres where rested the strangers. Even in the good town of Three Rivers a row of thickset houses are standing over one of these early cemeteries, whence the bodies have been removed. There were no headstones, only planks. These soon settled and the sleepers beneath passed into oblivion, their friends dead, gone away, or worse, indifferent. Everybody attended the funerals of forty years ago. The neighbors were sympathetic and helpful; there was no expense except for the plank coffin made by the nearest joiner and the white cambric shroud, which was the burial robe for man and woman alike. Mourning was put on by the women, even if it was nothing but a bit of black ribbon on a white straw bonnet. There were no flowers, no hearse, no undertaker. The body was carried in a common lumber wagon, the bearers riding in the same vehicle. The coffin was lowered into the grave by means of lines taken from the horses. All remained till the grave was filled up, the head and foot plank were in place and the mound had been rounded and smoothed into its suggestive shape. Then it seemed that all was done by kind friends, for each neighbor had taken a part in these duties. Now we turn away from the open grave and leave this work to the hireling. The tunes and the hymns sung at funerals seemed purposely designed to make the bereaved ones sadder. There was little hope or consolation in either. Who of us older ones does not remember "China" sung at all pioneer funerals? The sermon, too, seemed to arouse not allay sorrow. He was the eloquent preacher who made the mourners cry the hardest. People worshipped in schoolhouses and private dwellings. So far as I know the only church edifice in 1836 anywhere in the country was the Liberty Pole Church near Harrison's[181] on the north end of Prairie Ronde. There was not one in Schoolcraft, Three Rivers and I think not in Centreville.

Park was settled later than the surrounding country because of the Indian Reservation there, so we repeated our pioneer experiences when my father went there to live. We settled in the woods, saw herds of wild deer and flocks of wild turkeys, our neighbors were visited by bears; my sister saw a bear near a lonely road as she was coming home on horseback. In the winter we heard the wolf's howl, in the spring the thrum of the prairie hen, and in the summer the song of the whip-poor-will. We had unlimited range of pasture with the inconvenience of having our cows go off and our being without milk a week at a time.

Our fruit was picked from the field and the swamp, strawberries from the former and huckleberries and cranberries from the latter. Gardens and fields were luxuriant; melons were brought in by the bushel basket and when the corn was cut up in the fall there was a golden display of pumpkins. That almost forgotten fruit was made into pies, stewed for sauce, was dried, made into pumpkin butter, and a toothsome corn bread known as pumpkin Johnny cake made of it. All housewives cooked by open fireplaces, baked bread and pies in the old fashioned backkettle or in the tin baker. Not until the forties did cook stoves become common.

My mother spun, wove, colored and made up the wearing apparel for her whole family, until the invention of machinery and the incoming railroad changed everything and made home manufactures unprofitable. Suddenly all the female world found itself genteel in calico at twelve and a half cents, and delaine at twenty-five cents per yard, then the spinning wheel and loom were put aside.

There was no plaster, our plank walls were covered with newspapers. Oil for painting was scarce and high priced, so we mixed some red lead with common lard, and put the mixture on the doors and partitions, but it never got dry and was always rubbing off on our clothing. Before the era of rag carpets was the notable era of scrub brooms, those well remembered homemade splint brooms. Many a lady here present can recall the time when it was a disgrace to any housekeeper not to keep her floors "clean enough to eat off of,' and the rule for rinsing was to dash on and sweep off water till "it was clear enough to drink."

Most of the furniture had been brought on the immigrant's wagons. My mother's old armchair thus imported is my most valuable possession. Our bedsteads were the work of several hands, the posts had been done by the turner, the ruder hand had squared the rails and bored the holes for the ropes. The splint bottom chair was in every house; the greatest elegance was the Windsor chair, popularly know as the "Winzy." These wooden bottom chairs were painted in a variety of colors, usually dark, but I have seen them of a bright grass green. The grandest piece of furniture known was a mahogany bureau, which many went to look at as a great curiosity. People who had linen for the table made it themselves; not until late in the forties did the Irish peddler bring in a plentiful supply of table cloths.

Musical instruments were few, the fiddle, the most common. Some had accordions but few could play them. When the first organ grinder came through he was greeted with joy, and some wanted to know if that thing that he carried on his back were not a piano. We had much singing of songs, mostly English ballads and Scotch airs. The songs of Burns were as familiar to us as to the Scotchman in his native land but a few of American authorship were popular. Such a one was "Oh doubly mournful is the fate that I am called to relate," and "James Bird, the White Pilgrim" was another. These early songs were the seed which brought forth a crop of piano wrestlers and screamers of opera a few years later.

The old fashioned winter evening visits brought to your door at sunset a large wagon load of men, women and children. They remained until towards morning; a hearty meal was served about midnight. The time was filled with singing and stories. Ghost stories were most popular, but war stories had a part. There were still living not a few men who had seen Washington and Wayne, who like my father had fought in the War of 1812. We were told how Perry's heroes looked as they marched through western New York to reach the squadron being built on Lake Erie. We heard the story of men who fought at Tippecanoe or escaped the massacre at Frenchtown.[182] The War of 1812 was always spoken of as "the late war."

Ruth Hoppin, wolverine woman from St. Joseph County.

Jackson County:1837
by
Mrs. M.W. Clapp

Mrs. M.W. Clapp was 75-years-old when she took the time to recall her pioneer life in Jackson County's Hanover Township in the form of a letter written to the Michigan Pioneer Society in 1881. This wolverine woman's terse sentences and sparse descriptions leave much to be "read between the lines," yet her sincere recollections offer a refreshing relief from the flowery prose of the literary ladies.

In the year 1837, in the month of May, we left my native place (Farmington, Ontario County, New York) in company with Mr. Azariah Mallory and family, of Macedon, Wayne County, who were also bound for the same destination - the then far west - the state of Michigan, my husband having purchased three eighties in the southwest corner of Hanover Township, the year previous, where we now reside.

Emigration in those days was less expeditious than in these modern times. We went aboard the canal boat and jogged along at a slow rate, but as it ran both night and day, we made considerable progress. Arrived at Buffalo, we took the steamboat for Toledo, not much of a village at that time, there being but a few houses. We made out to climb the bank and then started by team for Adrian, Mr Mallory having transported his horses and wagon across the lake. We found the roads rough passing through the cottonwood swamp, through mud and muck, where many a wagon had been stuck, Mrs. Mallory and myself walking four miles on logs and rails.

We saw the first locomotive with cars making their first trip in Michigan.[183] My uncle, Daruis Comstock, and George Crane, from Farmington, New York, (who were stockholders) were on board. When the train stopped at Blissfield the old gentlemen alighted with buckets in hand and descended the bank of the River Raisin and up again as sprightly as young men, with their buckets of water to supple the tender. Both men are now dead.

We arrived at Moscow Plains, put up with an old

acquaintance of ours for six weeks, who made our stay very pleasant, until our house was finished, which was built of logs, of course. We then commenced keeping house. We experienced many privations, having to go thirty miles to mill, with an ox team, taking two days for the journey. Our neighbors were few and far between. No roads at that time except the main traveled road, three miles south, known as the "Chicago turnpike." Now and then we came across an Indian trail (though only one Indian called on us). Though our mode of conveyance for a few years was by ox-team, we could expedite by taking a bee line (nearly) to the different points, as there was no underbrush (the Indians kept them burned down). Afterward, by chipping the trees, or "blazing," the lines became established roads, until clearings obliged us to turn corners.

Jonesville had only one store at that time. Emigration was very great in 1837; it made very hard times, on account of the scarcity of provisions. Many were afflicted with ague, for which Michigan became proverbial. The first fall my husband had forty-nine "shakes" in forty-nine days; our daughter suffered from it at the same time, and none of us escaped it entirely. Mr. Mallory's people seemed like relatives, though living three miles away. On Sunday the old gray horse would bring the wife and youngest child, while he and one or two others trudged on foot. Then we appreciated the face of a friend, and the attachment thus formed has ever since existed.

In the spring the fire would run through the woods, which warmed up the ground and caused vegetation to spring up, beautiful to behold. The flowers covered the earth and yielded a fragrant perfume. The wild deer would gambol over the plains, and the turkey was also seen. Now and then a massassauga[184] put in an appearance, but the wolves and screech owls would sometimes make the night hideous. We soon had a flock of sheep, from which we spun and wove our own cloth, and had to be tailoress and dressmaker too, but clothes were made in plainer style then than now a days.

Where the village of Hanover is located, were only two or three residences, and one log school house, a few rods northeast of where the M.E. church now stands, where we used to attend meetings. The first tombstone in the cemetery marked the grave of our son. It was a brown sandstone, taken from the quarry at Stony Point, some ten years before its inexhaustible stores were developed.

And thus we might extend our review of pioneer life, but perhaps enough has been said. The improvements since "those days that tried men's souls," are before us. Our state being traversed by the numerous railroads, and the facilities we enjoy of communication enable us to see the progress in civilization. That which fifty years ago was an unbroken wilderness is now dotted with cities and village, with the advantages of modern improvements, and we truly "can sit under our own vine and fig tree."

A pioneer family surveys their hard won homestead.

Hastings: 1837
by
Mrs. A.M. Hayes

As a 17-year-old girl, Mrs. A.M. Hayes settled in the frontier settlement of Hastings. She would spend the remainder of her long life there, a witness to that city's evolution from a huddle of log cabins to Barry County's seat and largest city. Hers was the first marriage in the county and her home the first frame structure in Hastings. In 1894, 57 years after she first arrived in the newly created state of Michigan, she related her recollections to the Annual Meeting of the Michigan Pioneer Society.

She told her audience: "I will forget for the time the grey hairs, the wrinkles and the dim eyes, I will forget that I am the great grandmother of three children, and tell my story as if I were as young as I used to be." Then she began her narrative.

In the year 1837 my father, Daniel McClellan, and my uncle, James McClellan, hearing the praises of the young State of Michigan sounded throughout the eastern states, invested in land in the township of Hastings, Barry County, Michigan, and not waiting for their zeal to abate, we very soon left our pleasant home in Ithaca, New York, and started for the far west. The most rapid way of traveling then was by boat, and we arrived at Detroit on the third day out. At that time I thought it was the most dismal place I ever saw. The buildings were mostly old and low, and the streets dirty, and the accommodation we found, at what was said to be one of the best hotels in the city, were just about the same as you find now in any little back woods town. At that time there was no railroad[185] in the state, nor in fact any other road over which it was very pleasant to travel. A great part of the way was what they called "corduroy roads," and were made by cutting down trees and laying the trunks close together and parallel with each other; sometimes a little dirt was thrown over them, but more often the long marshes we crossed were laid with just the bare logs.

As it was not over comfortable riding, the older children walked a good share of the way, I was the oldest of seven children, being as I said, 17 years of age at the time. We had two teams and wagons, a spring seat on one for our mother and the younger children.

Many times we got fast in the mud, and then the men would put both teams on one wagon, and with poles cut from the forest, pry the wheels up so the horses could draw it out. Several times we came across an emigrant wagon fast in the mud, waiting for some one to come along and help them out, and they always got the needed assistance.

The road we came over was the old stage road from Detroit to Grand Rapids. Ann Arbor was the largest place on our route, and from there several stage lines were running to different points. My mother, wishing to visit a brother living in Clinton, Lenawee County, who had been in Michigan several years, father thought by taking the stage to Clinton they would travel much faster than we with loaded wagons and that they could make a short visit and get to Marshall as soon as we did. So we children, with uncle and the hired man, resumed our journey. After leaving Ann Arbor it was very difficult to get a place to stop over night, but we never were without some shelter, although sometimes we had hard times to get lodging place. One day right after noon, it began to rain. Uncle told us we would stop at the first house we came to. We looked for a clearing, for there we thought we would find shelter from the rain.

Soon we saw the looked for goal; there was a man and dog with an ox team, but we looked in vain for the house. Uncle asked him if we could stop with him, and he said, "You are welcome to all I have, but this is my house," pointing to the wagon-box by the side of a large tree. He had laid some brush over it to keep out the rain. He had left his family in Detroit and was there making a home for them in the wilderness. He told us there was a settler five miles further on, so we had to go on or stay without shelter.

It was after dark when we came to a little log house with one room below, and by climbing a ladder a low room above. They were willing to take us in, but it was a poor place for so many, as a family of six persons had got there before we did, and there were seven of us and five of their own family. There was a log stable for the horses, and our hired man slept there. We all felt very thankful for the shelter, but the house leaked so badly that I had to dry most of the children's clothes before they could dress in the morning. The next place was Jackson, which was then a small place without very few houses, and the hotel was even worse than the one at Detroit. There we saw our first Indians, there being about 1,500 of them there at that time, drawing their pay from the government, as Jackson, at that time, was a trading post. When we got to Marshall we expected to meet our parents, but we were sadly disappointed, and after waiting three days we went on our way without them.

When within about forty miles of the end of our journey, and, by the way, it was much farther then than now, on account of the round about way we had to take, we came to a piece of woods eighteen miles long and it took us from daylight until dark of that October day to get through, but there was a haven of rest, for we were at the famous Yankee Springs House, [186] of which we had heard so much since leaving Detroit. It seemed so pleasant to us, and more like what we had left far away in the east than anything we had yet found. Yankee Lewis, as he was called, told us he had plenty of room as his mansion was ten stories on the ground, made of logs, of course.

There were over forty persons staying there that night. I began to cheer up a little here, as our host and hostess were very kind and gave me encouraging words. I had been very homesick and discouraged at the dismal prospect before us, and because I was away from father and mother, but I had to keep my homesickness to myself, as I did not wish to mar the pleasure of my younger sisters, for they were very happy all the time, and everything was so new and novel to them that it seemed like fairyland.

The last day of our journey we found our way by marked trees as there was no road, and only one habitation between Yankee Springs and the county seat, where our journey ended and that was a little, shanty without a floor and a piece of bark for a door. The man had only been there a few weeks.

We had supposed as we were going to the county seat[187] we should find quite a little town, something like those through which we had passed, so when we met a man, uncle asked him how far it was to the center and he said, "You are right in the city." We all began to look for the buildings, and asked him if we could see it, and he said, "Can't you see that shanty through the woods there?" And sure enough, there was one small shanty and one quite good log house, and down under the hill was a sawmill. The house was occupied by Slocum Bunker and family and his brother Thomas, who had come there the year before to board the workmen for Hayes & Dibble, of Marshall, while building the saw mill, and were at that time getting out timber for a grist mill for the same men. It had taken us sixteen days to come from Detroit. My heart was heavy and I felt like crying but I did not. The people already there were so glad to have a family move in, and they treated us so kindly. I tried to be cheerful, but at night when all were asleep, I had my cry out and then and there resolved with the help of my father above to put away all homesickness and repinings, and make the best of my surroundings, and I did so from that time on. Dear Mrs. Bunker, she proved a mother to me in the eight long weeks my mother was away, sick at her brother's in Clinton.

Father had to leave my mother and come on without her when we had been in our new home two weeks. About that time quite a number of men came through looking for land, but Mrs. Bunker had lived there fourteen months without seeing a white woman. Indians were very plenty, one hundred lodges of them being camped on the north side of the Thornapple River. They were always ready to swap, as they called it, fish, cranberries, maple sugar and venison for flour, bread, pork or potatoes. The next day after we got to our new home, I invested in some honey. It was strained and looked very nice. In a few days Thomas Bunker came in and I was showing him what nice honey I had bought of the Indians. "How do you suppose they strain it" said he. I told him I had thought nothing about it; he said he saw them stain some though one of their old blankets. We did not eat any more honey after that; of course we like honey, but we could get along without it, and we did.

Their maple sugar was just the same, we thought it good until we saw them make it, but they were so dirty in their habits that we used no more of their maple sugar. The Indians often frightened us by putting their faces against the windows to look in, before they came in. They were all very kind when they were sober, but dishonest and treacherous when drunk. The traders that came through to buy their furs brought the fire water that was the curse of the red man, as it has ever been the greatest enemy of all mankind. One Indian that was always civil when sober came very near killing me one day when he was drunk; he knocked me down with a large iron fire shovel, and if help had not come immediately, he surely would have killed me. It was terrible the

Mrs. A.M. Hayes, one of Hastings' earliest settlers.

way they would fight with each other when they could get liquor; they would give anything they had for a pint of whisky, and were the terror of all white women when they could procure it. At one time they held what they called a medicine dance near us, and there were nearly 2,000 Indians gathered there.

They had two sick members of their tribe in a very tall wigwam of bark, and no one but the medicine men were allowed to go in. All of them joined in the dance and grunted out some guttural, unintelligible words.

They went through a great many heathenish performances that were a wonder to us who had never seen an Indian before in all our lives.

Our father's land was some four miles from the center, [188] and we went there and made us a home. We never lacked for food of some kind, for the country abounded in fish and game, and berries and wild fruits were plenty in season. Father went eight miles after our first potatoes to plant, and carried them home on his back. We had to go forty miles for flour and other provisions over bad roads; and sometimes the whole settlement would get out, and then you can imagine we were hungry. The first year we were here we had to go forty miles for our mail, too, and a letter from the east cost us 25 cents. We had to pay $20 per barrel for flour, and $40 per barrel for what was to be "one hog pork." The hog that was in one barrel we bought had three heads and feet to match.

The second year we were in Hastings, we thought we would like a turkey for Thanksgiving. The men were all too busy to hunt one, so the girls said they would try their luck, and to our great surprise, they brought in a full grown young wild turkey; they had run it down and caught it.

The first we knew we had a neighbor on the east of us. Father was hunting his cattle and had followed the ever to be remembered cow bell until about four miles from home; he heard some one praying, he went up and there was a man and his family who had just finished their breakfast off from a dry goods box, and were thanking God for his blessings. This was Mr. Mudge, and I must say right here that man always prospered and made a good home for himself and loved one. The new grist mill was all enclosed in the year 1840, and the citizens decided to celebrate the Fourth of July, and dedicate the new mills. So they came from miles around and danced all day in the new mill and ate their dinner on the banks of the Thornapple in a log tavern, which was about half a mile from the mill.

We had a great meeting and everyone enjoyed themselves. My father's family were the first to come into the township after the Bunkers. Several families moved in soon afterward, so we had quite a colony.

I had always thought I would not be married by a justice of the peace, but in the year 1839 I was married to Willard Hayes, by A.C. Parmater, justice of the peace; he was taken from my side by death in 1873. We were the first couple married in the county, and had the first frame house ever in the village. In the same year Mr. Hayes was appointed postmaster by Amos Kendall, postmaster general. Barry County was duly organized March 15, 1839, and the first Monday in the following April the first election was held and the first officers of Barry County elected. Thomas Bunker was elected county clerk, Mr. Spalding treasurer, A.C. Parmalee register of deed, and Willard Hayes sheriff. Nathan Barlow, Sr., was our first representative.

Death came in our midst and three were buried in the summer of 1838. The first minister we heard was at the funeral of a Mr. DeGroot; the Rev. Calvin Clark, a Presbyterian minister, rode in over fifty miles on an Indian pony. Whenever we wanted to hold any religious services we would all get together, and different ones would read sermons of different divines. We cared nothing for creeds in those days, God lived to us in the air we breathed, and we knew and loved Him who said on calvary, "I am the resurrection and the life." The majestic forest was our cathedral, the flowers of the woods our altar, and the sweet music of nature our choir.

The first church was organized in 1841 by the Methodists, Rev. Mr. Bush[189] the first pastor. If he wanted wood, he took his ax and went to the woods; if he wanted meat, he took his gun and went to the same place. We all called him "our pastor," and he was. The next church organization was the Presbyterian, in the year 1843, and the Rev. Hoyt[190] was the first pastor; he is now living in the east at the advanced age of 82.

The first schoolhouse was built and ready for use in 1841 and the first teacher was Sophia Spalding, now Mrs. Henry Knappen, of Kalamazoo.

In 1851 or 1852 we had a more commodious schoolhouse built, but the old one of pioneer days remained a good many years a landmark of the days that were gone. Our first court house was built in 1842 and 1843, and was burned in

1846.

Henry A. Goodyear kept the first store that was ever in the village and he has been there ever since. Dr. Wm. Upjohn was our first physician and lived there until he died at the age of 80 years.

I do not wish you to lose faith in my veracity, but I have seen the squaws spear sturgeon near by on the river that would weigh all the way from 60 to 100 pounds. This is no fish story. Of all that lived there is the year 1840, all are gone but H.A. Goodyear, Mrs. Esther Bennett, my sister and myself.

This is a brief history of my early life in the city where I have lived so long. There are many who remember the later years, and it would be useless to say more, so my story is done. When I came there that place was a vast wilderness, and where now the fine mansions of our citizens stand, then the majestic trees of the forest reared their heads and defied the storms of winter, and where now the boys and girls of our city play hide and seek, the wild denizens of the woods roamed unmolested.

Then we used the tallow dips to light up our log cabin homes, when night closed in upon us, while now the electric light make day of night and throws it gleams far into the heavens. Where now the beautiful farms of our surrounding country are green with grass and golden with the fields of waving grain, the wild Indians had their hunting grounds, chased deer and bear, and lived in all their savage freedom. It was not an easy life we old pioneers lived, but it was a happy one; clearing up land for our homes, working that our children might enjoy the fruits of our labor and also have better advantage of civilization and education than their parents had. Each year now thins the ranks of the old pioneers, and soon our children will be the only old settlers left, and we shall have crossed over the river to join those well loved pioneers who have gone before. I expect to have a grand reunion there in that happy promised land, where old hearts are ever young, and the weary are at rest.

Ionia: 1837
by
Polly Dye

Polly Dye was another of the women who left their comfortable homes in New York and traveled via the Erie Canal and Lake Erie steamer to begin a new life in the wilds of Michigan.

Born Polly Vine at Middleburg, New York, in 1813, she married Richard Dye at the age of 19. They resided in Herkimer County, New York, until immigrating to Michigan in the spring of 1837. Getting to her new home in Ionia, however, proved an adventurous and difficult travail as the narrative she delivered at the meeting of the Michigan Pioneer Society in 1885 documents.

The Dyes remained in Ionia for the rest of their lives, raising a family of eight children. Her husband died in 1886 and four years later she was buried by his side in the Ionia Cemetery. A memorial eulogy noted: "Few of the early pioneers were more widely known or more generally esteemed than 'Aunt Polly Dye,' whose kindly heart and cheerful disposition made her a universal favorite."

How clearly do I remember the day, in the month of May, 1837, on which I left my beautiful cottage home in Herkimer, New York, where I, in the spring time of life, had been blessed with plenty and happiness, and where the hospitality of friends was ever the characteristic of their lives. How sorrowful was the parting, as my friends came flocking in by groups to bid my adieu and to bring some little token of affection and remembrance. It seemed so hard to tear away from those I loved so much, knowing, as I did, that we would never meet again. On leaving my home, I was burdened with more anxiety and care than the average traveler is accustomed to meet, for the reason that my husband had started about ten days before me, leaving me, with two children, to follow. Fortunately, however, there were several persons besides my children who accompanied me, among whom were Mr. Dye's brother, mother and sister, all my father's family, except one brother and sister; thus making the company a pleasant one.

In those days we had not the accommodation of railroads, our only means of traveling being by canal. It was our fortune to secure passage on the first boat going west, which was owned by Captain Howell. It was a curiosity to me to ride on such a conveyance, as I had not done so before. After riding some time at that slow rate which such boats are noted for, it gradually grew very disagreeable, and I at last became completely disgusted, as I was confident that I could walk more rapidly myself. Soon, however, we were given a cause for greater complaint, for, as we moved down the canal, the report reached us that there was ice ahead, and that it would be several hours before it would be cleared so what that we could reach Buffalo.[191] It was, therefore, not without difficulty that we finally succeeded in reaching a port, for we found that the ice had worked into the canal from the lake, so as to render it almost impossible to land. At last, however, we succeeded in reaching land, and, learning from the captain that we could not leave until morning, we retired for the night. In the morning we were recommended to the *Daniel Webster* by a friend, Mr. Cospell, who had crossed the lake several times, and who stated that the boat mentioned was the safest one on the lake. Complying with his recommendation, we boarded it, but were surprised to behold the most obnoxious place I had ever witnessed. It was filled with foreigners of every description, and fairly alive with the "dregs of humanity," whose indulgence in tobacco and liquors fraught the air with an odor too vile to be described by human language. After some time we were informed that we could not leave that day, and it was thought, not that week, in consequence of the lake being filled with ice. Learning this, we determined to rent rooms on shore and to board together, which resolution we succeeded in putting in effect after some difficulty.

Day after day we awaited the time of our departure, but the ice still prevented our progress. At last, however, we learned of the determination of the captain to go through the ice, as he had made a wager of five hundred dollars that he could get through. Preparing for our departure, we had but little trouble in once more boarding the boat. Before us, as far as the eye could reach, lay a deep bed of ice, and behind us the city of Buffalo, with its many people pacing to and fro. At this moment the melodious strain of some far off band greeted our ears and sent a thrill of joy to our saddened hearts. At last our boat made one bold push and stood in the midst of ice as tight as a wedge. A feeling of intense agony came over me as I realized the still more hazardous situation in which we would soon be placed; for, after the combined efforts of crew and passengers had gradually forced our boat from its confinement among the broken columns of ice, the land gradually receding from sight, a fearful gale arose and we found ourselves surrounded by roaring waters and gigantic cakes of ice. On through the foaming billows we dashed, into the gloomy, turbulent waters of the lake, at last being hurled into the bed of fury, where we thought that surely we would be lost. But I had company in that melancholy hour. The men, becoming exhausted, at last sank down into the boat, while women wept and prayed for Divine assistance, imploring the Ruler of all storms to quiet the angry waters. It was but a short time, however before we began to feel the storm subsiding, and it soon passed over. At eleven o'clock at night we arrived at Dunkirk, where we had to stop for repairs, as the boat was very badly broke, having, at the time we reached port, only one paddle on the wheels. That night we rested well and in the morning enjoyed a good meal.

The boat being repaired, we started once more on our voyage, with a bright day before us and everything seeming favorable for its consummation without further danger or trouble. Again the sight of land left us, and once more we were surrounded with a dreary waste of waters, with no object to look at save the dark nimbus of heaven and the blue waters beneath At last we discerned a small object in the distance, which became larger and larger until we finally recognized a ship, known as the *Uncle Sam*, coming toward us at great speed, and before it could be mastered the two ships collided with such force that all on board feared they would be drowned, but from this spell we were soon relieved, as no serious injury had been done to either vessel. Again feeling secure and being quite exhausted, we retired for the night. In the morning we awakened to behold before us the grand old harbor of Detroit, and on the dock my husband. There was a great rejoicing then, and in a few hours we took our departure from the boat.

We next set about preparing for our journey to our future home. Enough provisions were secured before leaving Detroit to last, at least, two years. We loaded one barrel of flour on our wagon and shipped the rest of our provisions around the lakes, so that they would come to us by the way of Grand Rapids. The provisions that we loaded on our wagon we thought would last us to the end our Journey. Thus the day was passed in preparation and nothing else occurred worthy of recollection. The days flew away as we traveled through the almost unbroken country, seeing nobody save our little band of pilgrims, and hearing nothing save the howling of wild animals, in the dark primeval forest, where the echo would resound through the hollow quietude of nature and the world seemed hushed with the solemnity of death. At night we camped by the side of some stream, or stayed wherever we could, at some farm house, resuming our journey as early in the morning as possible.

The first village at which we stopped was Pontiac, where we remained overnight, at the house of an old friend, and spent a few of the most joyous hours of my life. We proceeded in the morning on our journey, through the unbroken wilderness, meeting meanwhile, some bands of Indians, with which we did some trading. We finally reached those terrible swamps which lay in the valleys of this country, the largest of which was about two mile across, and the only way we succeeded in crossing was, by having one of the men to take a long pole and, standing on the end of the wagon tongue, probe the water on either side and also in front, so as to ascertain the depth and thereby to prevent us from being drowned or otherwise injured. That night we stopped at the house of a Dr. Laing, taking lodging only, for which, in the morning we paid the usual fee of five dollars.

It was some time before we took shelter in another house and, meanwhile, our provisions becoming very scarce, we had to be as economical as possible, living chiefly on bread made of Indian corn. At last the crisis came; overcome by hunger, tired and exhausted, wet, cold and disheartened, we found ourselves at the very door of starvation. After traveling all day we were not able to obtain shelter or relief till very late in the evening, when we came to a log hut, where we partook very heartily of the hospitality of those living there and rested for the night. In the morning we resumed our way, very much refreshed. Our journey throughout was marked with hardship, toil, suffering, cold, hunger and almost starvation, and to add to our troubles there was an abundance of flies, gnats and mosquitoes, which were so numerous that the sky was completely darkened. The only way by which we were able to free ourselves from the mosquitoes was by cutting branches of small trees and using them as brushes. It would require too much time for me to describe in minute detail the scenes through which our journey led us, but they are nevertheless, as fresh in my memory as the events of yesterday or today.

At last, our journey ended where our little cabin stood surrounded by tall trees, through whose branches the rays of sun came pouring serenely down, and we thanked God for having brought us safely through our long and weary journey. The place where we settled was about six miles from the now beautiful city of Ionia, and as the custom among the settlers was to aid every one that came into the settlement, it was not long before we were provided with a comfortable home. We still met with some difficulty, however, for on several occasions we were at the edge of starvation in consequence of our provisions not reaching us promptly. But after many days of anxiety we received all our provisions, and were able to assist many of our needy neighbors, and received in return their heartfelt thanks and blessing. The Indians were all around us, and some of them caused us trouble by their treachery and stealing, and we had to take care that nothing was left around within their reach. As a rule, however, they were generally honest in their dealings, never taking advantage only when it was taken of them.

The years have rolled away. The country has become more thickly populated, and now we have before us all the benefits and blessings of the earth, with happiness for our portion instead of woe and want. No poisonous serpents hiss, no howling animals, fierce and wild, roam the fields where we were wont to find them on every side. Our youthful days are gone, our toils and privations are over, and now:

Honor comes, a pilgrim gray,
To bless the pioneers today;
While some have passed away to rest,
With all our greatest wishes blessed.

And thus it was and is, my friends. Where once was heard the howling wolf is now the peaceful home. Where once was seen the towering forest is now beheld the beautiful city, with its prosperous people, its many avenues, and its busy marts, and where the cold hand of starvation covered the weary pilgrim, now health, happiness, and abundance shed their mingled delights over the enchanting scene, while fields, teeming with their rich products now lend a helping hand to swell the streams.

New York Governor DeWitt Clinton ceremoniously wedded the waters of Lake Erie with the Atlantic Ocean at the opening of the Erie Canal in 1825.

Oakland County: 1846
by
Charity Stevens

Charity Stevens was nearly 90 when she wrote the following essay for the Pontiac Woman's Club in 1906. Like many Michigan pioneers she had originally lived in western New York. The first part of her narrative demonstrates that the hardships experienced in frontier Michigan mirrored similar circumstances encountered by those who had first settled western New York the generation before.

I was born in Cayuga village, New York, August 10, 1808. When three years old my mother died and left nine children, of whom I was the youngest. My father and one brother were drowned in Cayuga Lake when I was but five years old. When I was seven I came to western New York with my sister and her family. They settled on the Holland Purchase,[192] fifty miles east of Buffalo. It was wild country, with very heavy timber. They felled trees enough to make room for a house, which they built of logs and covered with oak shakes, which were held down by poles. We had no nails only those made by hand. Well do I remember the great wonder when cut nails were introduced.

They made the chimney of sticks and mud, the hearth and oven of stone, the floor of basswood logs, split and notched down to the sleepers. Chamber floors were made of bark peeled from large trees. I remember our buttery[193] was made by boring holes in the logs and putting in large sticks and laying a board across them on which to put our pewter plates and wooden trenchers. Our milk room was made in the same way.

The years 1817 and 1818 were cold seasons. The frost spoiled the corn. We lived six weeks without bread in the spring of 1818. Sometimes we could get wild meat such as deer, rabbits, etc. Our folks paid twenty shillings per bushel for wheat and twenty dollars per barrel for one hog pork. The men would feed their cattle by cutting down trees in the winter and the cattle would eat the buds. The hogs would fat on beechnuts.

When I was eighteen I went to Lawrenceville, Pennsylvania, where I had a brother living next door to the high school. Here I remained three years and attended school I had another brother in Cattaraugus County, New York. I went there to teach school. This was, at that time, a new and hard country, heavy timber, very frosty, a grazing country, would not produce wheat. At that time the principal way they got flour was to cut down timber, burn it to ashes, make salts, take it to Dunkirk, thirty miles through the woods with an ox team, and change it for flour.

The principal bread was of corn, and while teaching there and boarding around, as was then the custom, I have eaten it for my breakfast, carried it for my dinner and eaten it for my supper, yet one of the best schools and brightest scholars I ever had was there.

I came to Oxford fifty years[194] ago and settled on the farm on which I now reside. There were thirty acres of girdlings, forty acres of timber and 142 acres of stone. The buildings were just a barn and a comfortable house, no out building, not even a hen or hog house. There was but one small excuse for a store. Could not sell a pound of butter or a dozen of eggs in Oxford. Pontiac, twenty miles away, was our nearest market. Detroit can be reached now in less time and much easier, for it would take one day and part of two nights to go and return from there. There was no market for wool. We could not sell a sheep only to a hungry man.

I remember the first winter I spent in Oxford. I had six in my family and I had but six pounds of sugar in six months. Canned fruit, meat and vegetable had not been heard of them.

Pioneer life has its benefits as well as its disadvantages. One is, you can live plainer and nearer to nature which is conducive to good health and longevity as well. There is no aristocracy, all are on a level. Pioneer people are kind and obliging. It is here that self reliance is cultivated, that great essential to success in a person's character.

Although there are to me many pleasant recollections of pioneer life, yet no person is more deeply interested in the progress of the age or more able to see the contrast between then and now. I have watched the progress of the age, with the greatest interest, until I am convinced that man is not a condemned but a progressive being and if there is any limit to his progress it is yet far, very far out of sight. He can walk through he mountains, talk through the ocean, ride under the rivers and sail among the clouds already and the end is not yet.

Pentwater: 1854
by
Elvira Barber Lewis

Generally speaking, settlement of Michigan proceeded east to west along the southern most tiers of counties and then the frontier moved north. But there were many exceptions to this trend. Communities like Flint. Saginaw, Grand Haven and others got an early start. But pockets of wilderness remained within the lower tiers of counties well into the 1840s and 1850s. Lansing for example, did not exist prior to 1847. That same year Dutch colonists first settled Holland and they experienced all the vicissitudes suffered by the pioneers of the previous two decades. The pioneer era for Michigan, in fact, would continue well into the 20th century as succeeding waves of economic exploitation motivated settlers to immigrate to lumbering frontiers, mineral frontiers, railroad frontiers and other outposts on the periphery of civilization.

Many entrepreneurs, in particular, responded to the opportunities brought through the harvesting of Michigan's great stands of timber by establishing saw mills. At those sites pioneer communities often developed. Such was the case with the origins of Pentwater as described by Elvira Barber Lewis in a paper written for the Pentwater Woman's Club.

Very few, I think, would have recognized our charming village with its pleasant environments in the small settlement which I found here over fifty years ago. Imagine, if you can, this entire town instead of pretty lawns and grassy plats a barren sand covered place, not a blade of grass growing, a few ferns the only vegetation save the trees, that were mostly pine.

At the foot of what is now Hancock Street was a lumber mill erected by Messrs. Cobb and Rector.[195] This firm bought of the government the present site of Pentwater in the year 1849. A boarding house was built on the site of what is now known as the Reed House. A part of this boarding house was afterward moved and now stands the second house east on Second Street; this, then, is the oldest house in our village. These buildings, with a barn and work shop, comprised Pentwater. The only stock owned by the settlers was a single yoke of oxen. One of these was exceedingly useful as it often served as a ferryboat in crossing the channel. The name Pentwater was taken from the name the Indians had given the lake. [196]

The first families to locate here were those of Messrs. Cobb, Rogers, Barnes, Barber, and Rector; two other, Messrs. Glover and Harding, settled up the river and were engaged in cutting the logs for the mill. A Mr. and Mrs. Rosevelt [197] had been here in 1853, he being identified with the building of the mill. Mrs. Rosevelt was the first white woman to come to Pentwater. If we had any record of Mr. Rosevelt hunting the bear in these wilds we might, perhaps, think him a relative of the president. [198]

In the year 1854, July 4th was celebrated. We did not have an oration delivered, the Declaration of Independence was not read, we had not even a brass band, nor was there a gun fired, but it was Independence Day and our neighbors from the North Claybanks [199] came down in a small fishing boat, and when we saw at a distance the red and white sun bonnets worn by the ladies and the blue shirts worn by the gentlemen we almost imagined we could see "Old Glory." We certainly saw its colors. We passed the day very quietly, but never since has July 4th been more pleasantly celebrated in Pentwater.

In September of that year a sad accident occurred. Among the settlers was a man named Barnes, who, with his son, was usually employed about the mill. This day business took them up the river. Near nightfall their empty canoe came floating down. One of the bodies, their hats and an oar were found the next day, but we never knew how the accident happened. The interment of this body was the first burial; no funeral services were held.

That year late in fall, as in all years since, perhaps, frequent and severe wind storms prevailed. After such a storm it was the custom for some of the settlers to go to the lake to see if their assistance was needed in aiding unfortunate vessel or crew which might have been driven upon the beach during the storm. One morning upon going down they found a vessel on the south beach freighted with hardware. The men were all on deck and appeared nearly helpless, but upon seeing the men on shore they roused themselves and, writing a note they placed it in a bottle which they fastened to the cabin door and set it afloat. When it reached shore the men found the note to be in substance a prayer for those on shore to aid them in reaching land, that they were nearly exhausted, having been many hours without food, their provision box having been swept off at the beginning of the storm. They had worked hard the entire night trying to lighten the boat by throwing the cargo overboard. The settlers worked long and faithfully, at last a line was secured and the men were all saved - there were sixteen. It was near midnight when they reached the boarding house where we had prepared hot coffee and a good meal. The sailors remained several days with us, they finally went to Grand Haven, walking the entire distance. The name of the vessel was found to be the *Wright*.[200] Many of the nails used in our first buildings were from this wreck as kegs and kegs of them were found.

During the winter lumbering was carried on to some extent about half a mile from our main street. The wolves were quite troublesome to the workmen, gnawing the ax and saw handles if left during the night, and as winter advanced they seemed even dangerous. One time in particular the few settlers were frightened somewhat by them. It was night time and we were awakened by the howling of wolves in the distance. The noise became almost deafening as they drew nearer and on looking from the window we saw a great pack of them halted in front of the house as if about to attack it, but upon our placing lights in the windows they fled. You can hardly imagine the feeling of relief I experienced when I saw them disappearing across the lake. It was this year, 1854, that a daughter was born to Mr. and Mrs. Nelson Glover - the first white child born in Pentwater.

The first time the United States mail was brought to us was in February, 1855. Mr. E.R. Cobb was our first postmaster. Think of going, or rather sending to Chicago for our mail. In 1856 our settlement had grown from a mere handful to nearly a hundred people. A town meeting was held and the following officers elected: Supervisor, E.R. Cobb; Clerk, James Dexter; Treasurer, N. Rogers; Highway Commissioner, A. Rector. One hundred fifty dollars was voted for township expenses. It was in 1856 that Mr. Charles Mears came to our village and built a mill and boarding house just north of the ferry; in 1857 he built a store. Mr. Mears called his part of the village Middlesex. The first

Pentwater as it appeared ca. 1890.

manager of the Mear's House was our well known friend James Brooker and wife. Mr. H.C. Flagg, as Mr. Mear's general manager, came to Pentwater this year; also Dr. Wear, E.D. Richmond and many others. The natural channel from Pentwater Lake to Lake Michigan was at this time far to the north of what it now is, connecting with the big pond near the sand hills. This year it was made to lead perfectly straight from Pentwater Lake. This great improvement was accomplished mainly through the efforts and enterprise of Mr. Mears.

The first minister sent to this township was the Rev. Beard in 1858. Then came the Rev. Naylor, who was followed the following year, 1860, by the Rev. H.M. Joy, who encouraged the pioneers by frequent visits and word of cheer. The first semblance of a store was a trading hooker conducted by Mr. Chapin. From this could be bought many useful articles if the boat was in port when you wanted them.

In 1859 a change was made, J. Brillhart and H. Tower purchased the Cobb and Rector mill. This new firm opened a store at the corner of Third and Hancock Streets in what is known as the Turner building. The families of C.R. Whittington, William Webb and Captain E. Irons came to our village this year. These people have helped materially in making Pentwater the charming place it is. Mr. A. J. Underhill, T. Collister, the Craine family, J. Corlett, P. Labonta and many other came this year and were engaged in fishing; barrels and barrels were shipped from this port. The first school was taught by Miss. Emily Daniels, now Mrs. Croxson of Muskegon. The schoolroom was a part of a dwelling house where eight young urchins alternately whispered, chewed gum, went to the stove, got a drink, threw paper wads and whittled the seats as children have done in all time.

Pentwater had now increased to a settlement of sufficient importance to make the want of a newspaper apparent. The first was issued in 1861, the office being over the store of C. Mears. The editor was F. Ratzel, afterward a prominent journalist of Manistee. Mr Ratzel was a genuine newspaper man and issued a lively paper. [201]

I think many would smile if they could see the style of the hats worn by us in those early days. The new settlers bringing in the styles from outside made the female part of the population long for a milliner, and as we must be in style we were obliged to manufacture at least part of our bonnets. This we did by making the frames of starched mosquito netting, pressing the small back part over a pint basin, while the wide, flaring front was pressed over a two quart pan. These were decidedly stylish, but late in 1863 a milliner came. G.W. Faulkner and family came to Pentwater this year and Miss. Kate, a daughter, at once seeing the need, opened a milliner store, her capital was just five dollars. Early spring brought many new comers, houses were built, and our village seemed booming, but it was not until some years later that by a special act of the legislature the village of Pentwater became incorporated and held its first election, which was as follows: President, C.W. Dean; Recorder, E.B. Flagg; Treasurer, John Highland; Assessor, O.P.Cook; Trustees, D.C. Pelton, I.N. Lewis, J.J. Kittridge, A. Bryant, J. Bean, W.M. Merritt.202 It was a Republican victory and hailed as such. In the evening, jubilant over their success, they formed a procession and headed by a martial band, marched through the streets, cheering and firing guns. Thus ended the first election of the village of Pentwater, the first village of the County of Oceana.

Pioneer life anywhere must of necessity be rather trying, but I can say I truly enjoyed those early days, and it is with a feeling of satisfaction that I glance back to those pioneer times. They were years well spent by all of us; we were so helpful to each other, "sharing each other's sorrows, sharing each other's joys." Hospitality is to be found in a marked degree in all new settlements and Pentwater was indeed no exception. We always had plenty of room and enough to eat for all who came. Once, I believe, the supply of flour was rather short; in fact, the men for a time denied themselves white bread, but they were quite content with brown. The people seemed united in a sort of brotherhood with the same object in view, to make comfortable homes for their families rather than to acquire wealth.

I well remember the bright morning of June 18,1854, when I arrived in Pentwater on the *Spartan*, a sailing vessel which made regular trips between this port and Chicago for the purpose of bringing supplies to the settlers and in return taking to Chicago the lumber cut by the mill. The vessel anchored outside, as the natural channel was too shallow for the boat to enter. The passengers, four in number, went ashore in a small boat. I shall never forget how the great waste of sand looked to me, the like of which I had never seen before, my home having always been near the Green Mountains of Vermont

Benzie County: 1868
by
Martha Gray

For our final selection we travel to what has become one of the state's most renowned resort regions - the Grand Traverse country.

In a paper written for the Michigan Pioneer Society in 1912 Martha Gray described her experiences in Benzie County in the 1860s. At that time Civil War veterans and their families were flocking to a wilderness as rugged as the southern sections of the state had been four decades before.

The women who pioneerd this region experienced the same loneliness, isolation, fear of failure and danger as earlier pioneers. Gray's family struggled for survival in a strange land, attempting to cultivate the sandy soil while relying on a son's income earned in the lumber camps, maple sugar production and hunting passenger pigeons. Not until 1872 when the railroad reached Traverse City would the pioneer era in the Grand Traverse region begin to recede.

In 1863 northern Michigan was thrown into the market through the homestead law[203] and from that time on its future was assured. Men began flocking into the region and upon the close of the war nearly every quarter section was taken, many of them by the "boys in blue," and my father, Elijah Stata, was one who sought and found, for a time, a home in the wilderness. He was a born pioneer. His people left Holland at the close of the Spanish wars, crossed the Atlantic and settled at New Amsterdam. A generation or two later they left New York and migrated up the Mohawk Valley. In another generation or two, the country of the Mohawk becoming too settled, they moved again, this time into Canada. Still restless and roving, my father's generation started out, each taking a different direction. My father came into Michigan and owned a farm at Grand Ledge in an early day. He returned and made his home in New York for a time and there married my mother. Her parents had transmitted to their posterity the same roving inclination. They came from England, settled in Massachusetts and belonged to the Colburns, the Stowells and the Winchesters. Her grandfather was a paymaster in the Revolutionary War. They belonged to the stirring times when men were willing to lay down their lives for a good principle, to be sacrificed on the altar of the country they had chosen for the sake of freedom.

My father served through the Civil War and at the close went south to seek his fortune in that land that had been devastated by the War god. He found a more subtle foe lurking in the mud beds of the Missouri River flats than ever lay in ambush or was met on the battle field. He buried a part of his family who had fallen victims to the Asiatic Cholera and returned North the same year. On arriving at Chicago we took passage for Ogdensburgh and on that same steamer met a man named Johnson who was returning to Glen Arbor, having been "outside" to purchase supplies. He told father such glowing stories of the wealth of the wild, new country, the timber, the land for nothing, the ease in which one could become a well to do man that father would gladly have ended the journey at Glen Arbor but our mother would not. The next spring father returned and worked all summer for John Dorsey making fish barrels. Whitefish were abundant in Lake Michigan at that time in 1868. That autumn my father returned east and moved his family into Grand Traverse region. We children were delighted and happy that the change was to be made; for we like all children thought a new country and new people would bring us many things and we were not disappointed though the things brought were not expected.

One sunny day in September, *Oswegatchie* of the Western Transportation line, Capt. Rossman in command, landed us safely on the little dock at Glen Arbor. The only business the boat had at that dock was to take on wood and leave us, together with another family. Glen Arbor was like many other things one sees on maps, a name only. A dreary stretch of pure white sand, a few cabins completely hidden by small oak and pine trees, a hotel and no guests, a small general store owned by the Northern Transportation line, and a post office kept by George Ray in his home, completed the whole. The only industries, cord wood chopping to supply the steamers passing over the lakes and the taking of whitefish which were salted and shipped to outside markets. Here we began to hear the term "outside."

Anyone not living here, lived "outside." We thought this a very peculiar expression but in time its full significance grew upon us. We were to know some day that no other word could be used in its stead. It exactly expressed the condition, we were inside and the great world all outside.

Father decided we must get the things together again and finish our journey and be in the new home before winter would be upon us. We had been stopping in Glen Arbor until mother was strong enough to take the journey of twenty-five miles to the farm that father had chosen. Our baby was but three weeks old when we landed at Glen Arbor and that journey of twenty-five miles was considered more arduous than all the hundreds and hundreds we had come. Wagon journeys in the early days were difficult, and it took long hours to make short distances. Already father had gone with two loads and had taken two days for the journey and the next trip my brother Seth and I were to go. Mother and the little children would come last. One beautiful morning the wagons were again brought to the door and loaded and I took my seat by my father's side, Seth rode with the man who drew the other team, and we began that toilsome journey. The country was rough and hill upon hill rose before us. The patient horses kept climbing higher and higher. At every step we were jolted and nearly thrown from the wagon. But as often as we were jolted over a root on one side just so often were we jolted on the other and thus our equilibrium was preserved. When we had gone ten miles we came to the crest of the hills that formed the background to Glen Arbor and here we stopped to rest and feed the horses and eat our lunch. From here, the view was magnificent. Stretching away over miles and miles the country and great lakes lay before us and at the foot of the hills lay an inland lake nine miles across which was called Glen Lake. It was only one half mile from Lake Michigan and men had planned to open a channel so that vessels could seek a safe harbor there from storms that were frequently occurring on the great lake. Away over Lake Michigan we could see the great Manitous so far away that they could be seen only on a clear day. And to the northward lay old "Sleeping Bear." It was late in the day when we came to a place where father stopped the horses and calling to Seth told him to help me from the wagon. "Now," said he, "it is only two and one-half miles home and you two will run through the woods and get there much sooner than we can by the wagon road. Seth, be sure and follow the blazed trees and do not lose the trail, for if you do, you will perish in the woods." Father had six miles to make by road so Seth took my hand and we started on the trail.

Just as night fall was upon us, we emerged from the forest into a tiny clearing and Seth said, "This is home." There was a pond, a tiny dark pool, the forest leaves lying deep to the water's edge. Across the yard stood a log cabin and at the end of the pond another log cabin, and still another log building stood on a hill, the strangest looking building I had ever seen, just a square tower whose top was surmounted by a shaft with four great arms outspread. The solemn stillness of everything had begun to impress me and we were thankful that we were to have neighbors at least, for a family lived in a house at the end of the lake, and at the other was to be our future home. We crossed to the cabin. Seth lifted the wooden latch and we entered. Our cook stove was there, father having brought it with the first load, so that we could cook, and it was all up and ready. Seth built a fire and we sat in the light of it until some time after dark, when father came. He had lighted himself through the woods with a lantern. Soon after we had a light and supper. The old man whom we had met the year before and through whose influence we had been brought to our present condition came in the evening. It was his son who lived in the same clearing and was to be our neighbor. His name was Lije Johnson and his wife's name was "Marthy." "Lije" and "Marthy" it was from the from the beginning. Everyone was called by his first name. Older men were called "Old Man." The "Old Man" had married a second woman and she had left him and gone to her relatives "outside." He was going in the spring. Father had bought out the old man's improvement and that was how we had even this small beginning in the wilderness. In the evening the old man and his son Lije came in and the four, father and the teamster, fell into war reminiscences.

It was the first day of November when mother arrived and not a day too soon for the second day the snow began to fall gently, silently, without any warning whatever. It snowed fifty-one days, then the sun came out one day only, then the snow began again as it had done in the beginning, never any effort, never any noise, no sign of storm, no wind, no roar, no rush, just gently, silently fell; and mother sat in the cabin and wept all the time. We children did not run out to play for there was no place to play, nothing to play with and we could only stand by the two little windows and watch the snow fall and wonder if spring would ever come and it was not Christmas yet, that joyous time for children, a time lost to us now, and worst of all we had no books.

It was not long before we began to be acquainted with our new neighbors, the Johnsons. They lived in an adjoining township, the line was right through our clearing, they on one side, we on the other, our cabins but a few rods apart. "The "old man" Johnson was a tall thin man and had such an unkempt appearance that he might easily have passed for a denizen of the most remote part of "Arkansaw." I can never forget him for he sat by our fireside many a night during that dreary winter and told such queer stories as we had never heard before. He had taken up a homestead allowed soldiers of the Civil War. In time he could expect a pension and then hoped to make a home in a more civilized section. His son Lije could not be induced to become a worker and contrived a mill to be operated by the wind, which could not be relied upon. The forests failed to furnish sufficient wind to perform the task and so a huge coffee mill was successfully run by hand power, probably the first of its kind in Grand Traverse County. A part of the mill was used as a factory for making crude furniture. "Marthy" did not keep her cabin, her cabin kept her. She said she had not descended from working people and could not work. Such were our neighbors, the Johnsons.

Rev. Charles Williams, a homesteader living in the township of Kasson,[204] ten miles away, held services once in four weeks and wished to use the Stata cabin for this object, and in this way all the neighbors could meet the newcomers. The snow was over a foot deep and falling so fast that any road or path was impossible but nearly all were present.

A young woman whom the people called Melvina said she was going to have two "bees" at her house on Tuesday, a "chopping bee" and a "quilting bee" and she invited mother and told her to bring her daughter. Another woman whom the people called "Sary Ann" said she had been invited and would come for us if we could go and mother promised she would. The people took their departure and the next morning no one would have known that a footprint had been made in the snow.

The next Tuesday the neighbor came for us. Her husband, Harvey Noble, was the only man in the township who owned a team of horses. he had brought them hundreds of miles and knew if anything happened to them that they could not be replaced. He was raising a little corn and millet, had gathered some wild marsh hay and his sons purchased some feed at Glen Arbor which Mr. Noble had succeeded in getting home before the snow was too deep for travel. His two sons chopped cord wood at Glen Arbor to earn money to pay for the feed. The house where the "bees" were to be held was very small, made of logs, the roof covered with shakes, the floor made of puncheons and the cracks chinked with moss. There was an old fashioned elevated oven cook stove, one bed, a table made of boards and some chairs Lije Johnson had manufactured in his factory. There were holes bored in the logs in one corner and large wooden pins driven into them, then wide shakes laid across the pins to form the cupboard. When noon came she got out a loaf of bread and cutting a slice gave it to her child, a boy of two years, but no move was made toward dinner. We found out afterwards that the woman had food for one meal and that was to be at supper time and we had come too soon, and must go without dinner.

Soon after noon the people came to the "bees." The men went into the woods and by nightfall a large "slashing" had been made. The women began to work and the quilt was in a fair way to be finished, but there was only one window and long before the quilt was done they had to quit working as the room was too dark. The supper consisted of potatoes, pork, bread, tea, cornstalk pickles and sweet cake. The pickles were made of cucumbers salted with green cornstalks cut in pieces about the size of the cucumbers and tasted like the dill pickles on the market today. It was growing late and we ate hastily and started. The trail made by the horses could be followed and in good time we reached home. Then mother burst into tears and wept bitterly. What kind of a place had we come into? What kind of people were these? Father, ever hopeful, tried to tell her we would never be so poor, we would always have enough.

It was about Christmas time when mother decided to let Seth, now a healthy boy of seventeen go to Glen Arbor to work. The men were on the trail coming and going every week and the trail being through our clearing they were sure to stop both ways and tell stories. Father was a genial man and enjoyed seeing them, and mother's bread was good and the men were sure to get some thick slices if they were coming in from Glen Arbor. That walk of twenty-five miles was enough to sharpen any man's appetite. We had an abundance of food for the first year and mother dispensed it with a generous hand and the men were sure to stop. These men seeing Seth, a robust, rollicking youth just springing into manhood, thought he would enliven the camp and they persuaded mother to let him go. He could earn some clothing and his living, at least, and that would be of future use. The men declared he would have work for good and earnest by another winter and the present work would initiate him.

The cord wood camps were small flat-roofed shanties built of logs and sometimes the roofs were made of logs too. Basswood saplings were plentiful and the wood soft and easy to work up into long troughs and these troughs would be laid on for the roof and one tier of troughs fitting into the first row, completed and made the roof quite storm proof. A trough roof sounds queer but it was much easier to make the shallow toughs than split out shakes for a large roof and the troughs kept the storm out as well. Hemlock bark made a good serviceable roof and I have seen floors made of this material too. But in a new country anything that can be utilized must play a part in adding to the comfort of man, and the things that cost money must be avoided.

Seth's bundle was made ready and one Monday in company with three men he started over the trail. In coming and going they always had a company of three or more and walked single file. The first breaking the path for the rest, always with his eye on the blazed trees. When he became weary he fell out and dropped behind and the next man took the lead, and so on. Seth being the boy, fell in the rear and the path was a blessing, considering the heavy bundle, his youth and the twenty-five miles.

Our mother decided to go in search of a small store[205] that she had heard was located three miles from us in Almira Township, owned and conducted by Matt Burnett who had come into the country two years before and had brought some money with him. His father took up a homestead and built a small frame house, the lumber coming principally form Traverse City and a little mill on what was afterwards called Ransome's Creek. The sons, Matt and Sam, bought from the state, the school section,[206] and began operations on it. The Burnetts were real pioneers. They had brought into the country some money and a determination to win. Matt had married a woman of culture and their coming was a great uplift to the community. They built a good sized frame building all unfinished at the time and today after forty-four years it is unfinished still, and in this building they opened the store. The articles they had for sale were the common things, pork, flour, tea, sugar, matches and other simple supplies. Their goods were hauled from Traverse City fifteen miles to the east, and many times when someone had walked many weary miles to purchase these simple supplies they found Mr. Burnett 'out' or they must wait until he could get them in from Traverse City. It was to this store our mother decided to go. Our baby was four months old and she could not leave him, so she planned to carry him one mile on the way and leave me to care for him until her return. In this clearing lived two families, Mrs. Sally Fuller and her stepson Wesley. When she reached the next clearing she found no one living there. Levi Mansfield, a bachelor, owned the place and he was at Glen Arbor chopping wood. There were four roads leading out of this clearing and mother used her best judgment and chose the one she thought right, and plunged into the woods again. After what seemed an endless journey she came out into the strangest clearing she had ever seen, a strip four rods wide and extending both ways as far as the eye could reach. She had never seen or heard of anything like this before, and decided she was lost and would not see the little store that day, and began to return her steps. The snow was falling all the time and she was very weary and growing more faint and tired with each step forward. When she reached the last clearing where she lost the right trail, all trace of her tracks made in the morning were gone, but remembering the house and how she approached it she struggled through the snow and reached the woods to find the path again. When she came in sight of the log shanty she sank down exhausted and began to cry for help. It was growing late in the day and the evening shadows were gathering in the forest. Wesley Fuller chopping wood at his door heard her cry and hastened to her assistance and helped her into the shanty. His wife brewed some tea and gave her something to eat, helped her to dry her clothing and when she was somewhat refreshed Wesley ran over to Sally's house and got the child and carried him to mother. His joy know no bounds when he again rested on her bosom. When mother was ready to start, Wesley took the sleeping child in his arms and going before us breaking the path, carried the child all the way home. She had gone eight miles through that awful storm but it was the last time she ever undertook such a journey. Wesley Fuller told her that the queer place was the Allegan and Traverse City State Road[207] that had recently been opened up.

By the first of February the snow was so deep all traveling

was done on snowshoes and the men came over the trail carrying as much provisions as they were able to "back" home. Money was not to be had in large quantities at Glen Arbor and if they had received all money, supplies were not nearer to them than Traverse City or Glen Arbor. Everything at Glen Arbor was under the control of the Northern Transportation Company and good serviceable clothing and common staples could be obtained in exchange for work performed. But prices were high at the close of the awful Civil War, tea two dollars a pound; pork and sugar twenty-five cents a pound; flour eighteen dollars a barrel, and after the men had chopped cord wood to earn the necessities of life and then carried them home on their backs twenty-five miles they thought that they were doubly earned and that they had paid a high price for them.

In the month of March the men came home to make maple sugar and Seth came too, and doing as the rest did, he brought all he could carry and that was a large piece of salt pork. He had earned his living, some good stout clothes and had enough left to purchase the pork. When we saw him on the trail he was a funny sight. He was exhausted and could not carry the pork. He had cut a hole through the tough rind, fastened a stout string to it and was dragging it through the snow behind him. The cord wood camps were broken up. The men had come home. The sun shone out once more and when the days grew a little warmer the maple sap began to run up the trees and the sugar making was on.

Nearly all the settlers had some rude outfit for sugar making, troughs hewn from pine logs, large iron kettles for boiling the sap down, but occasionally a lucky man had a large sheet or galvanized iron pan and these came slowly into the country. It was almost impossible to get things at first. We had some kettles and father, doing as the others did, hewed out some troughs to catch the sap and we made sugar too. It seemed that there would never be an end to the sugar making. The snow was fully six weeks in going off and then long after it was gone the sap kept running. The last runs of sap were converted into sugar for beer making and some of the sap boiled just thick enough to turn into vinegar. For the manufacture of our beer we went into the woods and gathered princess pine, winter-green and squaw-berries, hemlock boughs, sarsaparilla and all things of this nature we could find and boiled them in plenty of water, strained and sweetened the mixture and put it in a wooden tub. Then mother made hop yeast and mixed; in a few hours later it would begin to ferment and a day or two later was ready for use. This was a good spring medicine and was a delicious drink, nearly all the settlers made this healthful beer and felt happy to treat a visiting neighbor to a copious draught.

We had commented on the great depth of snow, time and again and thought there would be heavy rains and a general breaking up and that the whole country would be flooded with water. But no such thing happened. The snow went as it came, silently, gently, no rush, no roar, just went. Things did not move in this new country at all like anything we had ever seen before and father would say: "The ground cannot hold all the water, there must be some outlet for it," and all in good time the outlet was found. The sun kept shining and it had stopped snowing. The moisture had all fallen from the atmosphere, a change had taken place, and finally the ground was bare and dry, no mud like we had seen in New York State, just dry ground.

As soon as the little pond was open in the spring, the frogs began to sing and a little later, toads came by hundreds from, no one could tell where, and hopped into the tiny pool and floated there day after day swelling their little throats and singing such happy songs of gladness that we thought no creature large or small was ever so happy to see spring come. After a few weeks the toads went as they had come, and a little later the whole clearing was alive with the tiniest little black toads that ever could be. We were not annoyed by the toads for we had seen them all our lives and the frogs were old friends too, but snakes were around the little pond in such numbers that father decided to try and destroy them. He and Seth cut stout poles and went around the pond several times each day killing all they could find and they killed as many as twelve in once going around. But they were there always, the bane of our lives; for at any time one was liable to come upon them and receive the shock that every individual experiences when encountering a snake.

The sugar things were finally gathered up and stored away for the next season and other work begun. A garden must be made and we started work at that. We began to find out something of the soil of this new country which we had come into. We thought we understood half of the climate and the summer would finish the acquaintance; we will see if it did. Father began to spade up the ground for lettuce and peas and lo and behold! the soil was only an inch or two thick on the top, the rest all sand and in patches pure white sand. No wonder the snow had gone off without visible signs. The whole country was like a great sieve and the water had run through it and away to feed the little ponds. In after years we found that the country had been at some remote time all under water and salt water at that. The fossil remains of coral and other evidences of salt seas were found n abundance. But at first we knew nothing of these things and gathered the coral to garnish tiny beds in the garden. In after years we were to know something of the world's history and this strange, new country was to have a deeper meaning for us. The country was new in every sense of the word, fresh from its long sea bath; and the soil, the accumulation of the few centuries that had elapsed since its baptism by the sea, could have no depth. How that magnificent forest ever grew in that soil is a mystery to all who know the country. Neither was the soil alike in all places; perhaps one quarter section would be all sand with giant pines and hemlocks, the next some depth of soil with beach and maple interspersed. Around the ponds was sand always and there were clearings, for men soon found that water could not be had on the highland without going to the level of the great lake - in after years, there were wells in the great country over two hundred feet deep.

There was another strange thing in this new country that same spring worth recording. The people had told us of the pigeons[208] and how they came there every year to nest, and that they had killed them for food. The had even gone into their nesting places and taken the squabs by the sackful, and told what fine eating they were. We had thought these stories might have some truth but were not prepared for the deluge that came upon us. As soon as the buds began to swell and weather to grow warm they came by the millions. I have seen flocks fly so low and so thick that Seth actually knocked them down with a stick. We finally did not try to shoot them, it was a waste of powder and shot. Once Seth killed nineteen at a single shot by firing into a flock that were flying through the clearing. So we put up the gun and set some traps by the little pond where they came down to drink and caught all we could use. They nested just a few miles from where we were located and Seth and I went to see them at home. Their homes were simplicity itself, a few sticks laid on a tiny crotch of a tree, that was all, and the trees were literally full of them. How the queer nests ever held the eggs and kept them from falling to the ground is a mystery.

The beech trees were the only nut bearing ones in the country and they bore abundantly. That was one reason why the pigeons came. Another reason was the solitude which they like for their brooding and food for their young. Some of the pigeons always lingered through the summer as though they were watching nature to see if food would be forthcoming another year.

Father, mother and Seth, worked out of doors, I did the work inside and took care of the baby, a boy nine months old by this time. Mother had declared over and over again that she would leave the country as soon as spring came, but now that spring had come, there were as many strange things, clearing land, etc., to do there was no time to move. Her Puritan spirit came to the front to assist her and she decided to stay and subdue one spot in the wilderness. She had brought an abundance of garden and other seeds from New York State and garden making together with other work was dear to her heart. There was sure to be an outlet for her energies, and I think she enjoyed the toil at first.

Lije Johnson would come over and help father and Seth roll logs together on our land; then they would go over and roll on his; and before the summer was ended the tiny clearing was enlarged by several acres. The Old Man Johnson lingered on waiting for a payment on the land, there was still some money coming from the sale of the old home, but he never got it when it did come, for our mother was a practical woman and kept the money to keep her children from starving while we were helping to develop a new country.

The garden was made, some potatoes and corn planted, new land being cleared for the latter, but no grain of any kind could be sown for there was no land for grain. Not a spear of grass growing on the tiny clearing could we find, but we began to explore the country some and when we found a bunch of grass, it grew in bunches, we always dug it up and carried it home and mother set it out in the yard, a beginning of what would take years to finish. It was years and years before grass seed would catch and grow evenly. It grew in stools or bunches as though nature was so perverted that she refused to perform her proper function and only sported. The garden seeds came up that we had sown, but the plants were sickly looking things as if they too were out of their natural element and refused to luxuriate in that virgin soil.

The sun kept right on shining ever since the snow had

stopped and continued to shine. We brought water from the little pond and watered the garden as best we could and wondered when the rain would fall. There was not a breath of air and the little clearing blazed like a furnace. The mosquitoes swarmed by millions and made the nights miserable, adding their stings to the intense heat. Occasionally we could see great thunder heads away to the west and hear the deep mutterings caused by the positive and negative forces of the upper air coming together, but the clouds rolled away, and the thunder died in the distance, and no rain fell on the parched earth. We almost thought we had come into a world of chance and if one thing chanced to be it kept right on, that was the way the snow had done, and now the sun had come and it seemed that the very heavens were turned to brass and everything would melt with heat. I could go on indefinitely in this strain for the sun shone all summer and no rain fell. Sometimes there would be a sprinkle but not enough to wet the thirsty earth. And the wind never blew. Everything seemed to be under a spell of an enchanter, silently waiting some magic touch to awaken to life the dormant nature that had been asleep through the centuries.

When spring opened we began to look around to see what the country offered for pleasure, instruction or maintenance. We found almost no flowers, we fished in the pond but found no fish. In after years, fish were planted and can be caught in many of the ponds now. We discovered that there were almost no animals there either; occasionally a bear, later some deer, but they are both gone long since. In the twenty-five years that I lived there, I never saw but two bears. There was nothing for animals to live on. It seemed that vegetation outside the magnificent forest was paralyzed, and ground hemlock was the only green thing in the woods. We were a quarter of a mile from a road and half a mile from the nearest neighbor, excepting the Johnson's. Many of the people were poor and uneducated, having no experience in life, only the male portion had been in the war. If we lived we must work, wait and suffer and then perhaps we could not see any of the results of our toil.

Fourth of July came and went but we scarcely thought of the day. We were out of the world and had enjoyed our last celebration of the nation's independence, for some years to come. Every four weeks the same minister came and preached what he called the gospel. I think he was orthodox but he had no theology. He did not understand the term at that time so he taught what he knew, and that was the stories he had heard in his childhood, and the conclusions he had come to in his early manhood. I had heard these stories all my life and could understand them, but the plan of salvation as laid down by some churches had always been such a mystery to me that I could not understand it then and just wondered what it was all about. But here in the wilderness was a man who told stories instead of teaching mysteries and they were such wonder stories that they took root in the fertile soil of the unfilled brains of the listeners. These meetings were the only things to remind us that it was Sunday. We had heard the last church bell ring that we should hear for years to come and everything of an intellectual nature was swept like a flood from us. All that was left for us was nature in its simplest form; no garnished nature with bud and bloom made beautiful, just unadorned nature, grim, silent and forbidding.

Occasionally some would set a slashing on fire and not watch it carefully enough and the fire would run through the forest and the clearings would be filled with smoke and the nights made fearful by the glare of the fire from the burning timber. But these fires were of great benefit for the undergrowth would be burned away and the next year the berry bushes would spring up as if by magic and the second year the berries would begin to come. There were none at first. Trees and ground hemlock seemed to be the garment chosen by nature to adorn herself in.

The first summer wore away as it had begun. There was nothing when it opened and there was nothing at its close, a few nubbins of corn, some potatoes, only a little money left and starvation seemed near. We had seen nothing but work with no results. Father was hopeful and would say, "The country is new and all will come right in time." One thing was sure, we could make arrangements and another season see how large a crop of maple sugar we could gather. The nubbins of corn were carefully gathered and carefully housed in the loft, the potatoes were stored in a deep hole under the floor, more corn was purchased - we must live on that now - and we got ready for when that awful snow was on and no one could get in or out. In the early fall father and Seth went to Lime Lake, a mile from us, and cut down some pine trees, sawed them into bolts, the proper length for sap buckets and piled them ready to be hauled home when the snow came. There was so little money left that it was decided that Seth should go to Glen Arbor the first thing in the fall and work all winter. It might be necessary to use his wages to keep the wolf away from the door and his clothes were made ready for his departure. We began to understand something of how we must proceed in order to keep soul and body together. The soul might shrivel until scarcely an atom of the Divine be left and the body grow gaunt and ugly for want of nourishment, yet they would cling to each other.

The summer had ended; we had worked, hoped and were not rewarded by any results from toil. We had heard from the old home once or twice. The nearest post office was six miles away. The mail was brought irregularly on the back of an Indian. When I was sent to get any mail that had come, I went with two or three other girls and it took a whole day. But there was one advantage in that, we had to stop and rest and we were sure to stop at some cabin and thus get acquainted with the people. The first time I met my mother-in-law, was on my first trip to the post office. I saw her a good many times after that, for when I was married I lived among my husband's people for twenty-one years and we got pretty well acquainted.

We were less prepared for the second winter. Father and I went over a mile to Lime Lake and brought home on a hand sleigh pine bolts which he split with a fro and made into staves for sap buckets. Our cabin was turned into a cooper shop and only on Sundays, the house being specially cleared up, had any semblance of a home. By this method we kept track of Sundays. Father made hundreds of buckets to gather the sap and tubs to hold the syrup which was strained through heavy woolen bags to eliminate the lime. Many of the pioneers had only sap troughs made from logs cut in two. He also made an iron pan in which to boil down the sap. These pans had sides of wood and were placed over arches which contained the fire. We made many hundred pounds of fine maple sugar. Food was scarce and the best mother could do was to contrive new methods of preparing the corn which was our only dependence. Mother suffered more than any of us as she was ill and hopeless. Seth worked at Glen Arbor and at long intervals came with tea and pork.

Father took the sugar with an ox team to Glen Arbor where it was shipped to a rich uncle of mother's in Detroit and sold to good advantage. With the money he bought a horse and wagon and many things needed. Our aunt sent a barrel of clothing and no present, past or future, can ever again be so acceptable.

Our sister Sarah who had been left in New York State came in July, and in August another sister was added to our family.

Dr. Wilson was our physician coming to us from Kasson Township, Leelanau County. He was an excellent doctor and fine scholar, teaching school during the winters. He continued this occupation after he became totally blind. He was to send us some medicine and I was sent on horseback to get it. On my return about a mile from home I met a big black bear which frightened me beyond measure. I screamed in my fright when the bear turned, looked at me and scampered off into the woods. I never saw but one after that and he ran one way as fast as I ran the other.

After mother's recovery Sarah went to Frankfort where she secured work and never made her home with us again. Things grew worse and worse and we knew all privations of direst poverty.

We missed Seth who was at work fifty miles away at a man's full wages, and we also missed the tea and pork he brought on his visits. Mother could only spare one slice of pork for a meal, using the drippings to season the water gravy for the potatoes and corn bread. The winter was awful with father sick most of the time and mother and I had to even chop all the wood. After the neighbors found this out they arranged a lug pile in such a way we could manage the logs better. No Christmas was observed.

The spring came and we hoped much from Seth's return with his winter's wages which would add to our comforts. He appeared, a full grown man dressed in a new velvet suit with ruffled white shirt, good shoes, felt hat and not a cent in his pocket. Everything spent for his Manistee finery. We children thought him a fairy prince but mother wept bitterly. Her starvation and suffering had culminated only in disappointment. Seth was now a man and did little for the support of the family. Sarah's few dollars saved from her small wages aided some, but all told it was hard to keep body and soul together.

Our sugar was sold in Frankfort and supplied only a few of our many necessities. That summer we found red raspberries and blackberries in abundance. The crops were very poor, a little buckwheat, corn, potatoes and "baggas." We killed our first pig. In our nine years stay on the place we never owned a cow. Someway they never thrived, perhaps they were too human and died of loneliness as well as insufficient food.

At one time a lake captain, who took up land in Platte Township, left his cow with us while he was on his summer trips. But though we gave her the best of care she grew thinner and really pined away and died. We could keep a very few chickens, a hog and pigs.

The townships were organized and the political machinery in full running operation when we reached Grand Traverse region. But office timber was scarce in the early day and many times very crude material had to be utilized. The first election of county officers for Benzie occurred on the first Monday of April, 1863. [209]

The choice of a location for a county seat was submitted to a vote of the electors in that early day but it was not an easy matter to settle on a permanent location. Frankfort and Benzonia contested the right of ownership for more than forty years and the county seat went like a will-of-the-wisp backward and forward from one place to another time and again. The newspapers of the early day, The *Banner of Benzonia* and the *Express of Frankfort,* in long elaborately wrought columns vented their spleen in vituperation of the unsuccessful party. Perhaps the people of Benzonia would be peacefully going about their daily avocation or sleeping quietly in their beds, never guessing anything out of the ordinary, when the summons would come for some of them to appear at the next term of the circuit court which would be held at the county seat at Frankfort. Then they would awaken to the fact that the county seat had literally taken legs and walked off, but it did not remain off for long, for the same mode of procedure would be used in reclaiming the stolen property. Finally Frankfort won out and for several years the county seat was fixed at the place, the discarded school building being used as a court house. People seemed afraid to invest money in a county building when the county seat was so insecure and liable to flit at any moment. In 1905, after more than forty years of contention the matter of a permanent location was again submitted to the voters and Honor, a new town on the Platte River near the center of the county, secured the coveted prize.

On the township board in Almira, in the early days, served two justices of the peace, Jack Burrell and William Rosa who could neither read nor write but each could make his mark. Jack Burrell's wife could read and was a person of some consequence for the township was named for her, and Jack said he got Almira to read for him and he could always compound the law "when Almira read it." But the silence was eternal and the peace almost unbroken and these men could serve as well as men of wider culture.

Calvin Linkletter came into the country as one of the earliest arrivals and started out on foot from Glen Arbor in company with his son Clarence in search of land to settle upon. The public highway was a meager affair, the brush simply cut away, but he followed on for many weary miles and finally settled upon a piece of land in the southern part of Almira Township. Everything was so deceiving in the early days. The soil covered by vegetable mold looked alike everywhere while giant trees grew just as luxuriantly in one section as in another, the only difference being in kind, not in quantity of growth. If a man was unacquainted with the country and taking land for the first time, there was no sure hand to go by for it was all fair to the eye.

I read a description of Benzie County written many years ago by a Benzonia man and he made this statement: "There is not a foot of waste land in Benzie County." I also read an article written by Horace Greeley at the time this region was thrown upon the market through the Homestead Law, stating: "The country is difficult of access, cold and cheerless, soil barren and unproductive and people will do well to consider the other sections before deciding upon Grand Traverse region." Both statements are incorrect. There are thousands of acres of land in this region not at all profitable for general farming purposes and on the other hand we are in one of the richest fruit belts of the United States and the Michigan potato is king. But these things could not be known at first sight. One must select and stand chances.

Mr. Linkletter made a small opening and built a log house; then he rolled the logs together and planted a potato patch right among the logs on that virgin soil. He took his ax and chopped the turf, lifted up the loose soil and placing the potato seed in the opening then turned the turf back in to place. That was the only work ever done on that potato patch. The sun was shining all the time and it continued to shine and never a drop of rain fell for four months. The potatoes did not need cultivation there was nothing to cultivate. Clarence Linkletter told me, that by the end of August all the stalks on that patch could have been gathered into a bushel basket. But the last day of August the rain came and continued to come and the potatoes touched by the magic influence of moisture sprang up and grew like "Jack's beanstalk" and in the end of October when they dug them up the yield was far and away above their expectations. When the potatoes were to be stored for the winter they put half in a hole under the log house and dug a pit in the yard, lined it up with hemlock boughs, put the potatoes in and covered them with boughs and earth. The next spring when they opened the pit the potatoes looked as though they had been polished. One thing was assured in their minds, they had found a region where potatoes grew to the highest perfection.

The first party I ever attended was the first spring that I lived in my new home and there I saw for the first time the youths and maidens who constituted what was called society. They were a good looking lot of youngsters as I remember them, robust and healthy and quite in keeping with the place and surroundings. When these parties were indulged in, they were always a finishing touch to a hard day's work, for anyone who wanted an extra amount of slashing done or logs rolled together would invite the youths to do the work and the maidens to help in the evening's jollification which was sure to last all night, for most of the youngsters came from long distances through the woods so they were obliged to remain all night. They always danced at the parties and sometimes during the evening a youth known by the name of "Big Jack" would entertain the company in his original way. This usually took place at midnight when the company was fatigued and waiting for refreshments to be served. These consisted of dried apple pie and sweet cake not frosted. "Big Jack's" party suit consisted of trousers, flannel shirt, shoes and a strap around his waist to keep his trousers in their proper place. He never wore suspenders which he said interfered with the set of his shirt and did not look well any way. He had a huge mustache and bushy curly hair. He carried a stick which he called a shillalah and when the time came for him to perform his part in the entertainment he would spring out on the floor, stick in hand his head up, and his shoulders back. Then he would sing some Irish melody in which Tim Finigan or Dennis McCarty played an important part. Perhaps it would be the songs of a wake or the sighs of a lovelorn youth, and in either case at the end of each stanza he would throw the shillalah about in the wildest manner and jig a clog. I recall the chorus of one song beginning with Tim Finigan:

"Whack for the day and dance with your partner,

On the floor your trotters shake,
Isn't it the truth I told you?
Lots of fun at Finigan's wake."

At the conclusion of the first song he met with such an enthusiastic encore that he was sure to favor the company with another. That part of the entertainment over, the supper was eaten, each youth choosing the maiden he liked best to eat from the same plate with him, and many times when seats were scarce the maiden sat on his knee. Much laughing and loud talking would be indulged in during the meal, some crawling across to others to trade pie for cake or offering pie in exchange for the privilege of the first dance of the fair one on the others' knee. When the company was refreshed the dancing would begin. It usually commenced by some youth and maiden taking the floor and dancing a jig until someone taking pity upon them stepped in and cut them out. A youth first then a maiden alternating until everyone was in humor for dancing. Then the cotillion would be called on, and the jollification would continue until morning. Then each youth would go home with the maiden he liked best and the party would be a thing of the past never to be forgotten. For many, an emotion was awakened that later was fanned into flame called love and these conditions usually resulted in Hymen's bonds.

I was so tired after the first party I decided never to go again and kept my promise good for a year then was induced to go again and this time a queer thing happened. It was at the end of one of those log rolling days and the woman had chicken for supper, the first chicken that was ever served at a log rolling in this new country. A youth and a maiden had laughingly broken the wishbone and put it over the door and the first maiden to come under the bone was to be his sweetheart and the first youth her beau. This youth played an important part in my life. His people, like mine, had come into the country from the state of New York and had been here four years. There were several sons in the family, all unmarried and working at home for their father, who consequently was getting on and had a large clearing and hoped for good things to come. This youth was keeping company with a girl named Polly Fuller and seemed very much enamored of her and my chance to win him seemed small indeed, but I was the first maiden to come under the wishbone. There was much laughing and teasing done but he paid no attention to me, not even once asking me to dance and took the

269

whole thing as a joke. So far as I was concerned, I was such a mere child that I gave him no further thought at the time. Polly Fuller (my rival) married a man in after years that she met at Frankfort.

The winter I was sixteen years old was the worst winter of my life so far as food and clothing were concerned. If we could get two new print dresses during the year, we thought we were well clothed and one summer mother and I had one pair of shoes between us. It is safe to say they were worn only on rare occasions. The next summer after I was sixteen years old I attended a Sunday school several miles from our house, the first since coming into this new country. There would be the same singing and praying we heard at all the meetings and the teaching consisted of our repeating as many verses from the Bible as we had learned through the week. I have, and have always had a remarkable memory, and that summer I committed the four Gospels to memory and would repeat to the young man who did not teach, just listened to us recite, as many as two hundred verses at a session. It was the same young man who had put the wishbone over the door. He must have been struck with this peculiar mental power and fell in love with me. I returned the affection and the winter I was seventeen years old, I was married. He owned eighty acres of timber land and so far as finances were concerned, nothing else. But he worked at Glen Arbor most of the time and earned food and clothing and some money. He had no home to take me to and I was to stay on with mother. I was fed and clothed and sometimes my good husband brought clothes for mother too. In May when the little eleven-month-old baby sister died it was buried in a little coffin made by some kind hearted man, a few neighbors gathered, a prayer was said, a hymn sung, some tears shed and the baby taken two miles away and laid to rest. People had begun to die in this new country and a little cemetery was started and already several graves gave evidence that one thing, the great Inevitable, could not be put off.

The exodus had begun. The first people in a new country seldom or never remain long enough to reap benefit from it and this held true in this new country, and many families were leaving, among the rest, 'Lije and Marthy Johnson. More than a quarter of a century has rolled away since then and no other family has ever tried to live there. The soil was very poor and 'Lije gave it up and went somewhere else. I lost trace of them years ago. Other people lured there by wealth supposed to be in the standing timber came and in many instances bought out the improvement of the first settler and thus a better class was located on some of the farms bringing with them higher ideals and a touch of the great outside world.

The summer after we were married my husband chopped and cleared about one acre and built a tiny log dwelling on our eighty acres of land. When one and a half years had passed away we went there to live. We were a half mile from water but were on level ground. I was now in my nineteenth year, happy in the love of my husband. I had married the finest youth in the country and our little dwelling was the best furnished for miles around. We had six rush bottom chairs, one walnut table, a cottage bedstead, a cook stove, two trunks, one rocking chair and some dishes, a few simple things to work with and enough bedding for one bed. Everything was new and at that time and in that place it had cost a large sum of money. I shall never forget the anguish I experienced over the first thing broken. We had a large lamp, the bottom of which got loose one day when I was washing it and the bottom fell out and struck the stove and broke all to pieces. I cried all day. There was a woman living a mile from me who listened to all sorrow and gave Christian advice and this being my first loss I went to her. She had lately come into the country and knew nothing of the privations of the people, that would come later. When she saw me she thought some awful calamity had befallen me, and really there had for the nearest lamp was twenty-five miles away. I told her my trouble, and she looked strangely at me and said. "You foolish child! Crying for a broken lamp bottom! You will cry for bigger things some day!" and going to a box she took out a lamp bottom prettier than the one I had broken and putting it into my hands said, "There take that and stop your foolish tears" and then she took some plaster of Paris and told me how to repair the damage done.

The only living things we had on what we termed our farm were a hen and brood of chickens mother had given me, and a pig we had purchased. Because we had these living things I had to stay there and watch and feed them. Hawks abounded and little pigs must be fed if they grow. There is nothing like living on a farm if you are to make a success of farming. Father had made me a very large rain water tub. It held several barrels and this was the only well we had for several years. It would be filled with snow in the spring and a good tight cover kept the water clean and with

271

the rain water we could catch were usually supplied. My husband had a neck yoke and buckets and sometimes he carried the water from a little pond a half a mile away. These things seem trivial in the recital, but they were not trivial matters at that time. When my husband chopped the trees down he left a little clump of maple saplings at one end and side of our dwelling and this gave the place a picturesque appearance and the very first spring we went there, two robins came and set up housekeeping in the young trees. I fed the birds and watched over their domestic plans and mode of life and we called them "Our Birds." They came the next summer and set up housekeeping in the same trees. But the third spring the robins made some mistake and came north too soon and were frozen to death. One man picked up twenty-seven dead birds around his clearing. A strange thing happened at our place. A robin came and hopped about our door. I threw out some crumbs which he ate but still remained, and I opened the door and it hopped inside and flew up and perched on the end of the cottage bedstead. It sat there watching me with its bright eyes and did not seem to be afraid of me in the least. I reached out my hand and stroked it, then took it up and laid it against my cheek. I was young and thoughtless at that time and did not know the birds were freezing and after a time I opened the door and held it in my hand. There was an upturned tree across the road and the robin flew straight over to the upturned sandy roots and went in out of sight. I could see where he went in. The next morning my robin failed to put in an appearance for crumbs. I went over and thrust my hand into the place where he had disappeared and found my pretty red-breasted harbinger of spring dead. I wept bitterly when I remembered that the bird had come to me for shelter and I in my thoughtlessness had let him out. That summer the robins did not build in our trees and we knew our birds were dead.

We planted some potatoes and corn and cleared some land for a wheat field and really thought we were getting along in the world. The following winter was the most terrible winter of my life. The family that lived a quarter of a mile, our nearest neighbors from us, moved to Glen Arbor to get work. They left me a half mile from the nearest people and a strip of woods between, walled me in and them out. I could not see a sign of life now that my neighbor was gone and I was only nineteen years old.

The snow always came early and by Christmas it would be

two feet deep. There were no roads and no stirring, only on snowshoes. I had a rude pair made from a piece of wood and mother lived two and one half miles away. Can you imagine the situation? The only book I had was the Bible and a young girl cannot read even that book all the time. I had no work, not even rags to sew for carpet against the day I should have an extra room to lay one down. I had no pieces to sew together to make extra quilts. I had nothing to do, nothing to look at, nothing to entertain or amuse myself with and night after night I lay awake and could not sleep. Day after day I stayed in that dwelling walled in by the trackless forest, the whole world, my world, wrapped in a mantle of impassable snow and more falling all the time. Once a month my husband came home on Saturday and went again on Monday.

I fell ill in February and kept growing worse and worse and finally lay too ill to speak aloud, some cold on my lungs, and my little brother growing alarmed went on the wooden snow shoes across the trackless two and a half miles to fetch mother. When he got home he found that she had been gone several days to care for a sick woman. Father went a mile, got a man to go for mother, and came to me. I was alone all this time. When he got there the fire was out and I could not speak. I remember he made me comfortable and it was late in the day, he sat Bible in hand reading. I wanted to say something and lay there and tried to say, "Father, father," but the words were not even a whisper. But my mind being so intensely fixed on attracting his attention he turned and came to me. Late after dark the man came with mother. She had walked six miles, most of the way on snowshoes, to get to her suffering daughter. Father went home and she remained with me until I was better. My husband came home in March. He had engaged father to make him two hundred sap buckets and now we were busy and happiness would come. Idleness kills more people than hard work ever could. The buckets were drawn on a big hand sleigh and after he had gone over the way several times he could draw a large load. I was never unhappy when he was home and now was busy watching his departure and return and finally the buckets were all drawn home. He had secured a large pan for boiling down the sap and when the time came we made over six hundred pounds of sugar. Father took three hundred pounds to Frankfort and sold it for us, and bought us the money and clothing we needed.

Looking over my life from this distance I set that winter

down as the loneliest one of my life. The next winter he took me with him and the next he stayed home and never left me again.

In 1869 George Aylsworth moved his cord wood enterprise from the Manitou Islands and established himself on the mainland at the point now called Empire. This opened a way for work to be obtained nearer than Glen Arbor or Frankfort. The blast furnace at Frankfort used thousands of cords of hard wood in their coal kilns and many men from our section spent a part of the winter working at that point. But it was much more difficult to get to Frankfort in the winter than to any other point where work could be obtained. They usually had to make a wide detour and go by way of Inland Township making the distance nearly forty miles. The snow was almost impassable and many settlers along the route would not see a traveler only on snow shoes during the entire winter.

No sooner had the country been opened up so that it was possible to get in and out with a wagon and work had been provided so that some money could be obtained, the settlers turned their attention to the founding of schools. The first schoolhouses were rude log huts sometimes right in the woods. The first teachers were often beginners and the instruction of the simplest kind. One teacher taught in Platte Township two summers who did not even know the parts of speech. Another taught in Almira who could carry the pupil through fractions but beyond that she could not go. But all this was a beginning and in a few years the young people from Benzonia College began to take schools and by their higher mental development stimulated many of the young girls of the section to attend the higher school at Benzonia and fit themselves for teaching. In time the schools of Grand Traverse region were noted for their efficient instructors.

It was a happy day when we knew the great outside world was connected with us by a reliable chain, a regular mail route. Sometimes it was difficult to keep the mail moving in the winter time, but men turned out with oxen and horses too and helped open the way. Now when the mail route was established there was always a road of some kind in the winter to Traverse City. Mr. Tweddle[210] of Empire had the contract form the government to carry the mail from Traverse City to Empire for several years. I remember his son, John, now a prosperous lawyer,[211] carried the mail on his shoulders walking on snowshoes one spring when one of those awful winters had blocked all travel for weeks.

Traverse City was beginning to have a great influence in the country for a railroad from the great outside world was gradually coming that way and in December, 1872, reached its destination, bringing a wave of immigration that was to influence the country for a time, in many ways. The coming of the railroad brought great changes to the country. It brought the mill men, speculators and the agents. The mill men planted themselves in any favorable spot, perhaps on some little lake or at the outlet of some winding stream and began converting the magnificent forest into lumber to be shipped to outside markets. This furnished employment to hundreds of men, for the great lumber camps were to be established and in time lumbering would be carried on in great proportions. The agents came and played their part. They brought into the country fanning mills, sewing machines and anything they could talk the people into buying on time. It was in this way through their influence that mortgages were attached to the few chattels the settler had succeeded in collecting together. One man established himself in Traverse City and began trading horses. He brought into the country all sorts of horses in different stages of decrepitude, disease and old age and sold them to the settlers and took mortgages on the land. It would be impossible to tell the number of these poor unfortunate creatures that enriched the soil with their decaying carcasses. The man made his "stake" and is living luxuriantly off the proceeds of his early investment, while the settler either lost his land or is still struggling, for mortgages are immortal.

The fruit tree agent with his dulcet tones, his persuasive smile and his highly colored sample book wandered into every clearing in the region and sold trees and shrubs by the thousands. Men early found that fruits of nearly all varieties grew to perfection here. The rough, hilly country afforded just the right natural environment for things that love to luxuriate and ripen on some sunny hillside. Thousands are covered with grapes and trees that bear heavy burdens of fruit of the finest flavor, richest color and first texture.

Speculators came looking up the timber. Thus a large part of the magnificent forest fell into the hands of the men who were destined to play their part in this drama of life. Some of the soil was so poor it would scarcely hold together, and the men laughingly said, "Put a mortgage on it and it will hold together." It produced a wonderful growth of timber which could be turned into valuable lumber in the market.

Too late to save any of the original forests the great State of Michigan is attempting to aid nature in the restoration of the lost wealth of trees which so often were wasted, not utilized. Here again man thwarts the purpose by his carelessness or greed. I could relate personal incidents of where thoughtless acts started fires which wiped out the work of years and hopes for future sustenance.

Leelanau's German settlement has done much for the country. The second crop of trees has been harvested in the county but whether wisely or not time will show. Persons searching for homes have traversed the west and south and returned to settle in the Grand Traverse region.

Gardening formed an important part of woman's work on the frontier.

Notes

1. Constructed near Buffalo in 1821 to replace the first steamboat on Lake Erie, the *Walk-in-the-Water*, which had been wrecked, the 346 ton *Superior* boasted but a 59 horse-power engine.

2. "On Sept. 23, 1813, (Col. Henry) Proctor abandoned the post at Amherstburg and ordered the fort and public storehouses burned by the soldiers before retreat. Four days later the Americans landed some distance below Amherstburg and constructed a fort which was called Fort Malden. It was not built on the exact lines of the other fort. The Americans held it until July 1,1815, when it was surrendered to the British. It was found necessary to make many repairs in order to render it useful but not until sometime about the Patriot War was the fort reconstructed. See *Early History of the Town of Amherstburg,* by C.C. James 1902." This annotation and others pertaining to Stewart's narrative, so noted, were appended to the second edition of Volume 18 of the *Michigan Pioneer Collection* (1911) edited by M. Agnes Burton.

3. "This was the Huron Mission Church called the Church of the Assumption, which was founded by the Jesuit Fathers de La Richardie and Potier. The exact date of its destruction is not known. The new church which is now standing, was planned in 1840, and built shortly after. R.R. Elliot." (Burton)

4. These famous pear trees which once lined the Detroit River and the River Raisin, were planted by the French. A century old at the time of Stewart's narrative, they grew to enormous size, 8 feet in circumference and up to 80 feet high. They bore great quantities of a delicious fruit.

5. Lewis Cass, one of Michigan's most distinguished statesmen, was a general in the War of 1812, Territorial Governor of Michigan, 1813-1831; Secretary of War under President Andrew Jackson; Minister to France, 1836-1842; U.S. Senator representing Michigan 1845-1857; Democratic candidate for president in 1848; Secretary of State, 1857-1860. He died at Detroit in July, 1866.

6. "Cass had three daughters who became Mrs. Canfield, Mrs. Henry Ledyard and the Baroness Von Limburg." (Burton)

7. "At this time there were at least three hotels in Detroit. The Mansion House stood on the northwest corner of Jefferson and Cass; Smyth's Hotel, which in 1823 was changed to the Sagina Hotel, and later to the Michigan Hotel, was on the west side of Woodward Avenue, between Jefferson and Woodbridge; Woodworth's Steamboat Hotel was on the northwest corner of Woodward and Randolph. Farmer's History of Detroit." (Burton)

8. Gen. William Hull, Revolutionary War veteran and governor of Michigan Territory, 1805-1813, ended his military career on a sour note when he surrendered Detroit to the British without firing a shot in 1812. Found guilty of cowardice and incompetence at his court martial in 1814, Hull was sentenced to be shot. But President James Madison pardoned him out of respect for his Revolutionary War record. Hull died in 1825.

9. "In 1824-25 Bethuel Farrand (father of J.S. Farrand) submitted to the Common Council of Detroit a proposition by which he could supply the people of the city with water. In May, 1825, he and Rufus Wells, a pumpmaker, commenced preparations for constructing the works. In the fall of that year Mr. Wells took Mr. Farrand's interest and proceeded alone. In 1827 the work was completed. A description of these first works was given in the Detroit *Daily Advertiser*, March, 1854. Mr. Wells continued on in the business taking in two or three partners until sometime in 1830, when he severed his connection with the works and went to Lexington, Sanilac Co. He came from Aurelius, Cayuga Co., N.Y., and was born about 1778." (Burton)

10. This is Mrs. Ira Bronson

11. Fort Shelby was abandoned on May 27, 1826, when the two companies which had been stationed there departed for Green Bay and during the year the fort and grounds were given to the city by Congress. (Burton)

12. "The allusion is to the author's uncle, Dr. Alexander Wolcott." This note and others pertaining to Kinzie which are so identified are taken from the 1932 Lakeside Classics edition of Wau-Bun edited by Milo Quaife, one of the most skilled and productive Great Lakes historians. All who work the fields of Michigan history follow the furrows he first plowed.

13. "Robert Stuart was a native of Perthshire, Scotland, who migrated to Canada in early manhood, studied law, and in 1810 joined the Astorian enterprise of John Jacob Astor. Although this terminated in failure, Stuart won the confidence of Astor, and in 1819 was sent to Mackinac as agent of the American Fur Company. Here he remained until about the year 1834 when he severed his fur-trade connections and became a resident of

Detroit. Here he remained a prominent citizen until his death, October 29, 1848. He died suddenly at Chicago, where he had gone some time before to supervise the construction of the Illinois and Michigan Canal. His widow died at her Detroit home, September 28, 1866. The biography of Stuart, here foretold, has not yet been written, although his career well deserves such a tribute." (Quaife) *Stuart Letters* (2 vols. privately printed, 1961) edited by Helen Stuart MacKay-Smith Merlatt, provides additional details concerning the lives of Robert and Elizabeth Stuart.

14. Washington Irving's *Astoria* (2 vols.) Philadelphia, 1836, deals mainly with the far western fur trade.

15. Gabriel Franchere's *Narrative of a Voyage to the Northwest Coast of America...* New York, 1854, is the first English translation of his classic account of the fur trade orginally published in French in 1820.

16. "This was the name which had been bestowed upon John Kinzie by the Indians in recognition of his practice of the art of silversmith. Following his death, apparently, the name was bestowed upon his son, John H. Kinzie." (Quaife)

17. "Reverend David Bacon, father of the noted Congregational divine, Reverend Leonard Bacon, had endeavored, unsuccessfully, to establish a Protestant mission at Mackinac in 1802. Twenty years later, Rev. William M. Ferry, a graduate of Union College, established the Presbyterian Church at Mackinac, and labored there until 1834. He subsequently founded the town of Grand Haven, Michigan, and in this connection accumulated a fortune. A son, Thomas Ferry, a child of three years at the time of Mrs. Kinzie's visit to Mackinac, served in the U.S. Senate in the 1870s and for two years was president of that body." (Quaife)

18. "A vivid picture of the activities of the American Fur Company in this period is contained in the *Autobiography of Gurdon S. Hubbard*." (Quaife) This was first published in Chicago in 1888 and reprinted as a Lakeside Classic in 1911 and in several later reprints.

19. "The remains of Fort Malden may still be seen in the outskirts of Amherstburg, on the eastern bank of the Detroit River just above its entrance into Lake Erie. The fort was established by the British upon the transfer of Detroit to American rule in 1796, and for several decades thereafter it continued an important center of British military and governmental power in the northwest." (Quaife)

20. "Corn which has been parboiled, shelled from the cob, and dried in the sun." (Quaife)

21. "Literally, *crazy oats*. It is the French name for the Menominees." (Quaife)

22. Writing in 1856, Kinzie is referring to the tragic Indian Removal policy of the 1830s.

23. "Madam Laframboise was born about the year 1780, her father being a French trader and her mother a native woman. The murder of her husband, mentioned by Mrs. Kinzie, occurred in the vicinity of Grand Rapids, Michigan, in the early summer of 1807. She was an aunt of Jean Bapiste Chandonnai, who figured in the Chicago massacre as the rescuer of the wife of Captain Heald. A daughter of Madam Laframboise in 1817 married Captain Benjamin K. Pierce, brother of President Franklin Pierce." (Quaife)

24. "The heads of the families enumerated were prominent American merchants of Mackinac in this period. Michael Dousman, a native of Pennsylvania, had been in the Northwest as early as 1796. In his later years he was reputed to be the richest citizen of Mackinac. Samuel Abbott was a member of the Abbott family, long prominent in Detroit. He was a younger brother of James Abbott, who in November, 1804, married at Fort Dearborn Sarah, daughter of Captain John Whistler. It was the first marriage of white people at Chicago of which any record remains. Edward Biddle was a brother of Nicholas Biddle of Philadelphia, statesman, financier and scholar. In 1819 he married at Mackinac a girl of French-Indian blood who was a step-daughter of Joseph Bailly, the Calumet River trader. A daughter of this union, Sophia Biddle, was educated in Philadelphia. Among her many admirers is reputed to have been a young army officer named Pemberton, who in 1863 surrendered his army and Vicksburg to General Grant." (Quaife)

25. Established to insure American possession of Prairie du Chien, Wisconsin, against rival British fur traders, the original Fort Crawford, named in honor of Secretary of War Wiliam H. Crawford, was constructed in 1816. That fort was abandoned in 1829 and another Fort Crawford built one mile to the southeast.

26. "The remains of Fort Holmes may still be seen, occuping the highest point in the interior of the island, overlooking Fort Mackinac, which the British captured in July, 1812, by dragging in the night time a couple of cannon to the elevation. Upon perceiving, next morning, the hopelessness of defense, Captain

Hanks surrendered Fort Mackinac without effort at resistance. The British later fortified the height, and when the Americans recovered Mackinac at the close of the war, they named the fortification Fort Holmes, in honor of Major Andrew H. Holmes of Virginia, who was slain in the battle of Mackinac Island, August 4, 1814." (Quaife)

27. "Here, as frequently throughout the narrative, Mrs. Kinzie is inaccurate in matters of historical detail. The Jesuit mission of St. Ignace was established by Marquette in 1670 on the mainland opposite the Island where the town of St. Ignace has since developed" (Quaife). More recent scholarship indicates Father Marquette did not establish the mission at St. Ignace until 1671.

28. The fort where the massacre of 1763 took place has been reconstructed at the original site in Mackinaw City. The best description of the event is found in witness Alexander Henry's *Travel and Adventures...* New York, 1809.

29. Titus Bronson founded the village he named after himself in 1829. In 1836 it was renamed Kalamazoo and the disgusted Bronson moved to the west.

30. First named Jacksonburgh in 1828, the village became Jacksonopolis in 1835 and finally Jackson in 1838.

31. This is a reference to John Milton's *Paradise Lost.*

32. This was probably near present day Marshall although the Territorial Road being traveled first crosses the Kalamazoo River near present day Battle Creek.

33. This is Prairie Ronde, the largest prairie that was in Michigan.

34. The Island Inn, named after the so called "big island" of trees in the middle of Prairie Ronde, was in the village of Schoolcraft.

35. A thirty-five mile ride from Kalamazoo would place this site in Cass County near Cassopolis. The old Kalamazoo Stage Trail passed through Gard's Prairie in Volinia Township. Gard's Prairie, also known as Dry Prairie was about 100 acres in size and is the only small prairie in the vicinity. See map in George R. Fox "Place Names of Cass County," *Michigan History Magazine.* Vol. XXVII (Summer, 1943) p. 463. However, I can find no evidence of a Nicholas B-- among the early land owners of Cass County in Howard Rogers' *History of Cass County* (Cassopolis, 1875).

36. Located at 190 Jefferson Avenue, the American Hotel was opened by John Griswold in May, 1836. The building which formed its nucleus had been constructed by the infamous Gov. William Hull in 1807. The American Hotel burned down May 9, 1848.

37. Charley was the six-year-old son of a pair of companions who accompanied Martineau on her trip across Michigan. Earlier she had described him as: "The great ornament of the party - our prince of Denmark - was Charley; a boy of uncommon beauty and promise, and fully worthy of the character given him by one of our drivers, with whom the boy had ingratiated himself by his chattter on the box; - 'An eternal smart boy, and the greatest hand at talk I ever came across'."

38. She means the Detroit River.

39. This is Stephens T. Mason, "the boy governor" of Michigan Territory at this time.

40. This is a synonym for linch-pin.

41. She probably means Dearbornville, now Dearborn.

42. This is a crossbar in a coach which supports the springs.

43. This had to be either the *State Journal* or the *Michigan Argus*, the two Ann Arbor newspapers being published at that time.

44. This was probably at the homestead of Daniel Wallace, located three miles west of Saline.

45. Originally called Sturgis Prairie after Judge John Sturgis of Monroe, the first settler, the name of this community became Sherman in 1832. It was renamed Sturgis in 1845.

46. Renamed simply, White Pigeon, in 1835, this community commemorates the name of Wakbememe, Chief White Pigeon, who, apocraphal local lore maintains, "about 1830 gave his life to save the settlement."

47. The population of Niles in 1838 was approximately 1,200 according to Blois' *Gazeteer of Michigan*.

48. The contention for Potawatomi land was sadly settled in the "squatters'" favor when most of the tribe was rounded up by troops and marched to the west of the Mississippi during the "Trail of Tears" in 1838-40.

49. Henry Schoolcraft's first wife, Jane, was the daughter of John Johnston, an Irish fur trader at Sault Ste. Marie and O-Shau-Gus-Co-Way-Qua, the daughter of a powerful Ojibwa chief. Famed for her beauty, Jane Schoolcraft was known as "the Northern Pocahontas."

50. Actually this is more like 45 miles, as the crow flies.

51. Alexander Henry wrote *Travel and Adventures... 1760-*

66. New York, 1809.

52. Located in the Les Cheneaux Archipeligo, this is a small island to the southwest of Marquette Island.

53. This is the site of present day DeTour village.

54. This is now known as Munuscong Lake.

55. On S. Augustus Mitchell's *Tourist's Pocket Map of Michigan* (1839) the entire Neebish Island is labeled Sailor's Encampment Island. Sailor's Encampment or Encampment Island (now called Rains) is a small island located at the southeast tip of Neebish Island adjacent the Canadian shore. It is found on many maps published through the 1950s but for some reasons no longer appears on the offical map of Chippewa County.

56. In 1833 Charlotte Johnston, Jane Schoolcraft's younger sister, married William McMurray, an Anglican missionary to the Chippewa stationed at Sault Ste. Marie, Ontario.

57. In 1641 the French Jesuit missionaries, Issac Jogues and Charles Raymbault, named Sault Ste. Marie after their patron saint.

58. This is a large old-time naval ship rated as carrying 74 cannons.

59. This is General Hugh Brady, who was in charge of the construction of the fort named in his honor in 1822.

60. This is now called Iroquois Point

61. This is undoubtedly the first literary reference to "Down Belowers."

62. Jameson adds a note that she is spelling this word phonetically. She probably is refering to siscowit, a deep water variety of trout.

63. This is John Tanner, whose story was told in Edwin James' *Narrative of the Captivity and Adventures of John Tanner.* N.Y., 1830. Tanner disappeared from the Sault following the murder of Henry Schoolcraft's brother, James, in 1846 and was blamed for the deed. His guilt was never proven, however.

64. Worse was to happen to this cemetery. When the first lock was being constructed in 1853-55 workmen cut directly through the burying place and unceremoniously carted away piles of bones.

65. This is an old spelling of Ottawa

66. Irish fur trader John Johnston, who died in 1828, had married Oshauguscodaywayquay, the daughter of the celebrated Chippewa chief, Waubojeeg, in 1792.

67. Portions of this dwelling survive as a museum.

68. Big George, the second son of John Johnston and Oshauguscodaywayquay, was born at the Sault in 1796.

69. Jameson's reference is to Andre Massena, "the greatest of Napoleon's marshalls." During his defeat and retreat from Portugal in the Peninsula Campaign of 1811 he lost approximately 30,000 men, chiefly due to starvation and disease.

70. The Tombs was the infamous city prison of New York.

71. The reference is to Charles Dickens' *Posthumous Papers of the Pickwick Club*, first published in 1836.

72. Ten shillings is $1.25 per acre, the established price for federal land at the time.

73. Constructed in 1818 by Father Gabriel Richard, the original St. Anne's Church was demolished in 1886.

74. Actually, Detroit was founded by Sieur de Cadillac in July, 1701.

75. The name of this railroad, which finally reached Chicago in 1852, was later changed to the Michigan Central.

76. The Detroit and Pontiac Railroad began service in 1843. The Shelby and Detroit Railroad was chartered in 1834. It was later renamed the Detroit, Romeo & Port Huron Railroad. However, its operations ceased about 1845.

77. Completed in 1838, this round water tank was 70 feet high and 60 feet in diameter. It was torn down in 1866.

78. This is the tulip poplar or whitewood tree.

79. William Darby, wrote *A Tour from... New York to Detroit.* New York, 1819.

80. First settled in 1805 and called Point du Chene, this community was renamed Plainfield in 1826, Clay, after statesman Henry Clay, in 1835 and finally Algonac in 1843.

81. First called Yankee Point, this settlement became Cottrellville in 1822. Later renamed Newport, it received its final name change in 1865 - Marine City.

82. Palmer is present day St. Clair.

83. This is now spelled Walpole Island. Obviously Steele is not narrating her impressions chronologically as she should have passed Walpole Island before Algonac, Marine City and St. Clair.

84. Built in 1814 and named in honor of Chief Engineer Captain Charles Gratiot, Fort Gratiot was occupied on and off until the Civil War. It was abandoned in 1879.

85. Steele is probably referring to what are now called the Thunder Bay Islands.

86. I can not identify this river. The author may have been misinformed.

87. These are, of course, religious tracts

88. This is a man's long close-fitting overcoat

89. Fuller had previously visited the Rock River region. Not far from Oregon, Illinois, she described a lofty Pine Rock, which is probably what is called Castle Rock today.

90. See note 51

91. This is Henry Rowe Schoolcraft, whose *Algic Researches.* 2 Vols. New York, 1839, Fuller had mentioned previously as being of great value.

92. See note 49

93. Alexander Mackenzie wrote *Voyages from Montreal... to the Frozen and Pacific Oceans...* London, 1801, which recounts his first crossing of the North American continent from ocean to ocean by a white man.

94. The Pillagers, at one time the most formidable robbing unit of the Chippewa, formerly lived in Northern Minnesota on Leach and Ottertail lakes and the intermediate region.

95. Shobal Vail Clevenger, an Ohio born sculptor of contemporary fame, executed in Rome in 1840 the "North American Indian," the first distinctive American piece of sculpture made there. He died at the age of 31 from a pulmonary disease caused by inhalation of stone dust.

96. Artist George Catlin's *Letters and Notes on... American Indians* (London, 1841, 2 vols.) was a popular book of the period.

97. Thomas L. McKenney, superintendent of Indian trade, 1816-22, and head of the U.S. Bureau of Indian Affairs, 1824-30, wrote *Sketches of a Tour to the Lakes...* (Baltimore, 1827) and a three volume *History of the Indian Tribes* (Philadelphia, 1836, 38, 44). Fuller echoes sentiments concerning the wrongs committed against the Indians similar to those articulated by McKenney in his books.

98. In 1820 some members of the Cherokee tribe adopted a regular form of government modeled on that of the United States. But when gold was discovered on their land in Georgia a powerful agitation for their removal developed. The tribe was removed to the west of the Mississippi in the winter of 1838-39. Approximately one-fourth of the Indians died en route on their "Trail of Tears."

99. This passage is a quotation from a Buffalo journal appearing on page 137 of Joseph Bouchette's *The British Dominions in North America.* 2 Vols. London, 1831. . Bouchette was actually a Canadian born in Quebec in 1774.

100. This was the burning of the *G.P. Griffith* on June 17, 1850, in which 250 to 295 lives were lost.

101. "Judge B" who met Bremer at Buffalo and escorted her from there through Michigan to his home in Niles was earlier described as an "excellent, vigorous old gentleman, yet quite youthful in spirit, one of the oldest pioneers of the West, and who had taken part in the founding or laying out of many of its flourishing cities, as Rochester, Lockport, and many others..." Most probably this is John G. Bond, orginally a native of Keene, New Hampshire, who moved to Rochester, N.Y., in 1815 and was one of the founders of Lockport. While residing there he was appointed one of the judges of Niagara County. In July, 1834, he immigrated to Niles with his family.

102. The Rev. S.A. McCosky, who arrived in Detroit in August, 1836, served as Bishop and rector of St. Paul's Episcopal Church there until 1863.

103. Father Gabriel Richard came to Detroit in 1798 and served as pastor there until his death in the cholera epidemic of 1832. In 1809 he established at Detroit the first newspaper west of the Allegheny Mountains. In 1823 he was elected to represent Michigan Territory in Congress.

104. See note 8

105. After Gen. William Hull surrendered to Gen. Issac Brock, Brock left Col. Henry Proctor in charge of Detroit while he returned to Niagara.

106. The Biddle House, a famous hotel erected in 1849, was located on the south side of Jefferson Avenue, just east of Randolph Street.

107. The "old" First Baptist Church stood on the northwest corner of Fort and Griswold streets.

108. The author's grandmother was Madame Therese Schindler, the daughter of Migisan, a full blooded Ottawa.

109. This should not be confused with the Point au Barques at the tip of the Thumb in Huron County.

110. The author would marry Henry S. Baird, then a Green Bay, Wisconsin, attorney, at the age of 14 in 1824.

111. High in the stern and bow, the vessel was about 140 feet long and 32 feet wide, with a displacement of 330 tons. Its masts were equipped with sails to supplement the two paddle wheels located midship.

112. Black Rock was a settlement on the Niagara River at the mouth of Scajaguada Creek. It then rivaled nearby Buffalo as a port.

113. Actually, this voyage began on August 23, 1818.

114. Abraham Edwards moved to Detroit in 1815, was active in territorial politics and from 1831 to 1849 was register of the federal land office, first at White Pigeon then at Kalamazoo. He died at Kalamazoo in 1860.

115. Actually, this was August 27, 1818

116. Thomas Palmer was born in Connecticut in 1789. He began business as a merchant in 1808 and in 1815 moved to Detroit. He married Mary Amy Witherell in 1821. Following the failure of his store in Detroit in 1824, he purchased a large tract of pine covered land in St. Clair County where he built a saw mill and operated a store. The site, first named St. Clair, became Palmer in 1826, but it was later renamed St. Clair. Palmer later moved back to Detroit where he died in 1868.

117. This is Capt. Jedediah Rogers.

118. First settled in 1823 by Benjamin Woodruff from Ohio, this ghost town had a post office from May 19, 1825 to Jan. 20, 1828.

119. John Allen, a Virginian, and Elisha Walker Rumsey, from New York, founded Ann Arbor.

120. This is a village on the west bank of the Maumee River south of Toledo which is now called Maumee.

121. Brownstown or Brown's Town was located at the junction of the Huron and Detroit rivers, near Gibraltar.

122. John Allen and Elisha Walker Rumsey first arrived at the site of the settlement they would name in honor of their wives - Ann Arbor - in February 1824.

123. See note 118.

124. This was a tribe residing in western New York. It was one of the five members of the Iroquois Confederation.

125. Judge Samuel W. Dexter was the first settler and the first postmaster in the community named after him.

126. By the terms of the Federal Militia Act approved April 2, 1825, "each and every free able-bodied white male citizen" between the ages of 18 and 25 was subject to enrollment in the militia. The militia was required to rendezvous for training the first Monday in June, the first Monday in September and once between September 1 and October 15 each year.

127. The author's brother, Eber Brock Ward, would be the first Michigander to become a millionaire through his interests in shipping, railroads, iron ore and steel production. At the time of his death in 1875 he was worth from $10 - $30 million.

128. This is the St. Clair River

129. George Catlin in *The Story of Detroit* (Detroit, 1926) states that Kishkawho and another Indian were arrested for hacking to death one of their own braves named Wauwasson. Three of Kishkawko's wives supposedly delivered the poison to him.

130. Named for pioneer John Baldwin, this prairie of approximately 500 acres was in sections 8,17 and 18 of Porter Township, just west of Baldwin Lake.

131. The author may be mistaken here. The first physician in St. Joseph County, Dr. David Page, settled near White Pigeon in 1827. Dr. Hubbel Loomis, also the first probate judge of the county, did not arrive in White Pigeon until the summer of 1829.

132. Asahel Savery also operated the first hotel in St. Joseph County at what is now Wade Park in White Pigeon.

133. "The first settlement in the town of Dexter was made in 1825 by Sylvanus and Nathaniel Noble, who had settled in Ann Arbor the year before. Judge Dexter - for whom the town is named - located land where the village is in October, 1824, so that the author is mistaken about Ann Arbor being the only settlement between Ann Arbor and Jackson."

134. Titus Bronson was known as "Potato" Bronson because he introduced a new variety of potato, the "Neshannoch," to Michigan and sold them in various communities in the 1820s. In 1829 he founded the community first called Bronson, later changed to Kalamazoo.

135. This is William R. DeLand.

136. The village of Barry, located on Sandstone Creek in Sandstone Township, was first settled in 1832. It is now a ghost town.

137. Now spelled Dixboro, this Washtenaw County community was founded by sea captain John Dix in 1825.

138. This disease is now known as tuberculosis

139. Stony Run was the site of a rural post office established in 1834 in Genesee County's Grand Blanc Township. It is now a ghost town.

140. Located on the west bank of the Saginaw River, Fort Saginaw had been first garrisoned in 1822, but was abandoned the following year.

141. George Nelson Smith was born in Vermont on October

25, 1807. In 1830 he married Arvilla Almira Powers. They immigrated to Michigan Territory three years later. The first Congregational minister to be ordained in the state of Michigan, Smith preached in Richland, Plainwell, Otsego and Allegan.

142. This is a form of cholera

143. Ague is now termed malaria

144. Plainfield was a ghost town that was located in Allegan County's Gun Plains Township.

145. In the pioneer era, Flavius J. Littlejohn of Allegan worked as a surveyor, engineer, geologist and lawyer. From 1850 - 1865 he served as a horseback circuit court judge, covering 20 counties in western Michigan. In the 1840s he represented Allegan County in the state legislature. He ran as a Whig candidate for governor in 1849 but was defeated. His book, *Legends of Michigan and the Old Northwest,* was published in Allegan five years before his death in 1880.

146. He was a chief of a band of Ottawas from Middle Village, located between Cross Village and Harbor Springs, who wintered between the Black and Kalamazoo rivers.

147. The author's cousin, Abigail McDonald McLaughlin, was the wife of James McLaughlin, a ship builder who lived in Newark, later renamed Saugatuck.

148. This is probably James R. Prickett, a half-breed government interpreter.

149. Platted on the south shore of the Black River, now Macatawa Lake, in 1836, this settlement lasted only four years. The resort community of Waukazoo was later developed at this site.

150. The Smiths would relocate to Fillmore Township, Allegan County, where they would operate the Old Wing Mission to the Ottawa until moving with their Indian followers to Waukazooville, now part of Northport, Leelanau County, in 1849.

151. The Rev. Mason Knappen was a Congregational minister.

152. Dr. David E. Deming, also from Vermont, had purchased land in Richland Township in 1833 and stayed temporarily on Gull Prairie before moving to Cooper Township where he became that township's first settler.

153. This is probably Philip Gray from Newport, Rhode Island, who settled on Gull Prairie in 1831.

154. First called Hinsdill's Hotel, this structure stood at the corner of Monroe and Ionia streets. Hinsdill opened it in 1836.

155. The Rev. Leonard Slater, a Baptist missionary to the Indians, was in charge of the Thomas Mission at Grand Rapids from 1827 to 1836. He preached and taught in Ottawa and English.

156. This would be the home of Luther Lincoln, a log frame dwelling located north of Pearl Street.

157. This is Sophia Page

158. Built in 1872, the Morton House stood at the site of Hinsdill's original hotel.

159. Bronson, the site of the federal land office, was renamed Kalamazoo in 1836.

160. Built in 1834, the structure known as the old yellow warehouse stood on the east bank of the river.

161. Sweet's Hotel stood on the northwest corner of Canal and Pearl streets.

162. Alva True, was the author's husband.

163. This is probably Stephen Towne, who settled in Rives Township in 1833.

164. This is probably Samuel Prescott, who moved to the township in 1831.

165. J. McQueen had purchased 160 acres in Eaton County in 1836.

166. This occurred in 1840.

167. This is a phonetic spelling of a colloquial pronounciation of the poplar tree.

168. This probably A. Sumner, who purchased 156 acres in Section 26, Eaton Rapids Township, in 1836.

169. The Patrick Gallery family arrived in Eaton Rapids Township in 1837.

170. The William Winn family settled in Eaton Rapids prior to 1837.

171. Jesse Munro purchased 160 acres of government land in Section 7, Eagle Township

172. This settlement was named after Capt. David Scott, who first settled the site in 1833.

173. This is probably the cabin of Anthony Niles, who had settled in Eagle Township in 1834.

174. She probably is referring to Philo Beers and his wife. Beers became a sawmill proprietor and blacksmith.

175. Born in Massachusetts in 1806, Lathrop settled on Prairie Ronde in 1830. He became active in state politics.

176. The murder referred to occured during the winter of

1839. Sin-ben-nim or Joseph Muskrat, his wife and two children had been allowed to seek refuge from the cold in Wisner's cabin. The Indian was drunk. He got into a wrestling match with Wisner and when he was bested suddenly stabbed him in the temple, killing him instantly. He fled, but was apprehended by Wisner's neighbors, bound and hauled to Schoolcraft. Tried and convicted of murder, the Indian was sentenced to be hung but that was later commuted to life imprisonment. He died after two years in the Jackson Prison.

177. The Potawatomi were rounded up by Col. Hugh Brady's dragoons and herded across the Mississippi on their "trail of tears" in 1840.

178. Indian agent Patrick Marantette operated a trading post near present day Mendon. The Nottawaseppe Reservation lay in northern St. Joseph and southern Kalamazoo counties. The Potawatomi lost it as the result of an 1833 treaty.

179. This was one of several explanations the pioneers put forth as the cause of the ague, now known as malaria, actually caused by the bite of mosquitoes.

180. This was a mercury compound used by many saddlebag doctors of the era as a virtual panecea. It was not.

181. Bazil Harrison was the pioneer settler in Kalamazoo County.

182. The River Raisin Massacre occurred at Monroe in 1813.

183. See note 185

184. The massasauga is a small rattlesnake once common in Michigan.

185. Actually the Erie and Kalamazoo Railroad had started horse powered service between Toledo and Adrian on November 2, 1836. On July 4, 1837, a steam locomotive made it's debut on that railroad.

186. The Yankee Springs Tavern was a famous hostelry operated by William Lewis. It was located two miles east of Gun Lake in western Barry County.

187. Hastings was not officially the county seat at this time as Barry County was not organized until 1839.

188. This is Hastings, "the center."

189. She refers to the Rev. Daniel Bush.

190. The Rev. Zerah T. Hoyt served as minister until 1855.

191. While May seems late for a great deal of ice to be encountered, the winter of 1836-37 has been described as being especially severe.

192. A Dutch group known as the Holland Land Company had purchased from Robert Morris approximately 3,300,000 acres of land in western New York and began selling it in 1801.

193. Buttery is an archaic term for pantry.

194. From internal evidence this would date approximately 1845

195. Edwin R. Cobb and Andrew Rector erected this mill.

196. Other sources claim the derivation of the name to be "pent up water" because of the small outlet of the lake, or that it is a corruption of "paint water," a name orginally given because of the dark color of the lake.

197. Charles A. Rosevelt and his wife came to Pentwater in 1853.

198. The reference is to President Theodore Roosevelt and his celebrated bear hunting adventures. Teddy bears resulted from him sparing a cub.

199. Claybanks Township to the south of Pentwater was the site of the first settlement in Oceana County in 1849.

200. The wreck of the schooner, *J.B. Wright*, occured in 1854.

201. The first issue of the *Oceana Times*, edited by Frederick W. Ratzel, came on April, 20, 1861.

202. This occurred in 1867

203. Passed on May 20, 1862, the Homestead Act offered any citizen or intending citizen who was the head of a family and over 21 years of age 160 acres of surveyed federal land after 5 years of continuous residence and payment of a registration fee ranging from $26 - $34. As an alternative, land under the act could be purchased at $1.25 an acre after a six months residence.

204. This is in Leelanau County

205. This was probably located at the little community of Almira, at the northeast corner of section 16, Almira Township. A post office operated there from 1864 - 1893. It is a ghost town now.

206. The proceeds from the sale of the one mile square, section 16, of each township were allocated for school purposes. Hence Section 16 came to be called the "school section."

207. Officially, the Allegan, Muskegon and Traverse Bay State Road, was first authorized by the legislature in 1859.

208. These were, of course, passenger pigeons. The last passenger pigeon on earth, a female named Martha, died in a

Cincinnati zoo in 1914.

209. Benzie County was attached to Grand Traverse County for civil and administrative purposes until 1869.

210. David Tweddle, with his wife Mary and family, settled in Empire in 1865.

211. John Tweddle later served as prosecuting attorney of Grand Traverse County.

Louise Therese Baird cherished her memories of growing up on Mackinac Island, 1814-1824.

SOURCES CONSULTED

Alward, Dennis and Pierce, Charles, compilers. *Index to the Local and Special Acts of the State of Michigan 1803 to 1927*. Lansing, 1928.

Baird, Elizabeth Therese. "Indian Customs and Early Recollections," *Collections of the State Historical Society of Wisconsin*. Vol. 9 (1882). p. 303.

Baird, Elizabeth Therese. "Reminiscences of Early Days on Mackinac Island," *Collections of the State Historical Society of Wisconsin*. Vol. 14 (1898). p. 17.

Barber, Edward W. "Report of Memorial Committee. Jackson County," *Michigan Pioneer Collections*. Vol. 32 (1903). p. 593.

Baxter, Albert. *History of the City of Grand Rapids*. N.Y., 1891.

Bayliss, Joseph E. and Estelle and Quaife, Milo M. *River of Destiny: The Saint Marys*. Detroit, 1955.

Blois, John T. *Gazeteer of the State of Michigan...* Detroit, 1839.

Bowen, Dana Thomas. *Shipwrecks of the Lakes*. Daytona Beach, Florida, 1952.

Bremer, Frederika. *The Homes of the New World...* 2 vols. New York, 1853.

Brunson, Catherine Calkins. "A Sketch of Pioneer Life Among the Indians," *Michigan Pioneer Collections*. Vol. 28 (1900). p. 161.

Catlin, George B. *The Story of Detroit*. Detroit, 1926.

Clapp, Mrs. M.W. "The Long Ago," *Michigan Pioneer Collections*. Vol. 3 (1881). p. 512.

Compendium of History and Biography of the City of Detroit and Wayne County, Michigan. Chicago, 1909.

Cutler, H.G. *History of St. Joseph County, Michigan*. 2 vols. Chicago, N.D.

DeLand, Charles V. *DeLand's History of Jackson County, Michigan*. (Indianapolis), 1903.

Deland, Mary G. and Stewart, Electa M.S. "The First Settlement of Jackson," *Michigan Pioneer Collections*. Vol. 5 (1884). p. 348.

Doll, Louis. *A History of the Newspapers of Ann Arbor*. Detroit, 1959.

Dunbar, Willis, *All Aboard! A History of Railroads in Michigan*. Grand Rapids, [1969].

Dunbar, Willis F. *Kalamazoo and How It Grew*. Kalamazoo, 1959.

Dunbar, Willis F. and May, George. *Michigan A History of the*

Wolverine State. Grand Rapids, (1980).

Durant, Samuel. *History of Ingham and Eaton Counties, Michigan.* Philadelphia, 1880.

Durant, Samuel. *History of Kalamazoo County, Michigan.* Philadelphia, 1880.

Dury, Wayne L. *White Pigeon, Prairie, Village, Township, Chief.* (Manchester, Tenn., 1987).

Dye, Mrs. Richard. "Coming to Michigan," *Michigan Pioneer Collections.* Vol. 8 (1886). p. 260.

Ellet, Elizabeth. *Pioneer Women of the West.* New York, 1852.

Farmer, Silas. *History of Detroit and Wayne County and Early Michigan.*2 vols. 3rd ed. Detroit, 1890.

Fox, George R. "Place Names of Cass County," *Michigan History Magazine.* Vol. XXVII (Summer, 1943). p. 463.

Fuller, George N., ed. *Historic Michigan. Vol. Three, Local Histories of Several Michigan Counties.* N.P., (1924).

Fuller, [Sarah Margaret]. *Summer on the Lakes, in 1843.* Boston, 1844.

Grand Rapids City Directory. 1883-84. Detroit, 1883.

Grant, Bruce. *American Forts Yesterday and Today.* New York, (1965).

Gray, Mrs. Martha. "Reminiscences of Grand Traverse Region," *Michigan Pioneer Collections. Vol. 38 (1912). p. 285.*

Hambleton, Elizabeth and Stoutamire, Elizabeth, eds. *The John Johnston Family of Sault Ste. Marie.* (Washington, D.C.), 1992.

Harley, Rachel Brett and MacDowell, Betty. *Michigan Women Firsts and Founders.* N.P., [1992].

Hartwick, L.M. and Tuller, W.H. *Oceana County Pioneers and Business Men of Today.* Pentwater, 1890.

Hayes, Mrs. A.M. "Reminiscences of Pioneer Days in Hastings," *Michigan Pioneer Collections.* Vol. 26 (1896). p. 235.

History of Allegan and Barry Counties, Michigan. Philadelphia, 1880.

History of Berrien and Van Buren Counties, Michigan. Philadelphia, 1880.

History of St. Joseph County, Michigan. Philadelphia, 1877.

History of Shiawassee and Clinton Counties, Michigan. Philadelphia, 1880.

History of Washtenaw County, Michigan. Chicago, 1881.

Hodge, Frederick Webb. *Handbook of American Indians North of Mexico.* 2 vols. Washington, 1907, 1910.

Hoppin, Ruth. "Personal Recollections of Pioneer Days," *Michigan Pioneer Collections*. Vol. 38 (1912). p. 410.

Howard, Nancy. "Mrs. Nancy Howard, of Port Huron, and Her Interesting Recollections," *Michigan Pioneer Collections*. Vol. 14 (1890). p. 532.

Howes, Wright. *U.S. Iana*. N.Y., 1962.

Hubach, Robert F. *Early Midwestern Travel Narratives An Annotated Bibliography 1634-1850*. Detroit, 1961.

Hubbard, Bela. *Memorials of a Half-Century in Michigan and the Lake Region*. N.Y., 1887.

Hubbs, Carl L. and Lagler, Karl. F. *Fishes of the Great Lakes Region*. Ann Arbor (1958).

Hurlbut, Frances B. *Grandmother's Stories*. Cambridge, 1889.

Illinois A Descriptive and Historical Guide. Chicago, 1939.

Jameson, [Anna B.] *Winter Studies and Summer Rambles...* 3 vols. London, 1838.

Jewett, Azubah L. "Saginaw County Pioneer Life in 1830," *Michigan Pioneer Collections*. Vol. 6 (1884). p. 426.

Jones, Mrs. George N. "Miss Emily Ward, Commonly Known as 'Aunt Emily,'" *Michigan Pioneer Collections*. Vol. 38 (1912). p. 581.

Kinzie, [Juliette]. *Wau-Bun. The "Early Day" in the North West*. Lakeside Classics reprints edition edited by Milo M. Quaife. Chicago, 1932.

Kirkland, Caroline M. "The Justice," *The Union Magazine*. Vol.1, No. 3 (September, 1847). p. 114.

Kunitz, Stanley J. *British Authors of the Nineteenth Century*. New York, 1936.

Lafever Margaret. "Story of Early Day Life in Michigan," *Michigan Pioneer Collections*. Vol. 38 (1912). p. 672.

Laws of the Territory of Michigan... Detroit, 1827.

Lewis, Elvira Barber. "Pioneer Life in Pentwater," *Michigan Pioneer Collections*. Vol. 35 (1907). p. 691.

Longyear, Harriet Munro. "The Settlement of Clinton County," *Michigan Historical Collections*. Vol. 39 (1915). p. 360.

Lorenz, Charles J. *The Early History of Saugatuck and Singapore, Michigan 1830-1840*. (Saugatuck, 1983).

MacCabe, Julius P. Bolivar. *Directory of the City of Detroit...* Detroit, 1837.

McKean, Eugene C, Harrison, Majorie M. and Mc Bride, Carol C. *Richland From Its Prairie Beginnings*. Richland, 1981.

Mansfield, J.B., ed. *History of the Great Lakes*. 2 vols. Chicago,

1899.

Martineau, Harriet. *Society in America.* 3 vols. London, 1837.

Meints, Graydon. *Michigan Railroads and Railroad Companies.* East Lansing, 1992.

Michigan Biographies. 2 Vols. Lansing, 1924.

Morris, Richard B., ed. *Encyclopedia of American History.* N.Y., (1953).

Mott, Frank Luther. *A History of American Magazines. 1850-1865.* Cambridge, 1938.

New York: *A Guide to the Empire State.* New York, (1940).

Ohio Guide. American Guide Series. N.Y., (1940).

Palmer, Mary A. Witherell. "Letter to Hon. E.C. Walker," *Michigan Pioneer Collections.* Vol. 4 (1883). p. 112.

Pierce, Gilbert A. *The Dickens Dictionary.* Boston, 1872.

Potter, William W. *History of Barry County.* Grand Rapids, [1912].

Rogers, Howard S. *History of Cass County From 1825 to 1875.* Cassopolis, 1875.

Rogers, Mrs. J.V. "An Incident of Pioneer Life," *Michigan Pioneer Collections.* Vol. 3 (1881). p. 299.

Romig, Walter. *Michigan Place Names.* Detroit, 1986.

Silliman, Sue I. *St. Joseph in Homespun.* Three Rivers, 1931.

Smith, Arvilla A. *A Pioneer Woman.* Lansing, 1981.

Steele, [Eliza R.] *A Summer Journey in the West...* New York, 1841.

Stephenson, O.W. *Ann Arbor The First Hundred years.* Ann Arbor, 1927.

Stevens, Charity H. "Pioneer Paper," *Michigan Pioneer Collections.* Vol. 35 (1907). p. 680.

Stewart, [Electa M.S.] "Childhood's Recollections of Detroit," *Michigan Pioneer Collections.* Vol. 18 (1892). p. 458.

Story, Norah. *The Oxford Companion to Canadian History and Literature.* Toronto, 1967.

Walling, H.F. *Atlas of the State of Michigan.* Detroit, [1873].

Wilbur, Lory, "One of the Early Settlers," *Michigan Pioneer Collection.* Vol 3 (1881). p. 515.

Withey, Marion Louise Hinsdill. "Personal Recollections of Early Days in Kent County," *Michigian Historical Collections.* Vol. 39 (1915). p. 345.

Wood, Edwin O. *Historic Mackinac.* 2 vols. N.Y., 1918.

Young, J.H. *The Tourists' Pocket Map of Michigan.* Philadelphia, 1839.

INDEX

Larry B. Massie is a Michigan product and proud of it. Born in Grand Rapids in 1947, he grew up in Allegan. Following a tour in Viet Nam as a U.S. Army paratrooper, he worked as a telephone lineman, construction laborer, bartender and in a pickle factory before earning three degrees in history from Western Michigan University.

He honed his research skills during an eight-year position with the W.M.U. Archives and Regional History Collections. He left in 1983 to launch a career as a free-lance historian, specializing in the heritage of the state he loves. An avid book collector, he lives with his wife and workmate Priscilla, and their 35,000 volume library, in a rambling old schoolhouse nestled in the Allegan State Forest. Sons Adam, Wallie and Larry Jr., as well as Maggie, Skippy, Jiggs and Ossie, pets canine and feline, insure there is never a dull moment.

Dressed as a voyageur, Larry Massie makes Michigan's past come alive through his storytelling.

Larry and Priscilla Massie's

MICHIGAN HISTORY BOOKS AVAILABLE FROM THE PRISCILLA PRESS

Birchbark Belles 310 pages, ill. bib. index. $10.95

Potawatomi Tears and Petticoat Pioneers 296 pages, ill. bib. index. $8.95

The Romance of Michigan's Past 270 pages, ill. bib. index. $8.95

Pig Boats and River Hogs 296 pages, ill. bib. index. $8.95

Copper Trails and Iron Rails 290 pages, ill. bib. index. $10.95

Voyages into Michigan's Past 298 pages, ill. bib. index. $10.95

From Frontier Folk to Factory Smoke 182 pages, ill. $8.95

Walnut Pickles and Watermelon Cake: A Century of Michigan Cookery 354 pages, 8 1/2 x 11, ill. bib. index, hardbound. $24.95

Warm Friends and Wooden Shoes:
An Illustrated History of Holland, Michigan 128 pages, 8 1/2 x 11, ill. bib. index, hardbound. $19.95

Shipping on individual books $1.50
Two or more books ordered retail—shipping is free
Michigan residents please add 4% sales tax

Order from Larry B. & Priscilla Massie
2109 41ST STREET
ALLEGAN FOREST, MICHIGAN
(616) 673-3633

Please indicate if you would like the author to inscribe the books.

Erratum: The events recorded by Anna Jameson on pages 57-77 occurred in July, 1837.